S. Eddy Bell's

LULU & MITZY

Best Laid Plans

PUT A
DOLLAR IN
THERE.

Published by SLG Publishing

Matriarch and Publisher
Dan Vado

Editor-in-Chief
Jennifer de Guzman

Book Design & Cover
S. Eddy Bell

SLG Publishing
P.O. Box 26427
San Jose, CA 95159
www.slgcomic.com

First Printing: November 2008
ISBN-10: 1-59362-137-X
ISBN-13: 978-1-59362-137-7

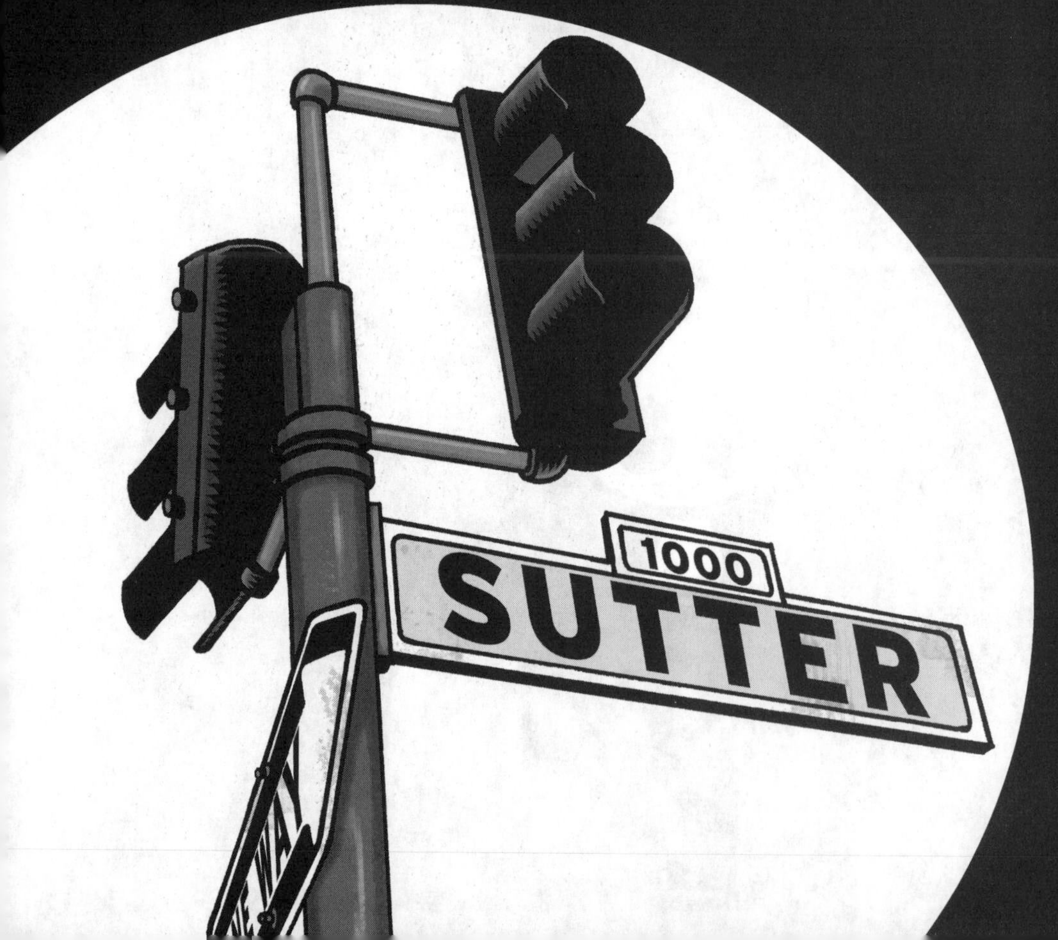
1000
SUTTER

AG
BEL

FOR OCHAN, WITHOUT
WHOM NONE OF THIS
WOULD BE POSSIBLE.

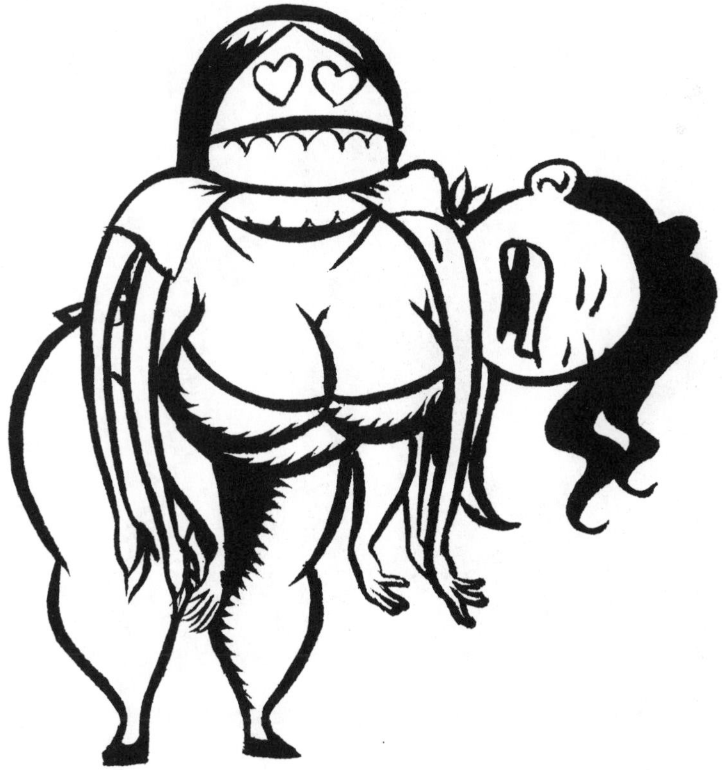

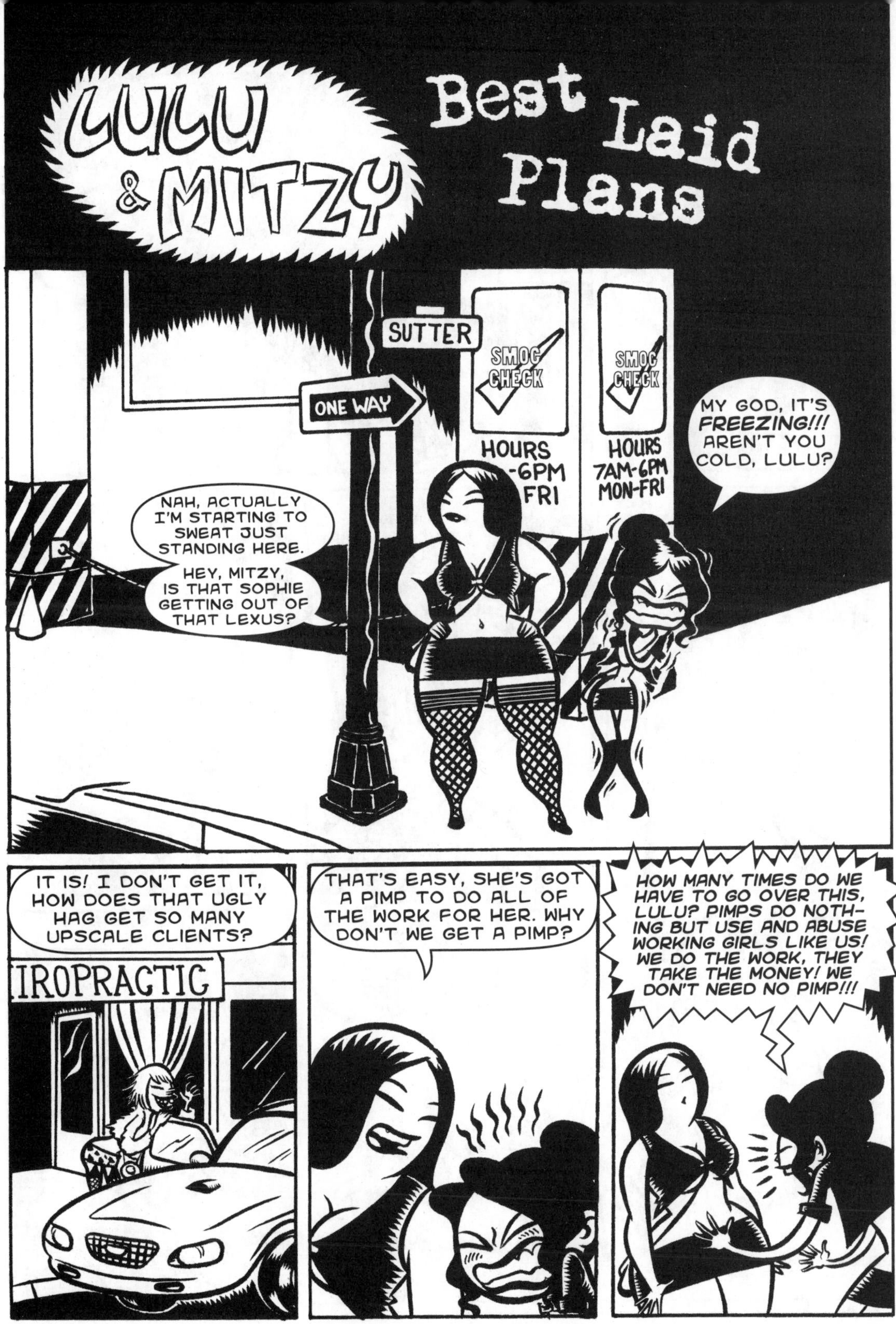
LULU & MITZY
Best Laid Plans
SUTTER
ONE WAY
SMOG CHECK
HOURS
SMOG CHECK
HOURS 7AM-6PM MON-FRI
MY GOD, IT'S FREEZING!!! AREN'T YOU COLD, LULU?
NAH, ACTUALLY I'M STARTING TO SWEAT JUST STANDING HERE.
HEY, MITZY, IS THAT SOPHIE GETTING OUT OF THAT LEXUS?
IT IS! I DON'T GET IT, HOW DOES THAT UGLY HAG GET SO MANY UPSCALE CLIENTS?
IROPRACTIC
THAT'S EASY, SHE'S GOT A PIMP TO DO ALL OF THE WORK FOR HER. WHY DON'T WE GET A PIMP?
HOW MANY TIMES DO WE HAVE TO GO OVER THIS, LULU? PIMPS DO NOTHING BUT USE AND ABUSE WORKING GIRLS LIKE US! WE DO THE WORK, THEY TAKE THE MONEY! WE DON'T NEED NO PIMP!!!

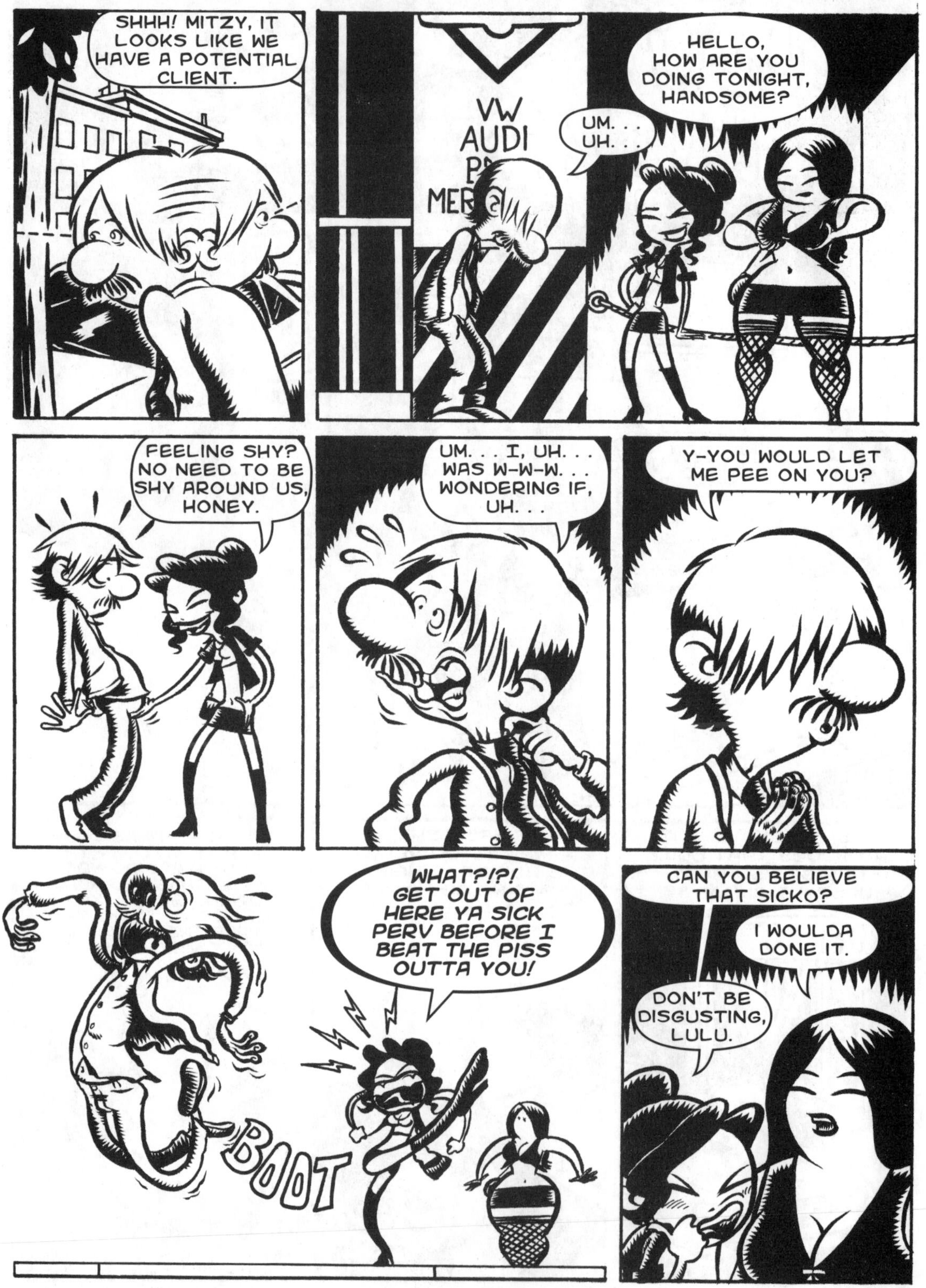
SHHH! MITZY, IT LOOKS LIKE WE HAVE A POTENTIAL CLIENT.
VW
AUDI
HELLO, HOW ARE YOU DOING TONIGHT, HANDSOME?
UM. . . UH. . .
FEELING SHY? NO NEED TO BE SHY AROUND US, HONEY.
UM. . . I, UH. . . WAS W-W-W. . . WONDERING IF, UH. . .
Y-YOU WOULD LET ME PEE ON YOU?
WHAT?!?! GET OUT OF HERE YA SICK PERV BEFORE I BEAT THE PISS OUTTA YOU!
BOOT
CAN YOU BELIEVE THAT SICKO?
I WOULDA DONE IT.
DON'T BE DISGUSTING, LULU.

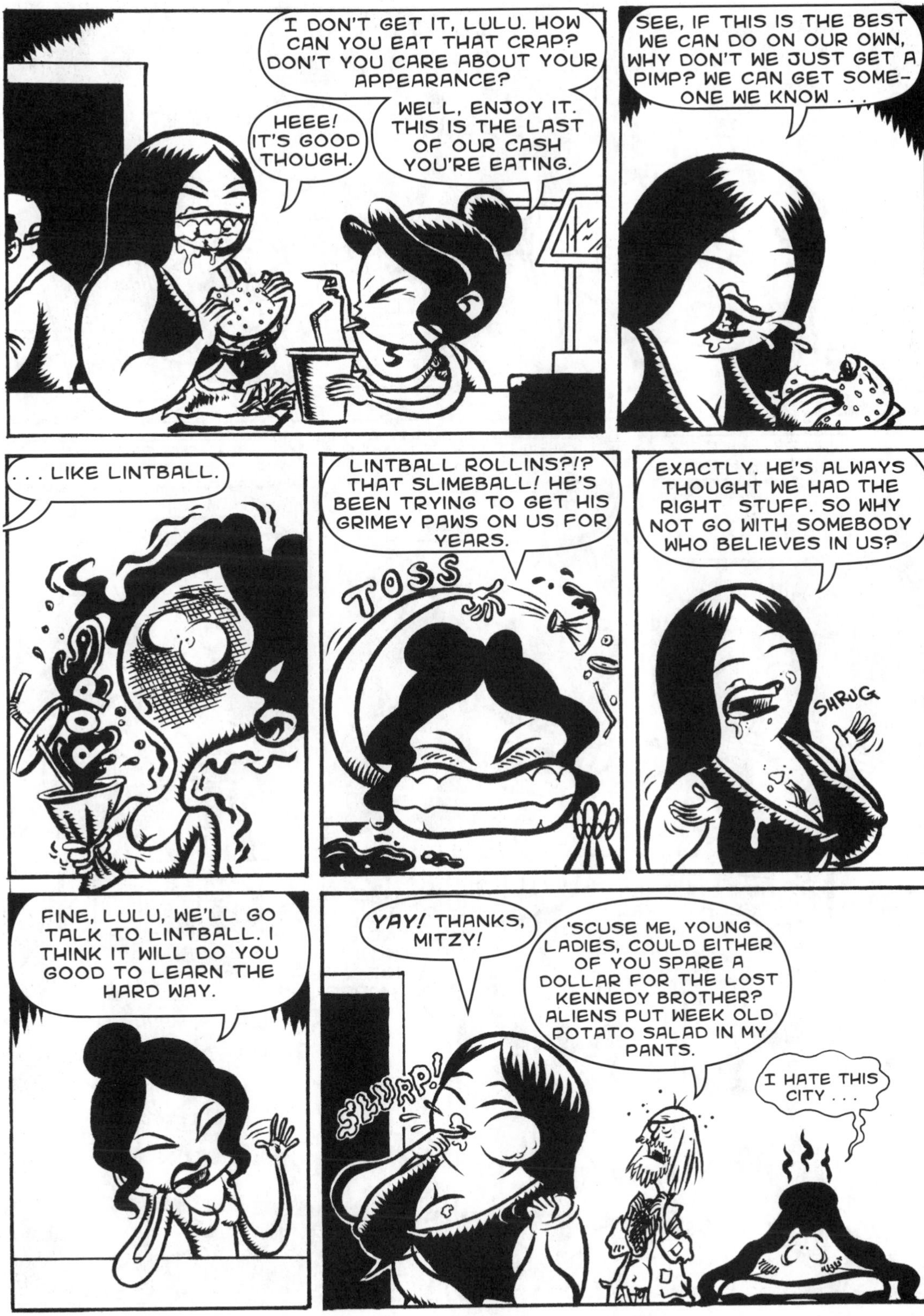
I DON'T GET IT, LULU. HOW CAN YOU EAT THAT CRAP? DON'T YOU CARE ABOUT YOUR APPEARANCE?
HEEE! IT'S GOOD THOUGH.
WELL, ENJOY IT. THIS IS THE LAST OF OUR CASH YOU'RE EATING.
SEE, IF THIS IS THE BEST WE CAN DO ON OUR OWN, WHY DON'T WE JUST GET A PIMP? WE CAN GET SOME-ONE WE KNOW . . .
. . . LIKE LINTBALL.
POP
LINTBALL ROLLINS?!? THAT SLIMEBALL! HE'S BEEN TRYING TO GET HIS GRIMEY PAWS ON US FOR YEARS.
TOSS
EXACTLY. HE'S ALWAYS THOUGHT WE HAD THE RIGHT STUFF. SO WHY NOT GO WITH SOMEBODY WHO BELIEVES IN US?
SHRUG
FINE, LULU, WE'LL GO TALK TO LINTBALL. I THINK IT WILL DO YOU GOOD TO LEARN THE HARD WAY.
YAY! THANKS, MITZY!
'SCUSE ME, YOUNG LADIES, COULD EITHER OF YOU SPARE A DOLLAR FOR THE LOST KENNEDY BROTHER? ALIENS PUT WEEK OLD POTATO SALAD IN MY PANTS.
SLURP!
I HATE THIS CITY . . .

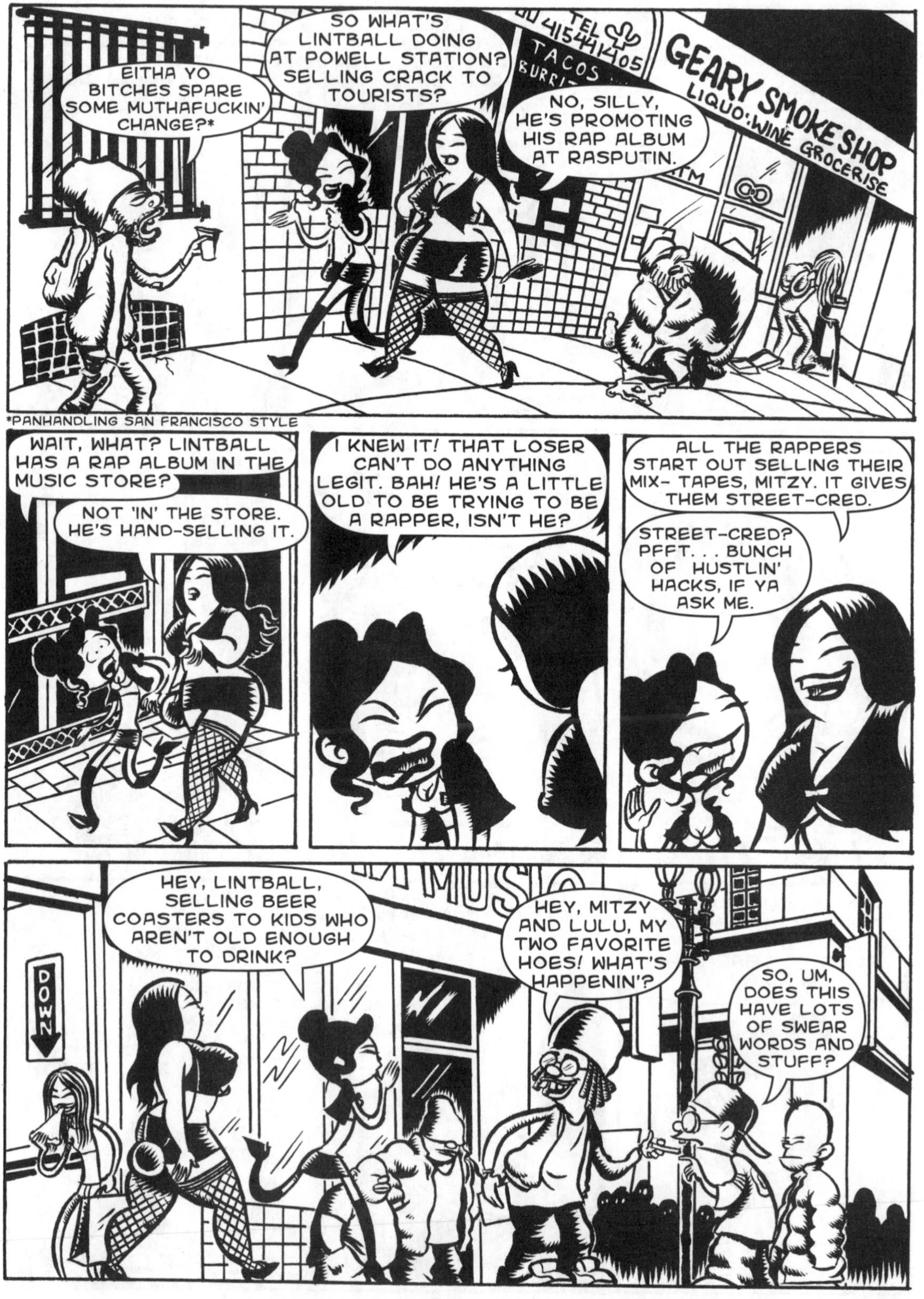
EITHA YO BITCHES SPARE SOME MUTHAFUCKIN' CHANGE?*
SO WHAT'S LINTBALL DOING AT POWELL STATION? SELLING CRACK TO TOURISTS?
TACOS
GEARY SMOKE SHOP
LIQUO: WINE GROCERISE
NO, SILLY, HE'S PROMOTING HIS RAP ALBUM AT RASPUTIN.
*PANHANDLING SAN FRANCISCO STYLE
WAIT, WHAT? LINTBALL HAS A RAP ALBUM IN THE MUSIC STORE?
NOT 'IN' THE STORE. HE'S HAND-SELLING IT.
I KNEW IT! THAT LOSER CAN'T DO ANYTHING LEGIT. BAH! HE'S A LITTLE OLD TO BE TRYING TO BE A RAPPER, ISN'T HE?
ALL THE RAPPERS START OUT SELLING THEIR MIX- TAPES, MITZY. IT GIVES THEM STREET-CRED.
STREET-CRED? PFFT. . . BUNCH OF HUSTLIN' HACKS, IF YA ASK ME.
HEY, LINTBALL, SELLING BEER COASTERS TO KIDS WHO AREN'T OLD ENOUGH TO DRINK?
DOWN
HEY, MITZY AND LULU, MY TWO FAVORITE HOES! WHAT'S HAPPENIN'?
SO, UM, DOES THIS HAVE LOTS OF SWEAR WORDS AND STUFF?

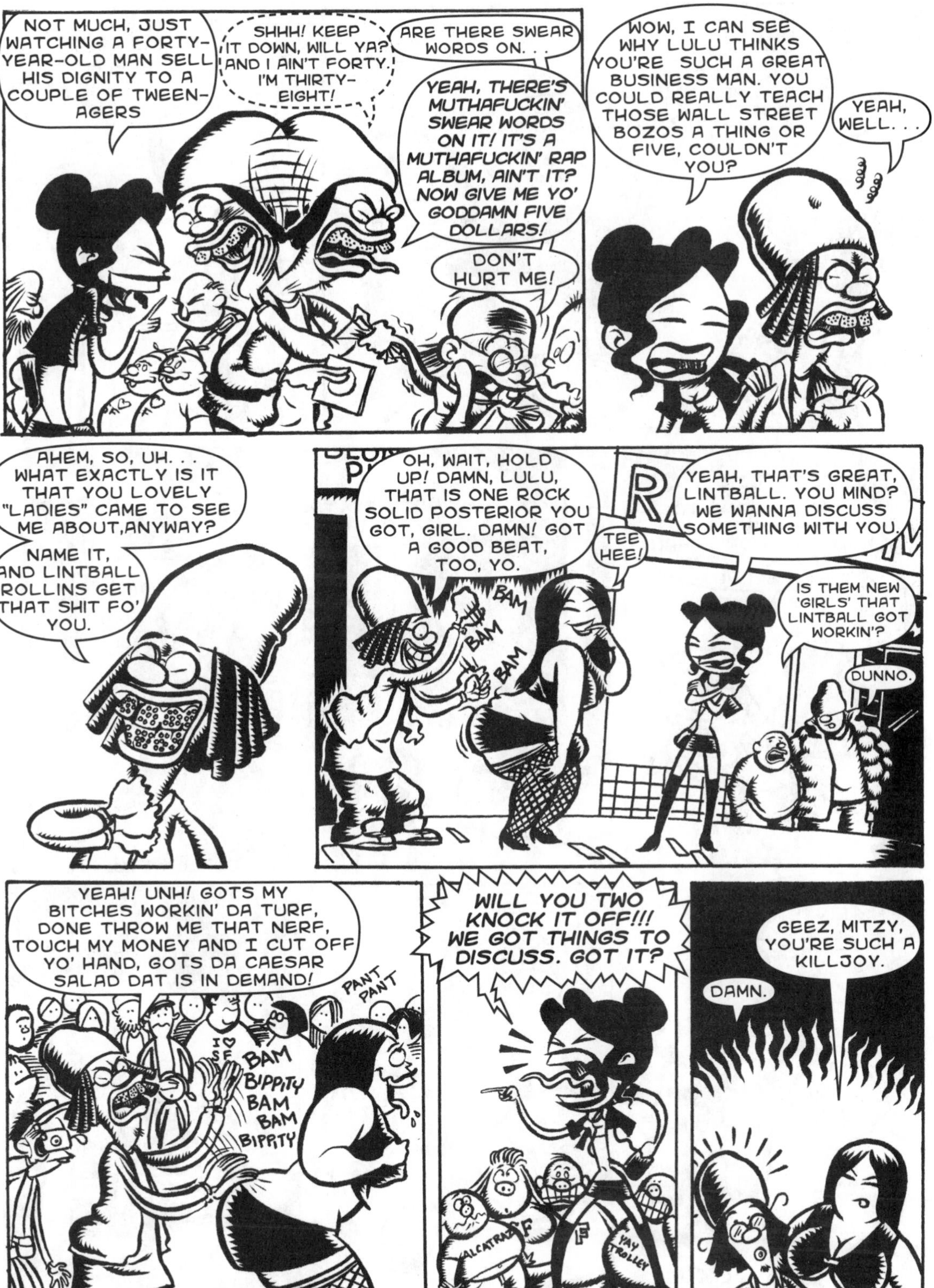
NOT MUCH, JUST WATCHING A FORTY-YEAR-OLD MAN SELL HIS DIGNITY TO A COUPLE OF TWEEN-AGERS
SHHH! KEEP IT DOWN, WILL YA? AND I AIN'T FORTY. I'M THIRTY-EIGHT!
ARE THERE SWEAR WORDS ON. . .
YEAH, THERE'S MUTHAFUCKIN' SWEAR WORDS ON IT! IT'S A MUTHAFUCKIN' RAP ALBUM, AIN'T IT? NOW GIVE ME YO' GODDAMN FIVE DOLLARS!
DON'T HURT ME!
WOW, I CAN SEE WHY LULU THINKS YOU'RE SUCH A GREAT BUSINESS MAN. YOU COULD REALLY TEACH THOSE WALL STREET BOZOS A THING OR FIVE, COULDN'T YOU?
YEAH, WELL. . .
AHEM, SO, UH. . . WHAT EXACTLY IS IT THAT YOU LOVELY "LADIES" CAME TO SEE ME ABOUT,ANYWAY?
NAME IT, AND LINTBALL ROLLINS GET THAT SHIT FO' YOU.
OH, WAIT, HOLD UP! DAMN, LULU, THAT IS ONE ROCK SOLID POSTERIOR YOU GOT, GIRL. DAMN! GOT A GOOD BEAT, TOO, YO.
BAM
BAM
BAM
TEE HEE!
YEAH, THAT'S GREAT, LINTBALL. YOU MIND? WE WANNA DISCUSS SOMETHING WITH YOU.
IS THEM NEW 'GIRLS' THAT LINTBALL GOT WORKIN'?
DUNNO.
YEAH! UNH! GOTS MY BITCHES WORKIN' DA TURF, DONE THROW ME THAT NERF, TOUCH MY MONEY AND I CUT OFF YO' HAND, GOTS DA CAESAR SALAD DAT IS IN DEMAND!
PANT PANT
I ♡ SF
BAM BIPPITY BAM BAM BIPPITY
WILL YOU TWO KNOCK IT OFF!!! WE GOT THINGS TO DISCUSS. GOT IT?
ALCATRAZ
SF
YAY TROLLEY
GEEZ, MITZY, YOU'RE SUCH A KILLJOY.
DAMN.

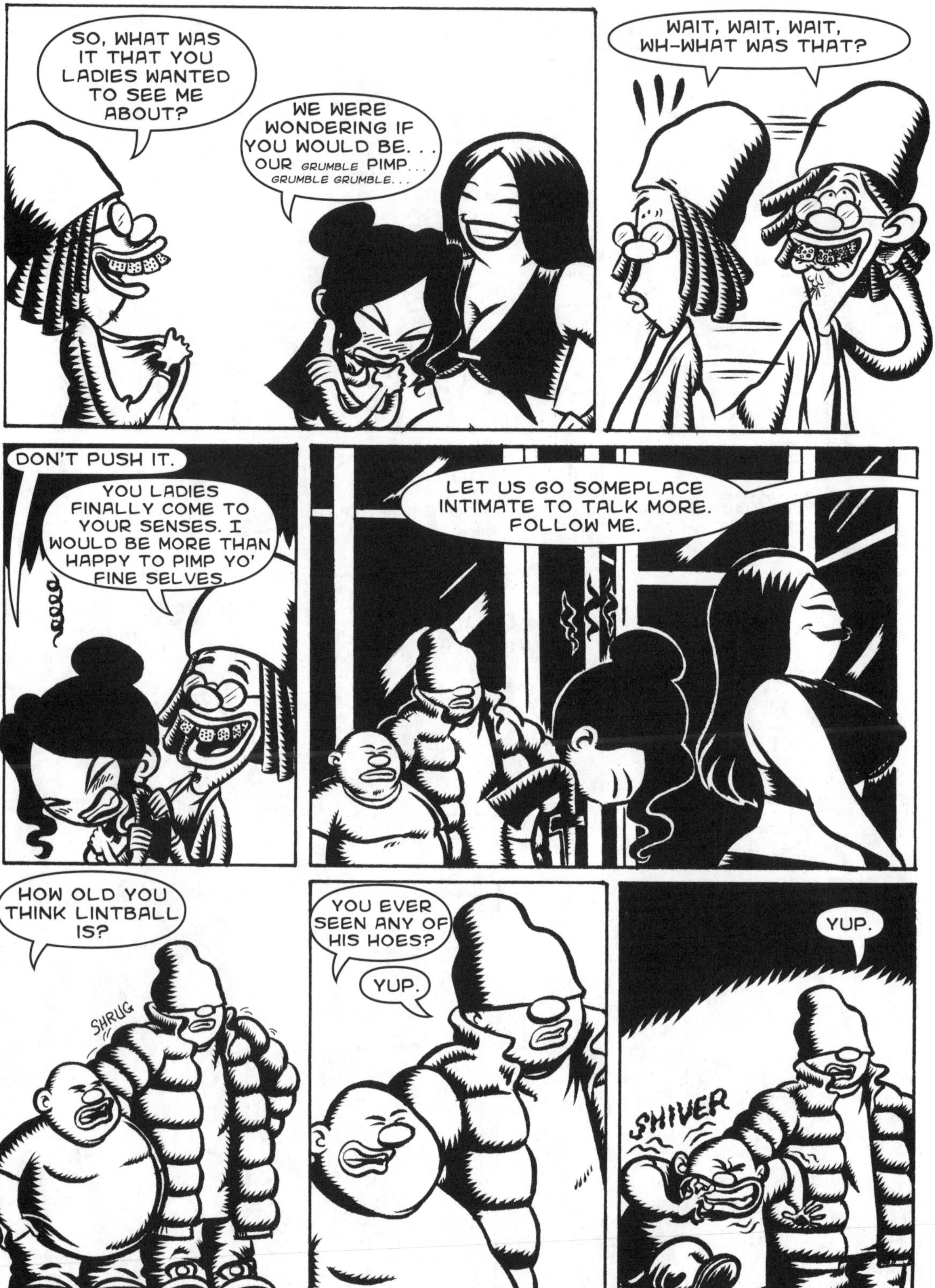
SO, WHAT WAS IT THAT YOU LADIES WANTED TO SEE ME ABOUT?
WE WERE WONDERING IF YOU WOULD BE. . . OUR GRUMBLE PIMP. . . GRUMBLE GRUMBLE. . .
WAIT, WAIT, WAIT, WH-WHAT WAS THAT?
DON'T PUSH IT.
YOU LADIES FINALLY COME TO YOUR SENSES. I WOULD BE MORE THAN HAPPY TO PIMP YO' FINE SELVES.
LET US GO SOMEPLACE INTIMATE TO TALK MORE. FOLLOW ME.
HOW OLD YOU THINK LINTBALL IS?
SHRUG
YOU EVER SEEN ANY OF HIS HOES?
YUP.
YUP.
SHIVER

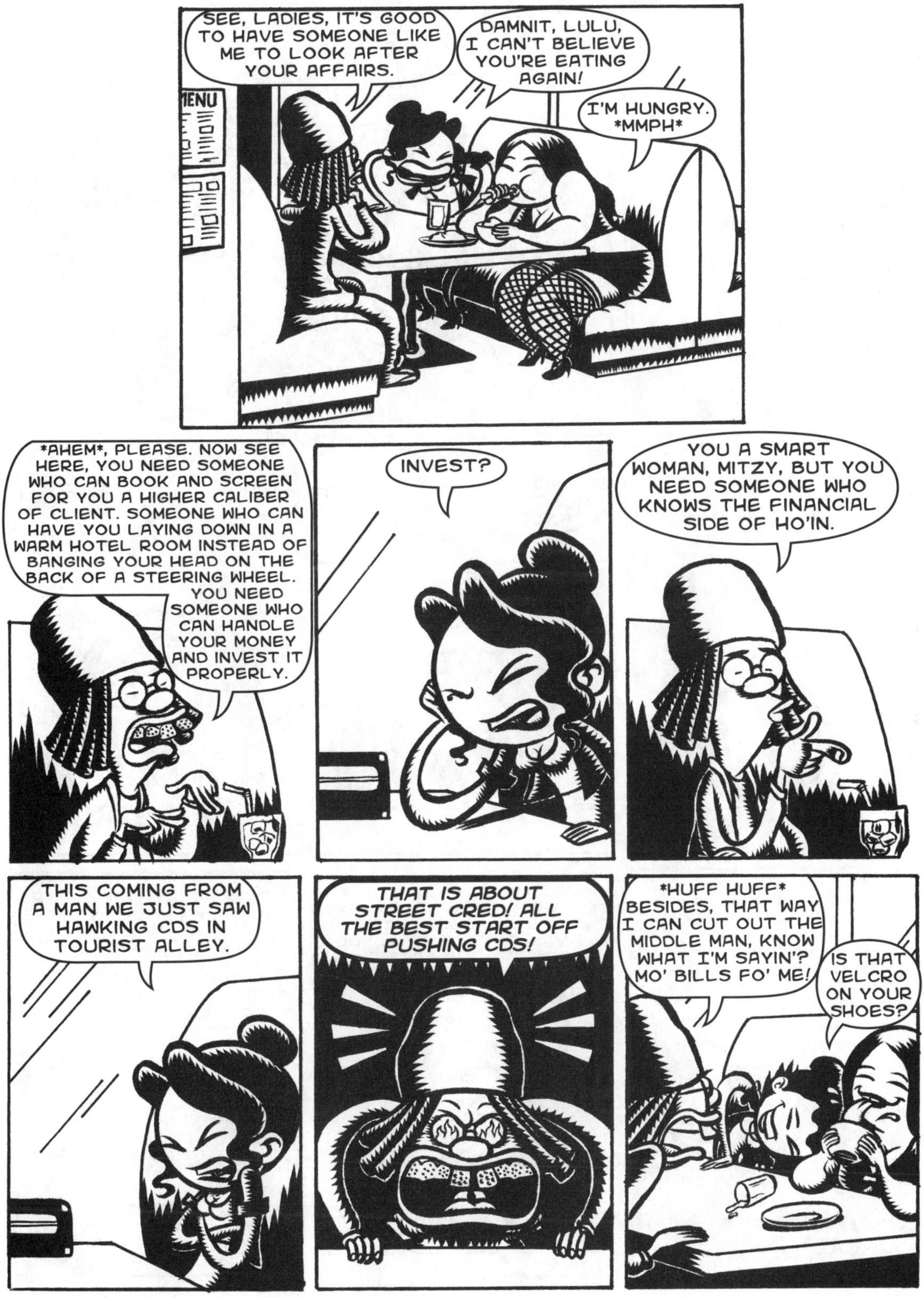
SEE, LADIES, IT'S GOOD TO HAVE SOMEONE LIKE ME TO LOOK AFTER YOUR AFFAIRS.
DAMNIT, LULU, I CAN'T BELIEVE YOU'RE EATING AGAIN!
I'M HUNGRY. *MMPH*
MENU
AHEM, PLEASE. NOW SEE HERE, YOU NEED SOMEONE WHO CAN BOOK AND SCREEN FOR YOU A HIGHER CALIBER OF CLIENT. SOMEONE WHO CAN HAVE YOU LAYING DOWN IN A WARM HOTEL ROOM INSTEAD OF BANGING YOUR HEAD ON THE BACK OF A STEERING WHEEL.
YOU NEED SOMEONE WHO CAN HANDLE YOUR MONEY AND INVEST IT PROPERLY.
INVEST?
YOU A SMART WOMAN, MITZY, BUT YOU NEED SOMEONE WHO KNOWS THE FINANCIAL SIDE OF HO'IN.
THIS COMING FROM A MAN WE JUST SAW HAWKING CDS IN TOURIST ALLEY.
THAT IS ABOUT STREET CRED! ALL THE BEST START OFF PUSHING CDS!
HUFF HUFF BESIDES, THAT WAY I CAN CUT OUT THE MIDDLE MAN, KNOW WHAT I'M SAYIN'? MO' BILLS FO' ME!
IS THAT VELCRO ON YOUR SHOES?

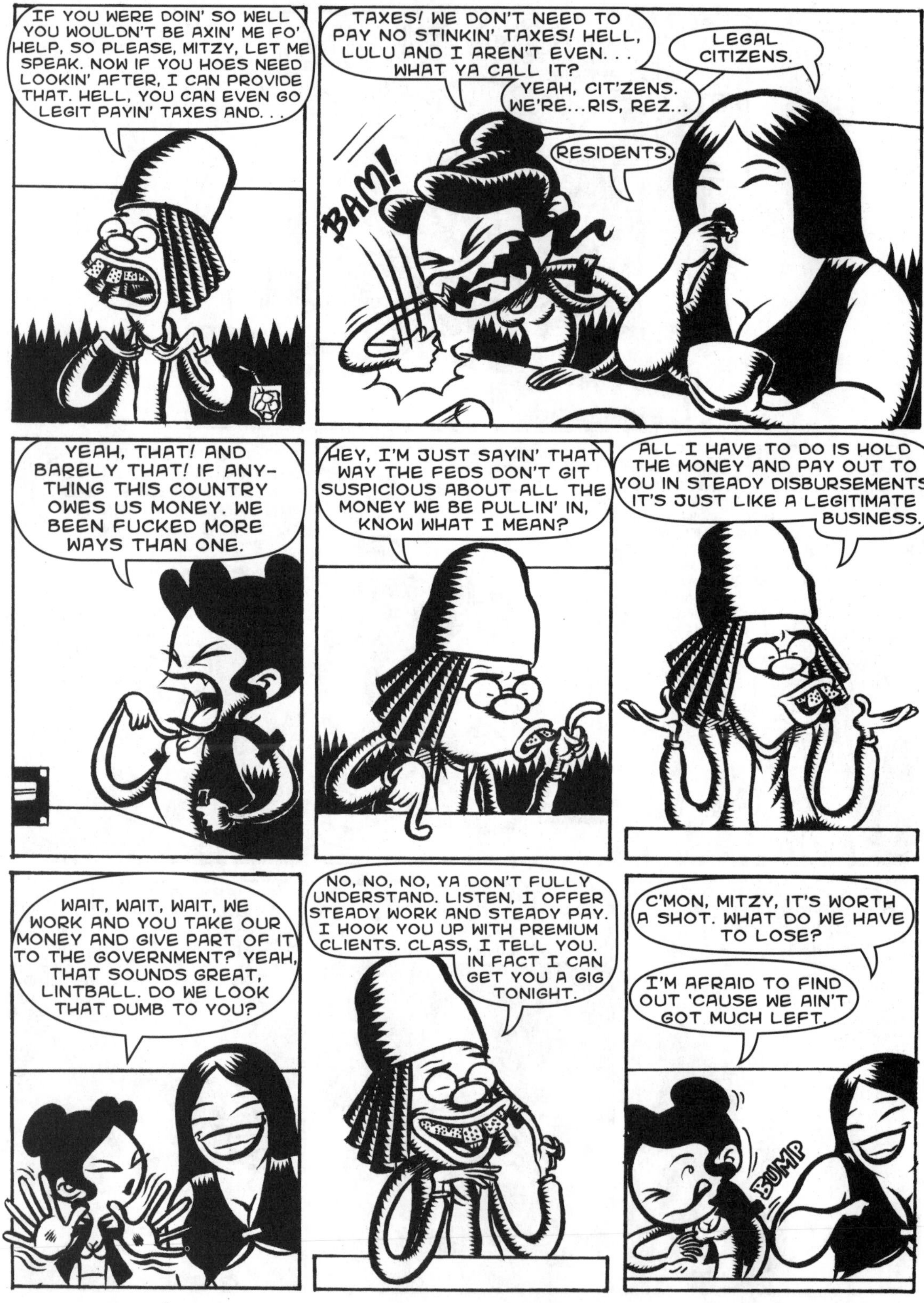
IF YOU WERE DOIN' SO WELL YOU WOULDN'T BE AXIN' ME FO' HELP, SO PLEASE, MITZY, LET ME SPEAK. NOW IF YOU HOES NEED LOOKIN' AFTER, I CAN PROVIDE THAT. HELL, YOU CAN EVEN GO LEGIT PAYIN' TAXES AND. . .
TAXES! WE DON'T NEED TO PAY NO STINKIN' TAXES! HELL, LULU AND I AREN'T EVEN. . . WHAT YA CALL IT?
LEGAL CITIZENS.
YEAH, CIT'ZENS. WE'RE...RIS, REZ...
RESIDENTS.
BAM!
YEAH, THAT! AND BARELY THAT! IF ANY-THING THIS COUNTRY OWES US MONEY. WE BEEN FUCKED MORE WAYS THAN ONE.
HEY, I'M JUST SAYIN' THAT WAY THE FEDS DON'T GIT SUSPICIOUS ABOUT ALL THE MONEY WE BE PULLIN' IN, KNOW WHAT I MEAN?
ALL I HAVE TO DO IS HOLD THE MONEY AND PAY OUT TO YOU IN STEADY DISBURSEMENTS. IT'S JUST LIKE A LEGITIMATE BUSINESS.
WAIT, WAIT, WAIT, WE WORK AND YOU TAKE OUR MONEY AND GIVE PART OF IT TO THE GOVERNMENT? YEAH, THAT SOUNDS GREAT, LINTBALL. DO WE LOOK THAT DUMB TO YOU?
NO, NO, NO, YA DON'T FULLY UNDERSTAND. LISTEN, I OFFER STEADY WORK AND STEADY PAY. I HOOK YOU UP WITH PREMIUM CLIENTS. CLASS, I TELL YOU.
IN FACT I CAN GET YOU A GIG TONIGHT.
C'MON, MITZY, IT'S WORTH A SHOT. WHAT DO WE HAVE TO LOSE?
I'M AFRAID TO FIND OUT 'CAUSE WE AIN'T GOT MUCH LEFT.
BUMP

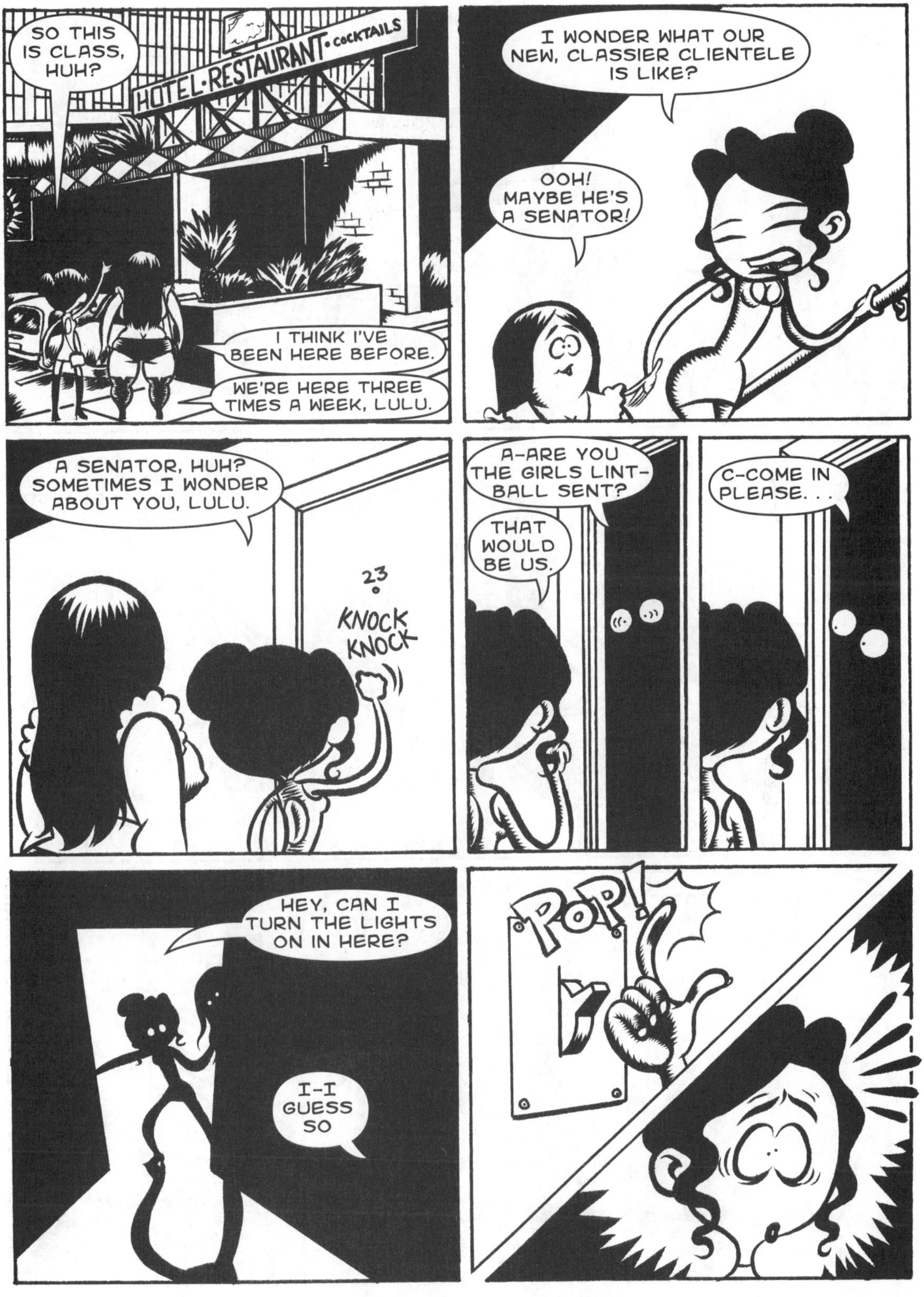
SO THIS IS CLASS, HUH?
HOTEL • RESTAURANT • COCKTAILS
I THINK I'VE BEEN HERE BEFORE.
WE'RE HERE THREE TIMES A WEEK, LULU.
I WONDER WHAT OUR NEW, CLASSIER CLIENTELE IS LIKE?
OOH! MAYBE HE'S A SENATOR!
A SENATOR, HUH? SOMETIMES I WONDER ABOUT YOU, LULU.
23
KNOCK KNOCK
A-ARE YOU THE GIRLS LINT-BALL SENT?
THAT WOULD BE US.
C-COME IN PLEASE. . .
HEY, CAN I TURN THE LIGHTS ON IN HERE?
I-I GUESS SO
POP!

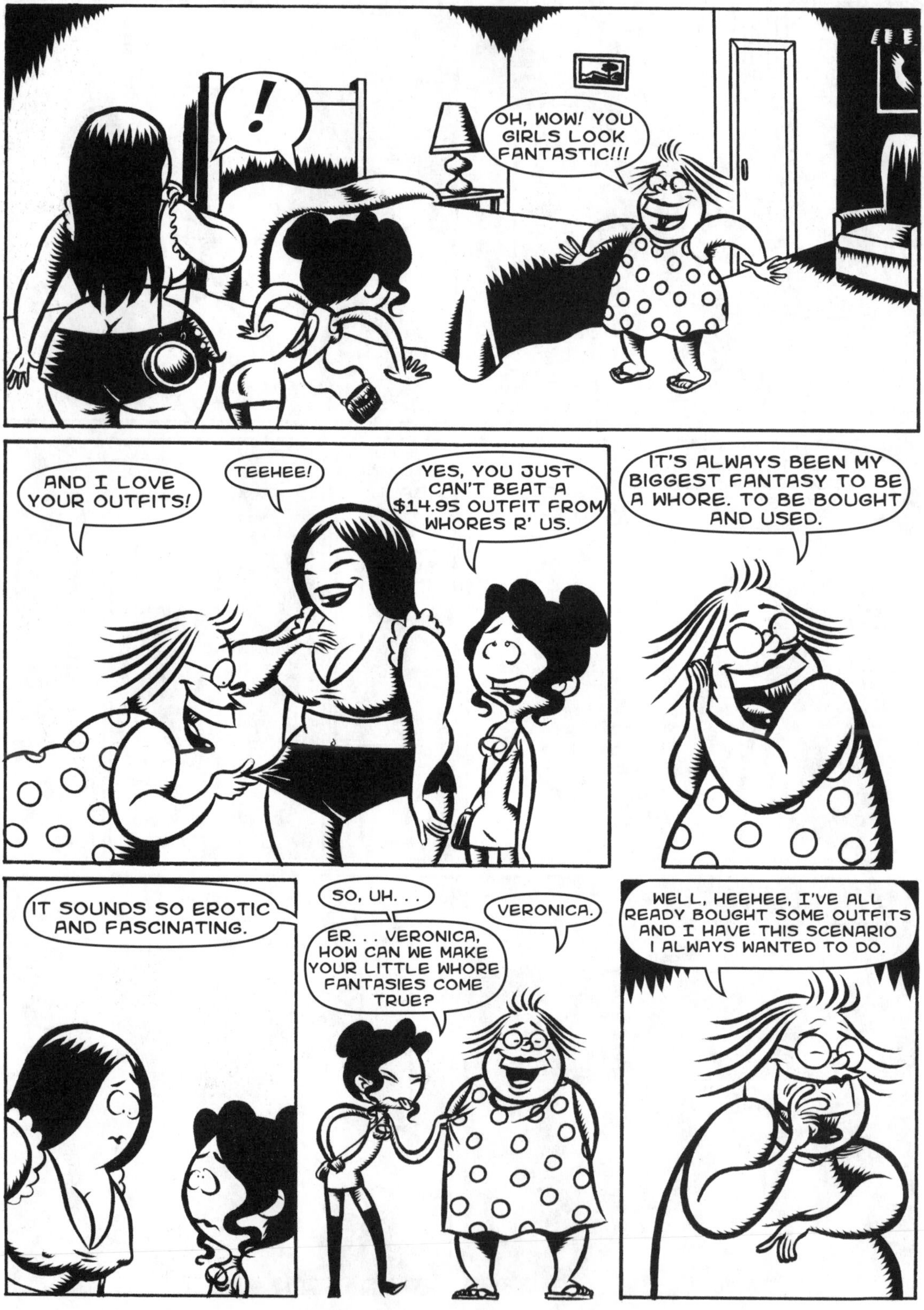
!
OH, WOW! YOU GIRLS LOOK FANTASTIC!!!
AND I LOVE YOUR OUTFITS!
TEEHEE!
YES, YOU JUST CAN'T BEAT A $14.95 OUTFIT FROM WHORES R' US.
IT'S ALWAYS BEEN MY BIGGEST FANTASY TO BE A WHORE. TO BE BOUGHT AND USED.
IT SOUNDS SO EROTIC AND FASCINATING.
SO, UH. . .
VERONICA.
ER. . . VERONICA, HOW CAN WE MAKE YOUR LITTLE WHORE FANTASIES COME TRUE?
WELL, HEEHEE, I'VE ALL READY BOUGHT SOME OUTFITS AND I HAVE THIS SCENARIO I ALWAYS WANTED TO DO.

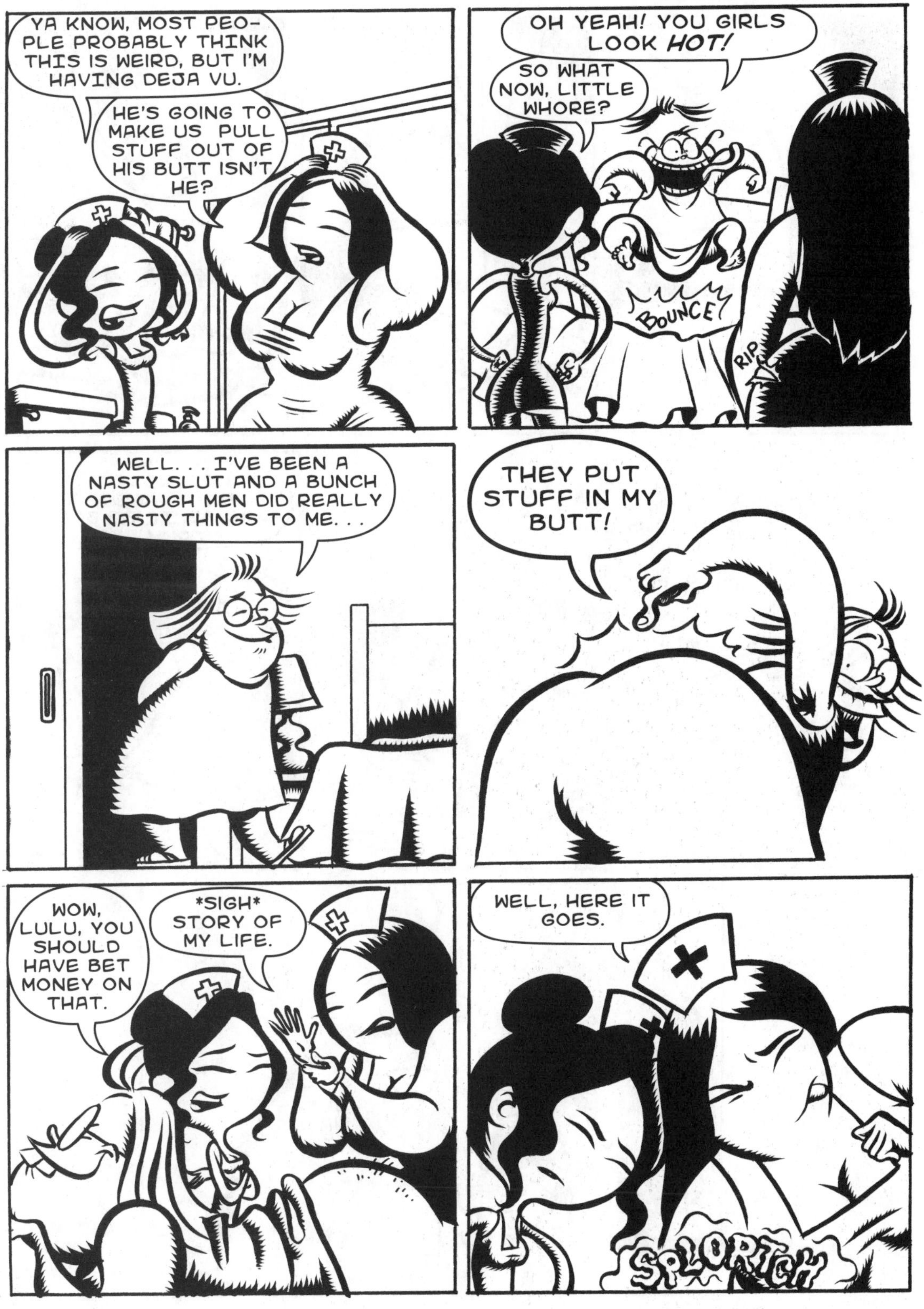
YA KNOW, MOST PEOPLE PROBABLY THINK THIS IS WEIRD, BUT I'M HAVING DEJA VU.
HE'S GOING TO MAKE US PULL STUFF OUT OF HIS BUTT ISN'T HE?
OH YEAH! YOU GIRLS LOOK HOT!
SO WHAT NOW, LITTLE WHORE?
BOUNCE!
RIP
WELL. . . I'VE BEEN A NASTY SLUT AND A BUNCH OF ROUGH MEN DID REALLY NASTY THINGS TO ME. . .
THEY PUT STUFF IN MY BUTT!
WOW, LULU, YOU SHOULD HAVE BET MONEY ON THAT.
SIGH STORY OF MY LIFE.
WELL, HERE IT GOES.
SPLORTCH

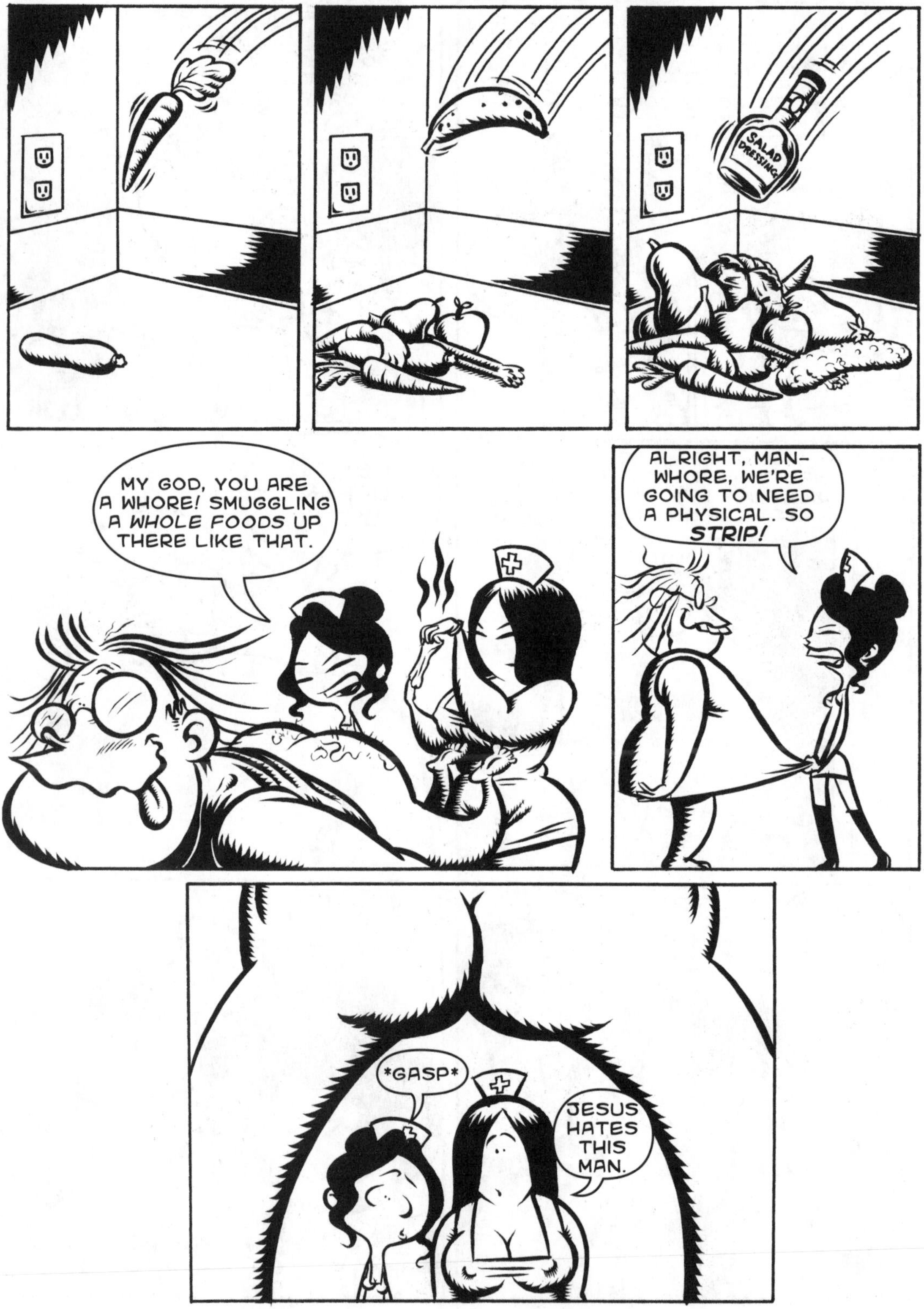
SALAD DRESSING
MY GOD, YOU ARE A WHORE! SMUGGLING A WHOLE FOODS UP THERE LIKE THAT.
ALRIGHT, MAN-WHORE, WE'RE GOING TO NEED A PHYSICAL. SO STRIP!
GASP
JESUS HATES THIS MAN.

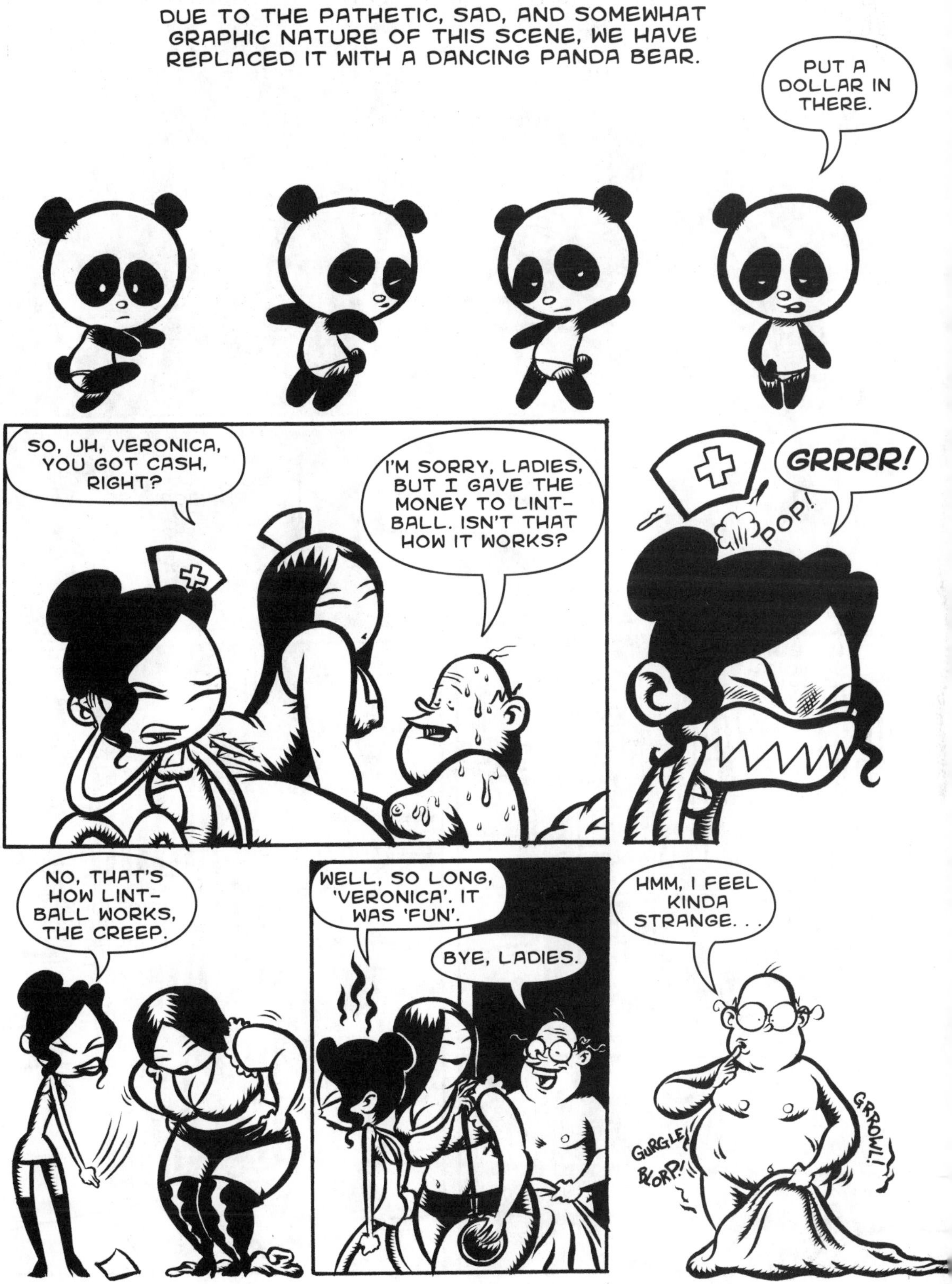
DUE TO THE PATHETIC, SAD, AND SOMEWHAT GRAPHIC NATURE OF THIS SCENE, WE HAVE REPLACED IT WITH A DANCING PANDA BEAR.
PUT A DOLLAR IN THERE.
SO, UH, VERONICA, YOU GOT CASH, RIGHT?
I'M SORRY, LADIES, BUT I GAVE THE MONEY TO LINT-BALL. ISN'T THAT HOW IT WORKS?
GRRRR!
POP!
NO, THAT'S HOW LINT-BALL WORKS, THE CREEP.
WELL, SO LONG, 'VERONICA'. IT WAS 'FUN'.
BYE, LADIES.
HMM, I FEEL KINDA STRANGE. . .
GURGLE!
BLORP!
GRROWL!

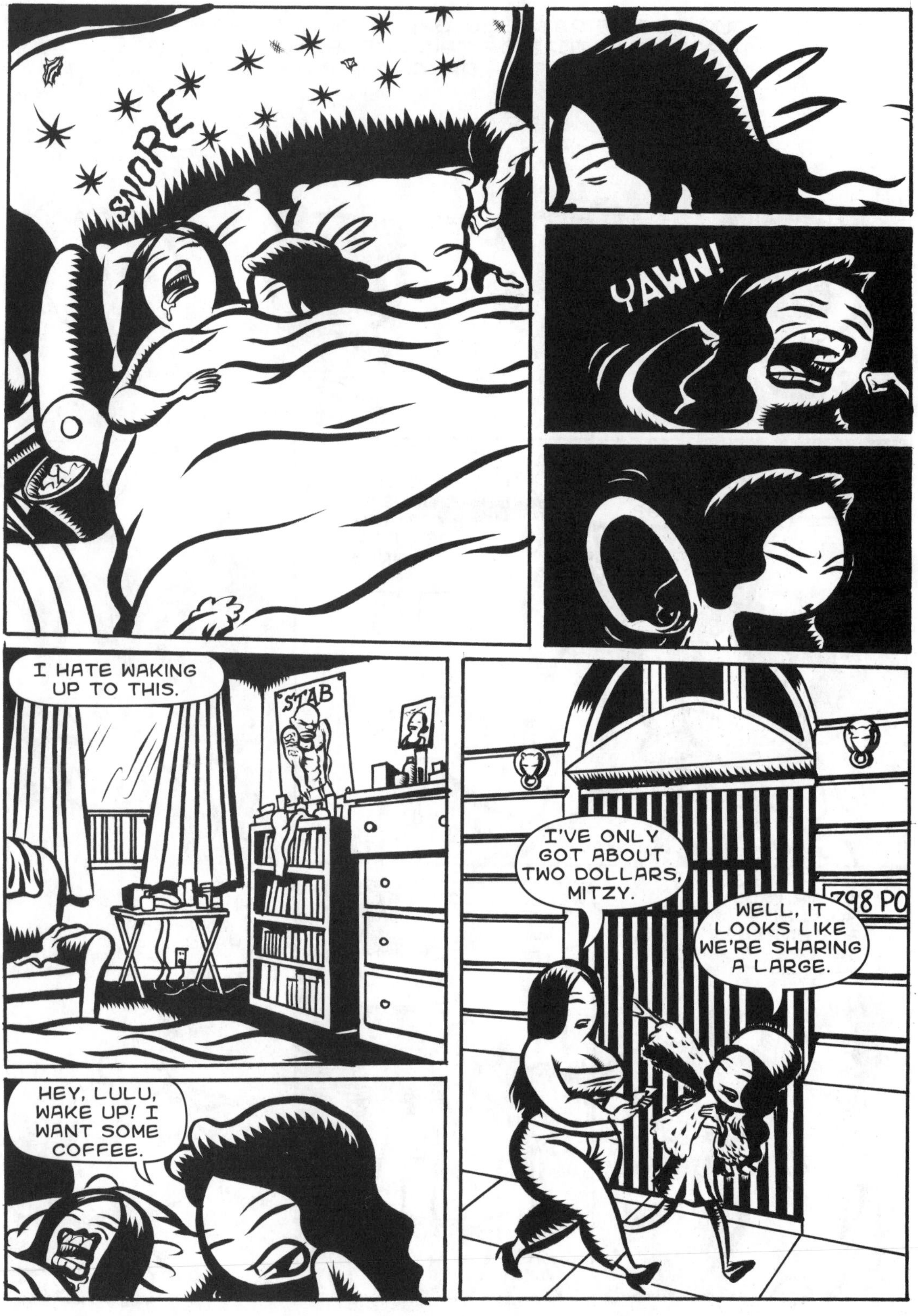
SNORE
YAWN!
I HATE WAKING UP TO THIS.
STAB
HEY, LULU, WAKE UP! I WANT SOME COFFEE.
I'VE ONLY GOT ABOUT TWO DOLLARS, MITZY.
798 PO
WELL, IT LOOKS LIKE WE'RE SHARING A LARGE.

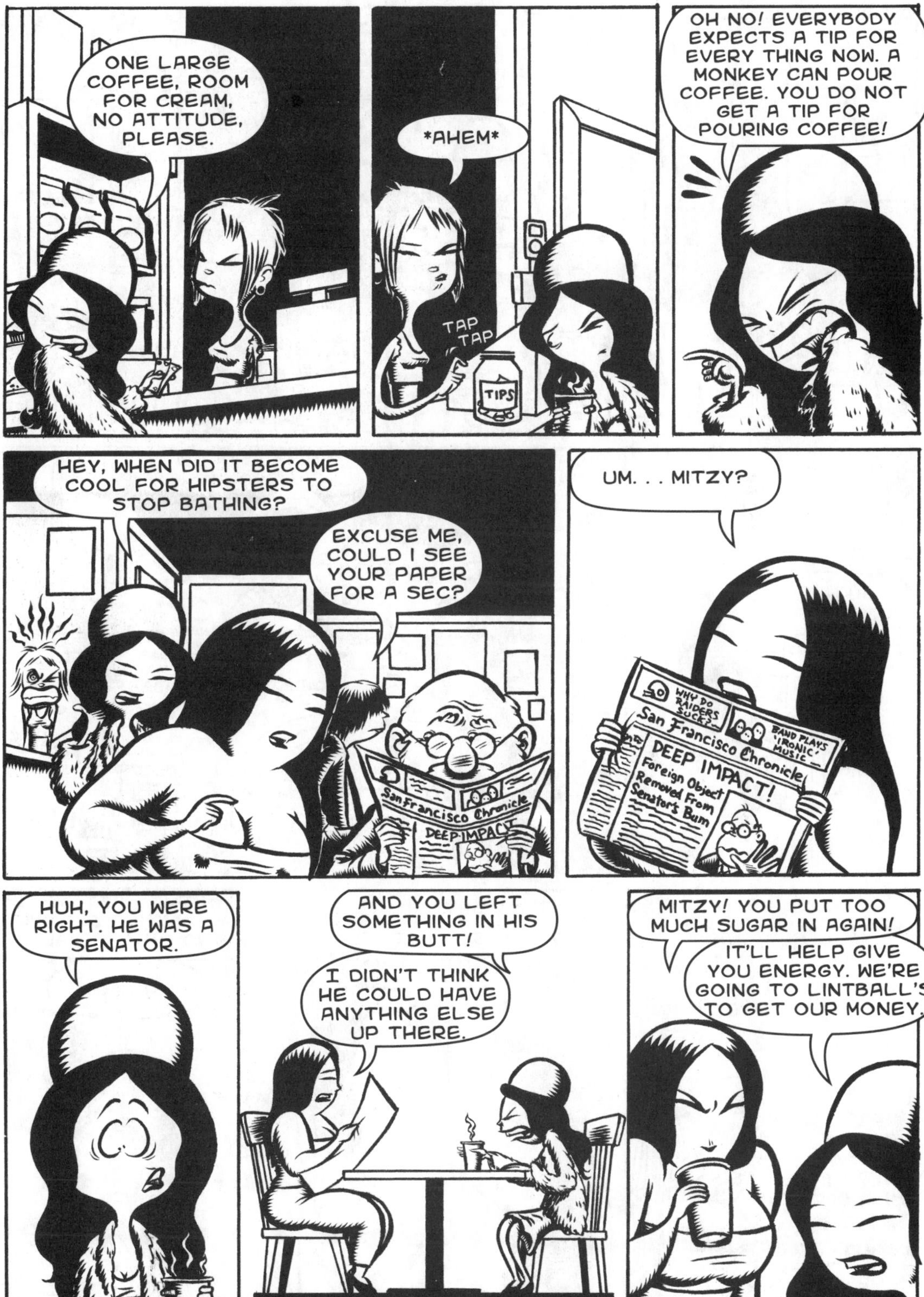
ONE LARGE COFFEE, ROOM FOR CREAM, NO ATTITUDE, PLEASE.
AHEM
TAP TAP
TIPS
OH NO! EVERYBODY EXPECTS A TIP FOR EVERY THING NOW. A MONKEY CAN POUR COFFEE. YOU DO NOT GET A TIP FOR POURING COFFEE!
HEY, WHEN DID IT BECOME COOL FOR HIPSTERS TO STOP BATHING?
EXCUSE ME, COULD I SEE YOUR PAPER FOR A SEC?
San Francisco Chronicle
DEEP IMPACT
UM. . . MITZY?
WHY DO RAIDERS SUCK?
BAND PLAYS 'IRONIC' MUSIC
San Francisco Chronicle
DEEP IMPACT!
Foreign Object Removed From Senator's Bum
HUH, YOU WERE RIGHT. HE WAS A SENATOR.
AND YOU LEFT SOMETHING IN HIS BUTT!
I DIDN'T THINK HE COULD HAVE ANYTHING ELSE UP THERE.
MITZY! YOU PUT TOO MUCH SUGAR IN AGAIN!
IT'LL HELP GIVE YOU ENERGY. WE'RE GOING TO LINTBALL'S TO GET OUR MONEY.

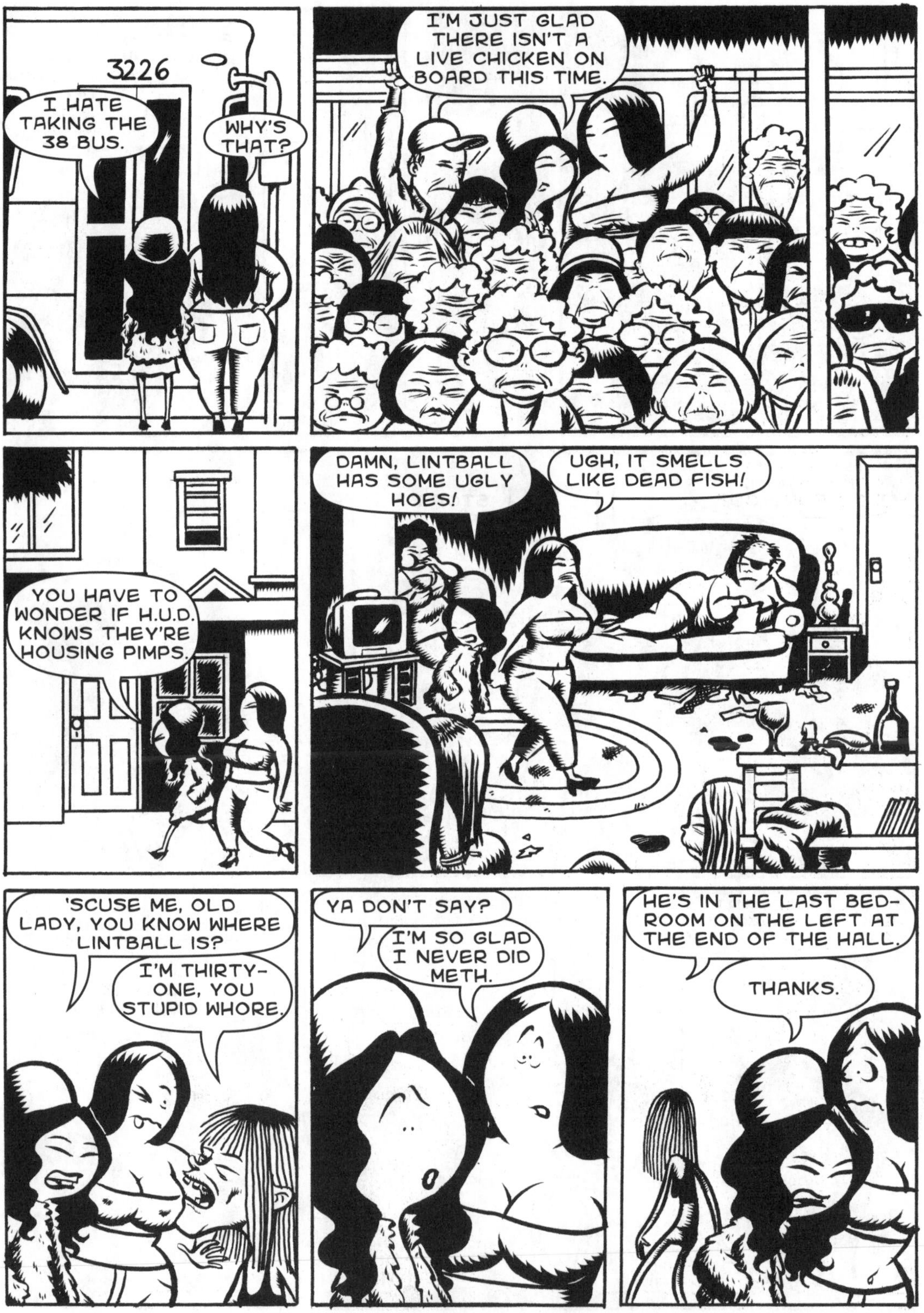
3226
I HATE TAKING THE 38 BUS.
WHY'S THAT?
I'M JUST GLAD THERE ISN'T A LIVE CHICKEN ON BOARD THIS TIME.
YOU HAVE TO WONDER IF H.U.D. KNOWS THEY'RE HOUSING PIMPS.
DAMN, LINTBALL HAS SOME UGLY HOES!
UGH, IT SMELLS LIKE DEAD FISH!
'SCUSE ME, OLD LADY, YOU KNOW WHERE LINTBALL IS?
I'M THIRTY-ONE, YOU STUPID WHORE.
YA DON'T SAY?
I'M SO GLAD I NEVER DID METH.
HE'S IN THE LAST BED-ROOM ON THE LEFT AT THE END OF THE HALL.
THANKS.

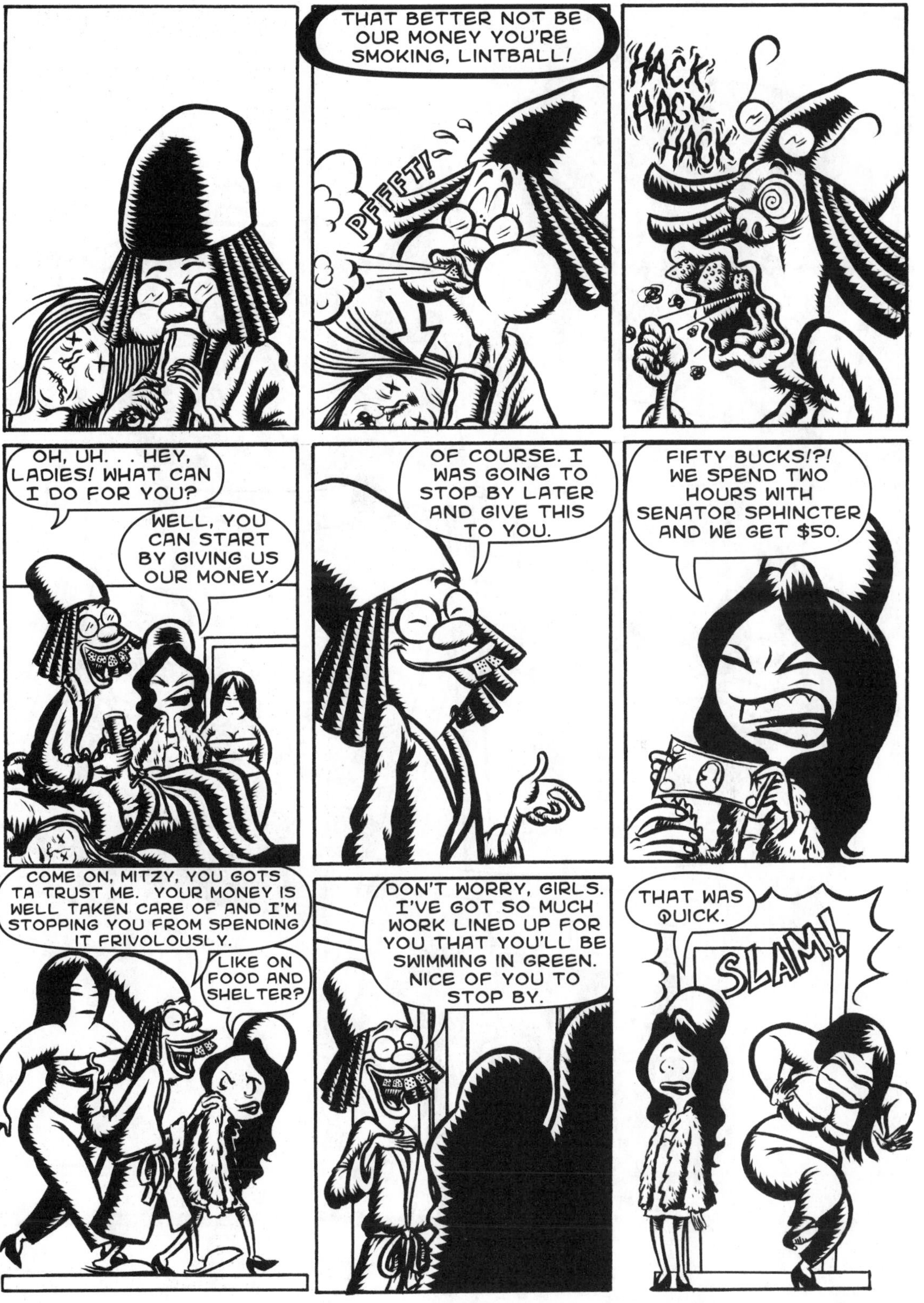
THAT BETTER NOT BE OUR MONEY YOU'RE SMOKING, LINTBALL!
PFFFT!
HACK HACK HACK
OH, UH. . . HEY, LADIES! WHAT CAN I DO FOR YOU?
WELL, YOU CAN START BY GIVING US OUR MONEY.
OF COURSE. I WAS GOING TO STOP BY LATER AND GIVE THIS TO YOU.
FIFTY BUCKS!?! WE SPEND TWO HOURS WITH SENATOR SPHINCTER AND WE GET $50.
COME ON, MITZY, YOU GOTS TA TRUST ME. YOUR MONEY IS WELL TAKEN CARE OF AND I'M STOPPING YOU FROM SPENDING IT FRIVOLOUSLY.
LIKE ON FOOD AND SHELTER?
DON'T WORRY, GIRLS. I'VE GOT SO MUCH WORK LINED UP FOR YOU THAT YOU'LL BE SWIMMING IN GREEN. NICE OF YOU TO STOP BY.
THAT WAS QUICK.
SLAM!

AND SO. . .

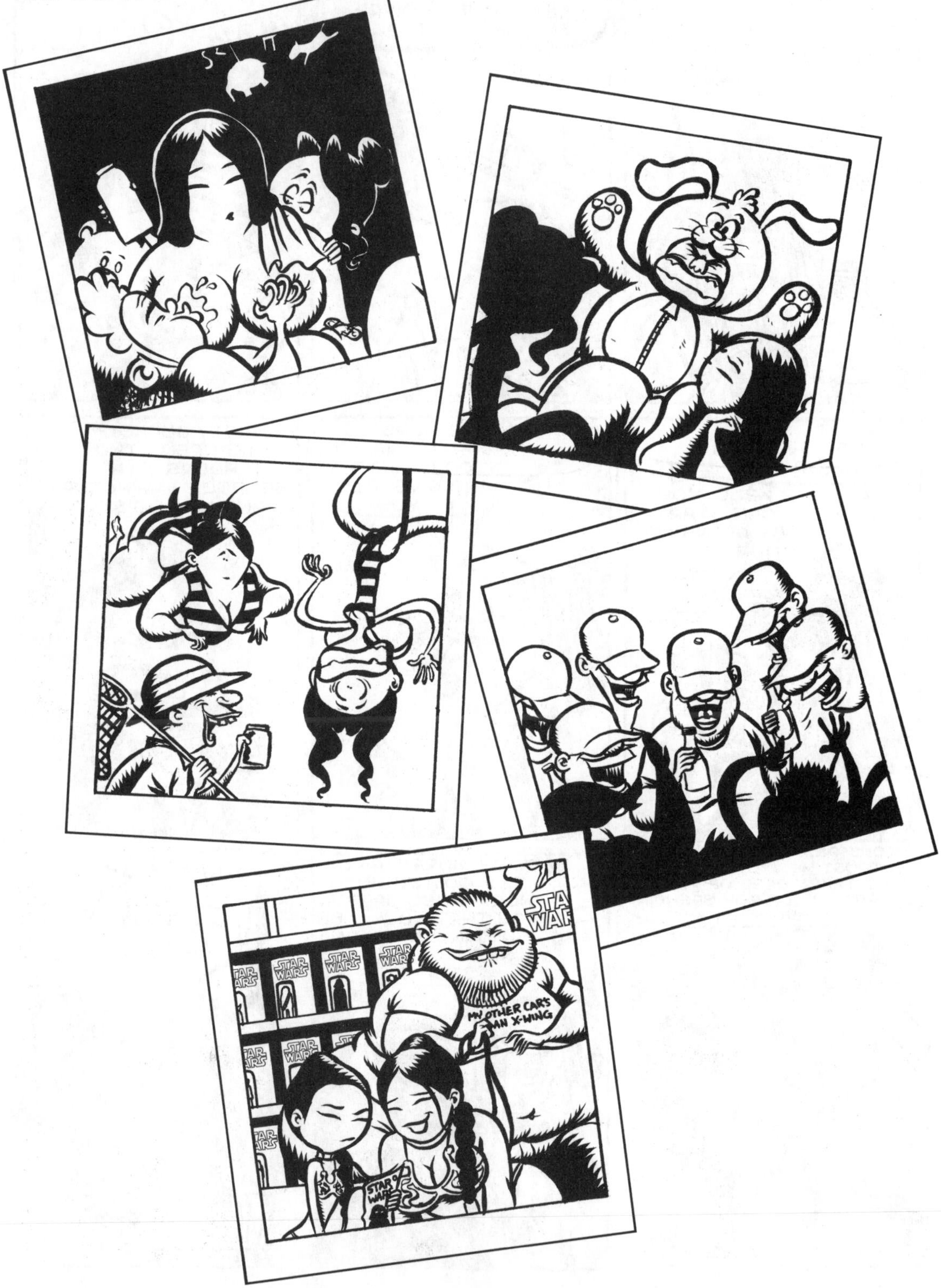
STAR WARS
STAR WARS
STAR WARS
STAR WARS
MY OTHER CAR'S AN X-WING
STAR WARS

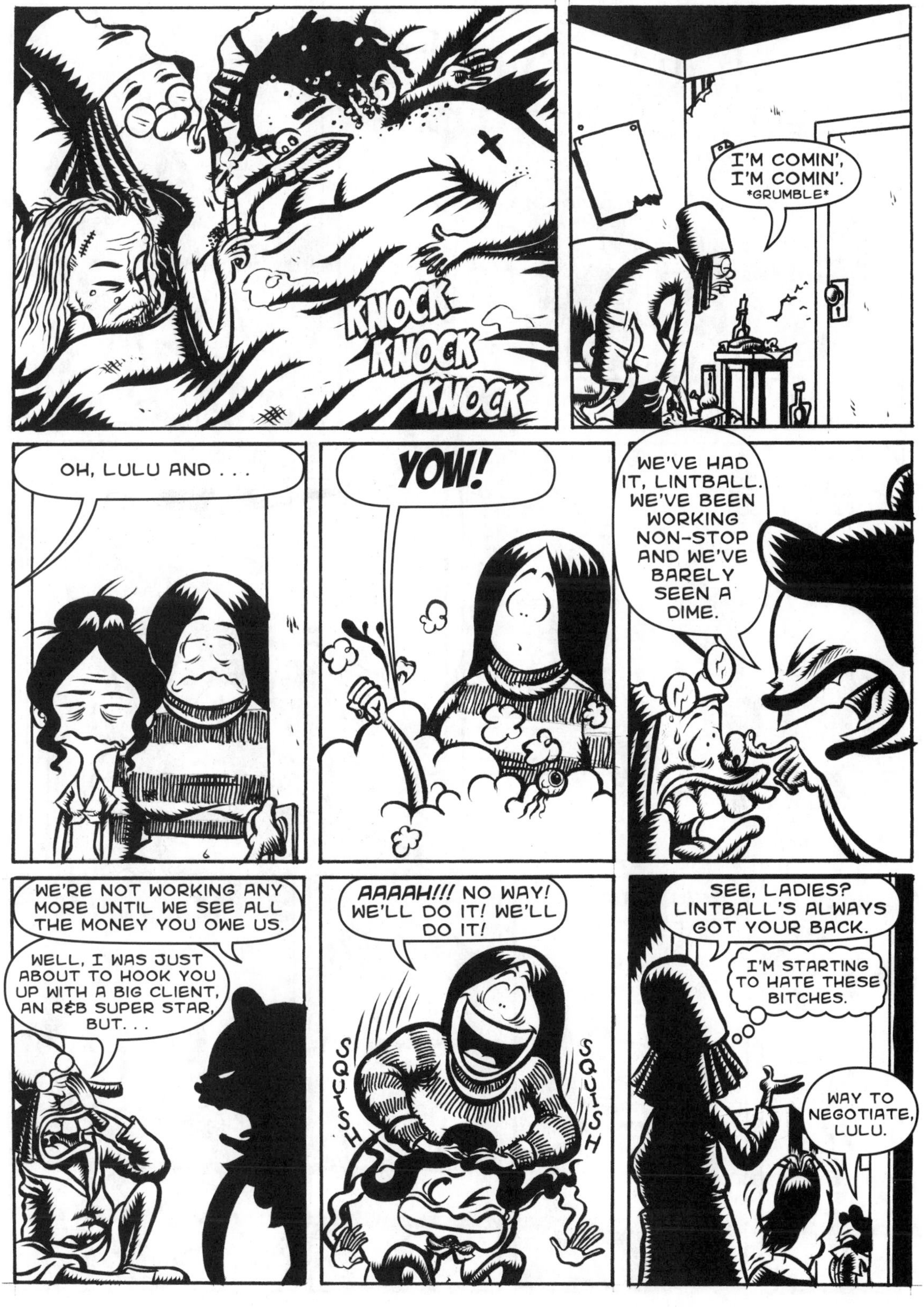
KNOCK KNOCK KNOCK
I'M COMIN', I'M COMIN'.
GRUMBLE
OH, LULU AND . . .
YOW!
WE'VE HAD IT, LINTBALL. WE'VE BEEN WORKING NON-STOP AND WE'VE BARELY SEEN A DIME.
WE'RE NOT WORKING ANY MORE UNTIL WE SEE ALL THE MONEY YOU OWE US.
WELL, I WAS JUST ABOUT TO HOOK YOU UP WITH A BIG CLIENT, AN R&B SUPER STAR, BUT. . .
AAAAH!!! NO WAY! WE'LL DO IT! WE'LL DO IT!
SQUISH
SQUISH
SEE, LADIES? LINTBALL'S ALWAYS GOT YOUR BACK.
I'M STARTING TO HATE THESE BITCHES.
WAY TO NEGOTIATE, LULU.

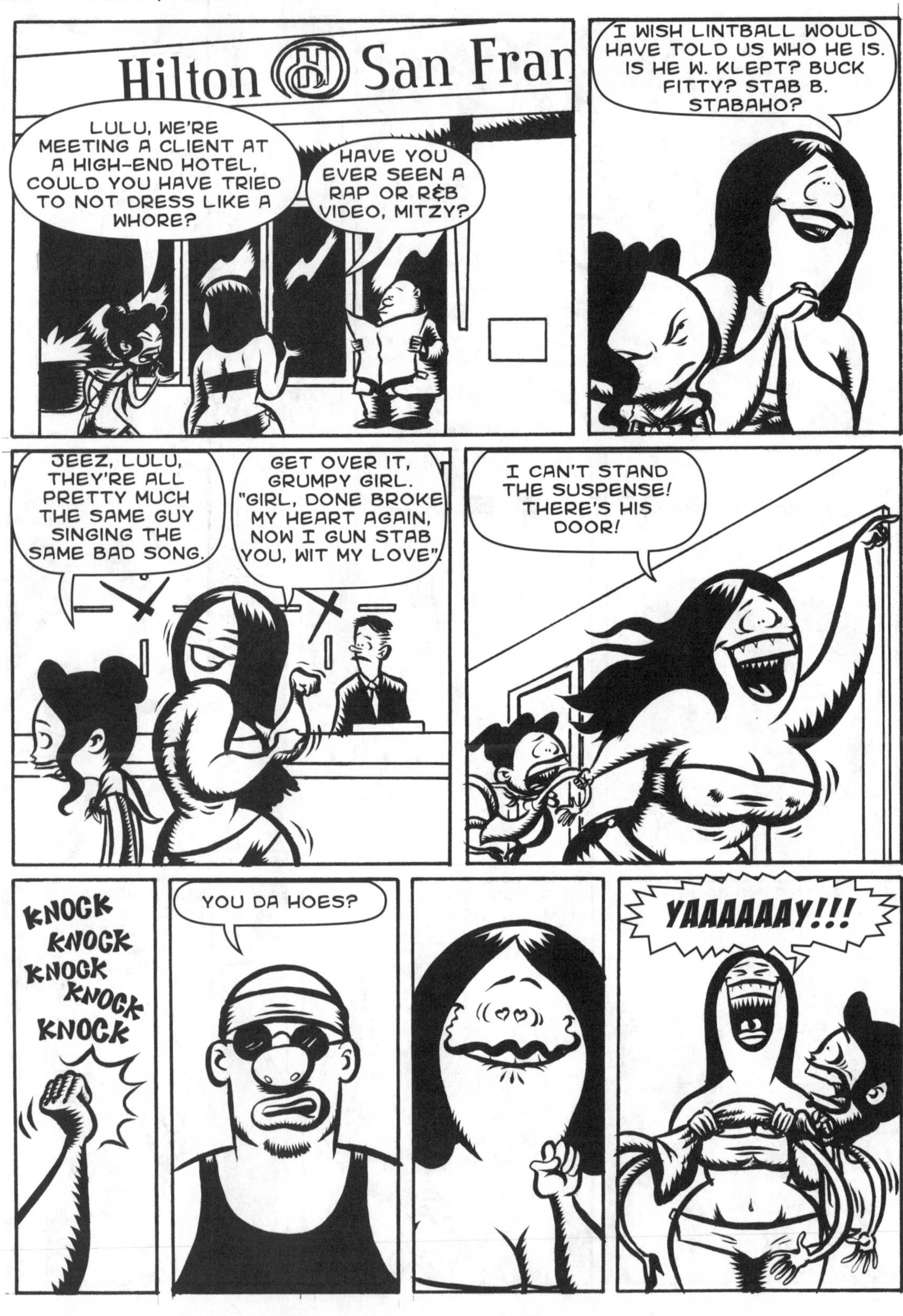
Hilton San Fran
LULU, WE'RE MEETING A CLIENT AT A HIGH-END HOTEL, COULD YOU HAVE TRIED TO NOT DRESS LIKE A WHORE?
HAVE YOU EVER SEEN A RAP OR R&B VIDEO, MITZY?
I WISH LINTBALL WOULD HAVE TOLD US WHO HE IS. IS HE W. KLEPT? BUCK FITTY? STAB B. STABAHO?
JEEZ, LULU, THEY'RE ALL PRETTY MUCH THE SAME GUY SINGING THE SAME BAD SONG.
GET OVER IT, GRUMPY GIRL. "GIRL, DONE BROKE MY HEART AGAIN, NOW I GUN STAB YOU, WIT MY LOVE".
I CAN'T STAND THE SUSPENSE! THERE'S HIS DOOR!
KNOCK KNOCK KNOCK KNOCK KNOCK
YOU DA HOES?
YAAAAAAY!!!

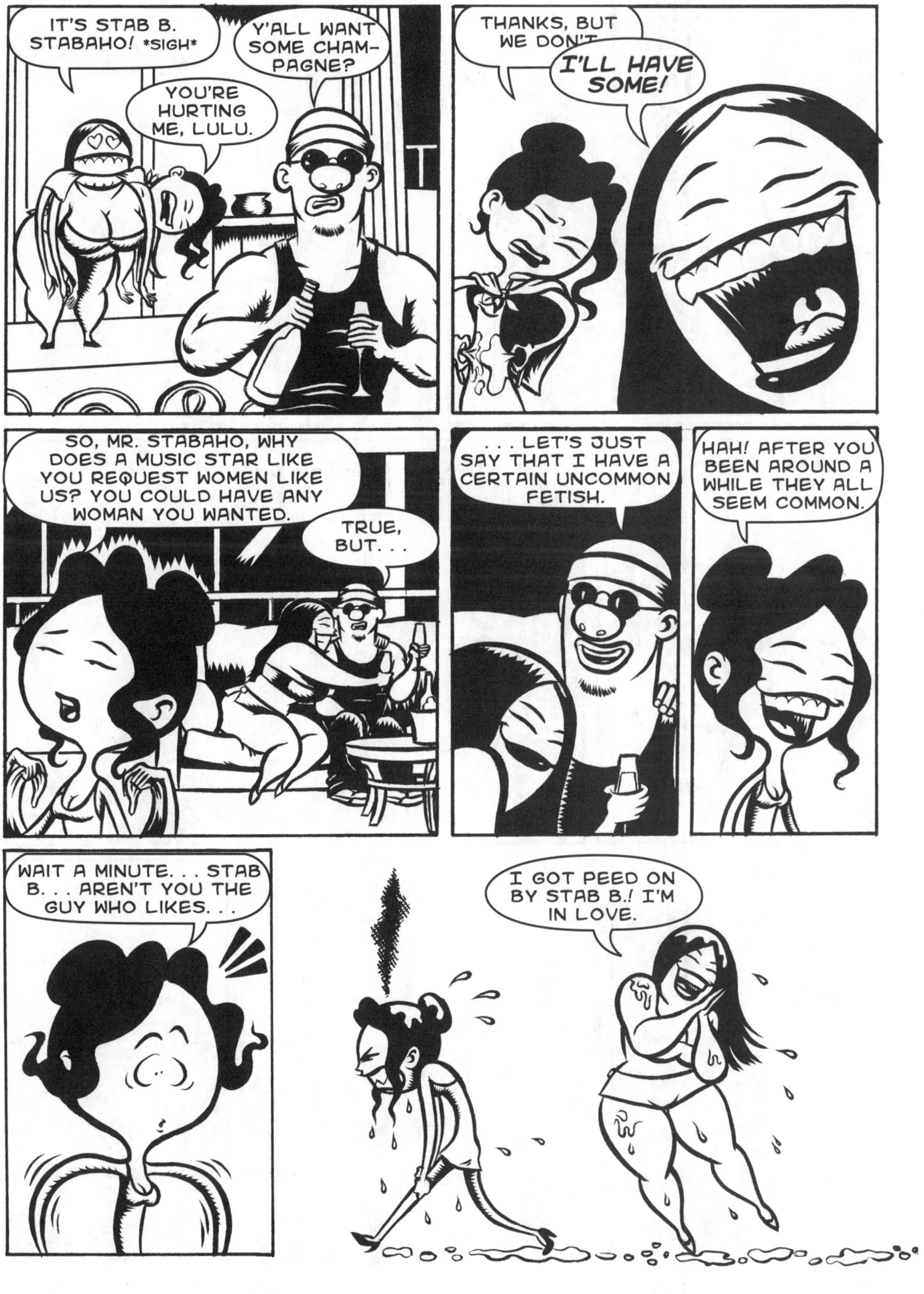
IT'S STAB B. STABAHO! *SIGH*
YOU'RE HURTING ME, LULU.
Y'ALL WANT SOME CHAMPAGNE?
THANKS, BUT WE DON'T
I'LL HAVE SOME!
SO, MR. STABAHO, WHY DOES A MUSIC STAR LIKE YOU REQUEST WOMEN LIKE US? YOU COULD HAVE ANY WOMAN YOU WANTED.
TRUE, BUT. . .
. . . LET'S JUST SAY THAT I HAVE A CERTAIN UNCOMMON FETISH.
HAH! AFTER YOU BEEN AROUND A WHILE THEY ALL SEEM COMMON.
WAIT A MINUTE. . . STAB B. . . AREN'T YOU THE GUY WHO LIKES. . .
I GOT PEED ON BY STAB B.! I'M IN LOVE.

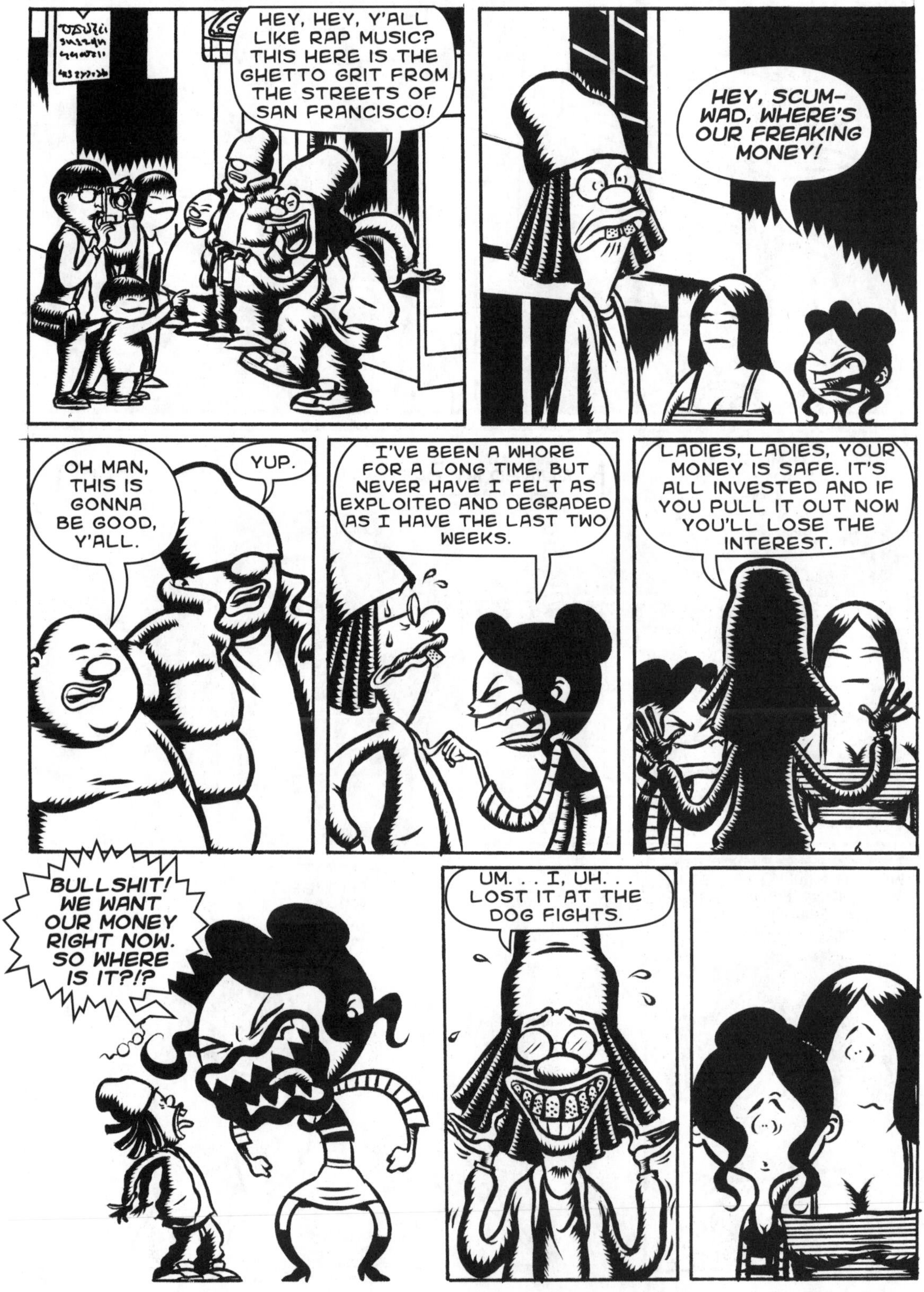
HEY, HEY, Y'ALL LIKE RAP MUSIC? THIS HERE IS THE GHETTO GRIT FROM THE STREETS OF SAN FRANCISCO!
HEY, SCUM-WAD, WHERE'S OUR FREAKING MONEY!
OH MAN, THIS IS GONNA BE GOOD, Y'ALL.
YUP.
I'VE BEEN A WHORE FOR A LONG TIME, BUT NEVER HAVE I FELT AS EXPLOITED AND DEGRADED AS I HAVE THE LAST TWO WEEKS.
LADIES, LADIES, YOUR MONEY IS SAFE. IT'S ALL INVESTED AND IF YOU PULL IT OUT NOW YOU'LL LOSE THE INTEREST.
BULLSHIT! WE WANT OUR MONEY RIGHT NOW. SO WHERE IS IT?!?
UM. . . I, UH. . . LOST IT AT THE DOG FIGHTS.

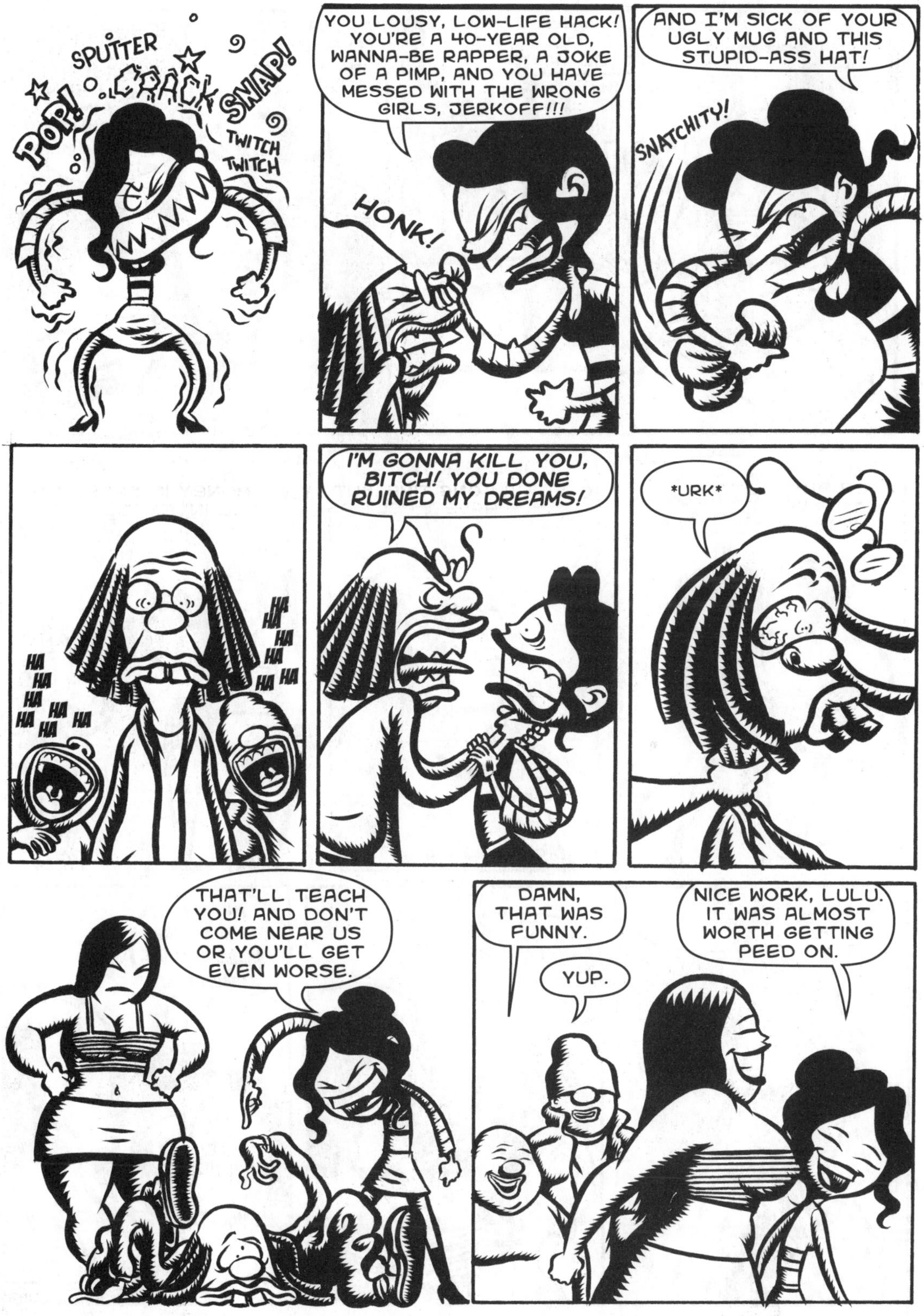
SPUTTER
POP!
CRACK
SNAP!
TWITCH
TWITCH
YOU LOUSY, LOW-LIFE HACK! YOU'RE A 40-YEAR OLD, WANNA-BE RAPPER, A JOKE OF A PIMP, AND YOU HAVE MESSED WITH THE WRONG GIRLS, JERKOFF!!!
HONK!
AND I'M SICK OF YOUR UGLY MUG AND THIS STUPID-ASS HAT!
SNATCHITY!
HA HA HA HA HA HA HA HA
HA HA HA HA HA HA
I'M GONNA KILL YOU, BITCH! YOU DONE RUINED MY DREAMS!
URK
THAT'LL TEACH YOU! AND DON'T COME NEAR US OR YOU'LL GET EVEN WORSE.
DAMN, THAT WAS FUNNY.
YUP.
NICE WORK, LULU. IT WAS ALMOST WORTH GETTING PEED ON.

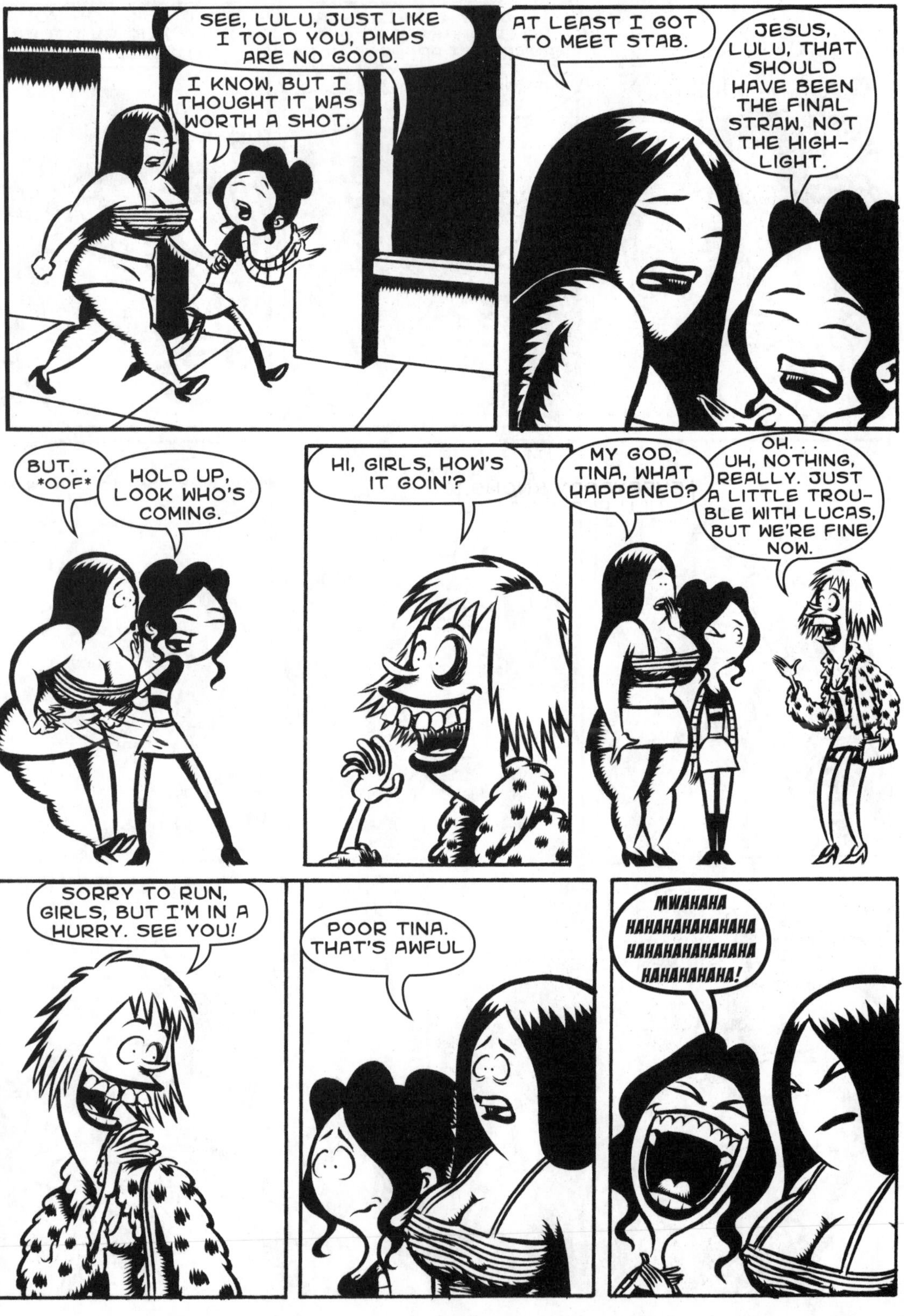
SEE, LULU, JUST LIKE I TOLD YOU, PIMPS ARE NO GOOD.
I KNOW, BUT I THOUGHT IT WAS WORTH A SHOT.
AT LEAST I GOT TO MEET STAB.
JESUS, LULU, THAT SHOULD HAVE BEEN THE FINAL STRAW, NOT THE HIGH-LIGHT.
BUT. . . *OOF*
HOLD UP, LOOK WHO'S COMING.
HI, GIRLS, HOW'S IT GOIN'?
MY GOD, TINA, WHAT HAPPENED?
OH. . . UH, NOTHING, REALLY. JUST A LITTLE TROU-BLE WITH LUCAS, BUT WE'RE FINE NOW.
SORRY TO RUN, GIRLS, BUT I'M IN A HURRY. SEE YOU!
POOR TINA. THAT'S AWFUL
MWAHAHA HAHAHAHAHAHAHA HAHAHAHAHAHAHA HAHAHAHAHA!

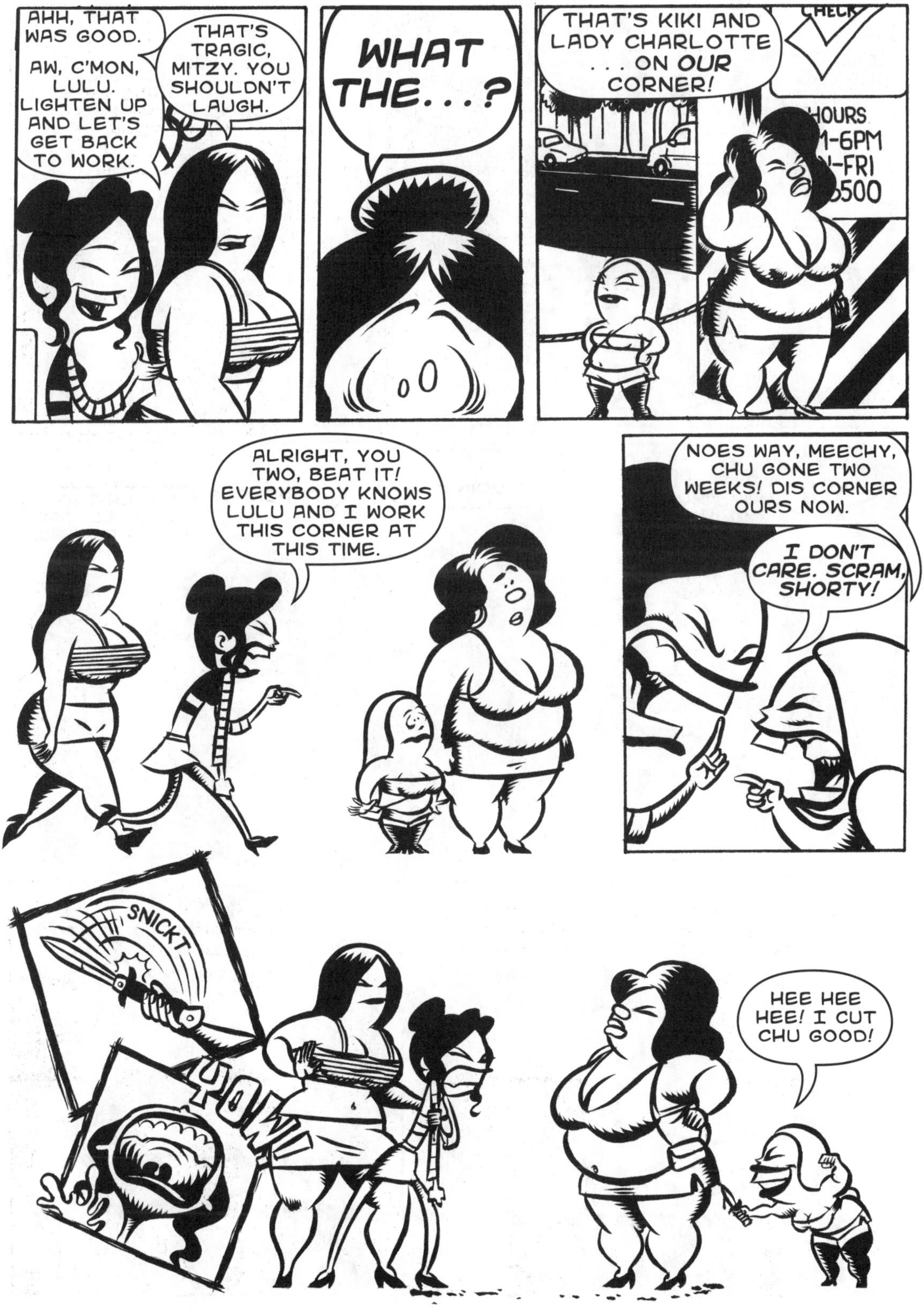
AHH, THAT WAS GOOD.
THAT'S TRAGIC, MITZY. YOU SHOULDN'T LAUGH.
AW, C'MON, LULU. LIGHTEN UP AND LET'S GET BACK TO WORK.
WHAT THE...?
THAT'S KIKI AND LADY CHARLOTTE . . . ON OUR CORNER!
CHECK
HOURS
1-6PM
-FRI
5500
ALRIGHT, YOU TWO, BEAT IT! EVERYBODY KNOWS LULU AND I WORK THIS CORNER AT THIS TIME.
NOES WAY, MEECHY, CHU GONE TWO WEEKS! DIS CORNER OURS NOW.
I DON'T CARE. SCRAM, SHORTY!
SNICKT
YOW!
HEE HEE HEE! I CUT CHU GOOD!

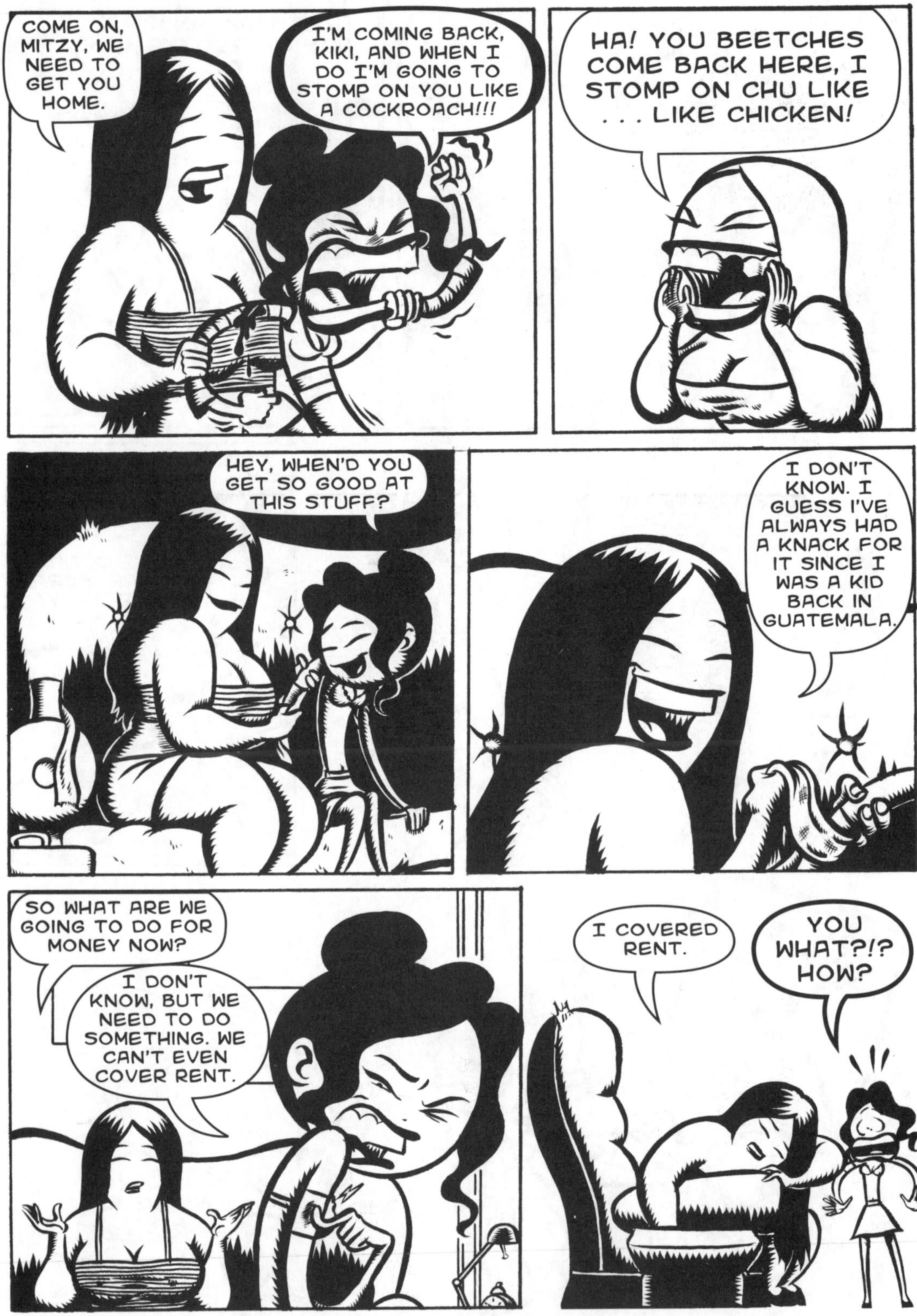
COME ON, MITZY, WE NEED TO GET YOU HOME.
I'M COMING BACK, KIKI, AND WHEN I DO I'M GOING TO STOMP ON YOU LIKE A COCKROACH!!!
HA! YOU BEETCHES COME BACK HERE, I STOMP ON CHU LIKE . . . LIKE CHICKEN!
HEY, WHEN'D YOU GET SO GOOD AT THIS STUFF?
I DON'T KNOW. I GUESS I'VE ALWAYS HAD A KNACK FOR IT SINCE I WAS A KID BACK IN GUATEMALA.
SO WHAT ARE WE GOING TO DO FOR MONEY NOW?
I DON'T KNOW, BUT WE NEED TO DO SOMETHING. WE CAN'T EVEN COVER RENT.
I COVERED RENT.
YOU WHAT?!? HOW?

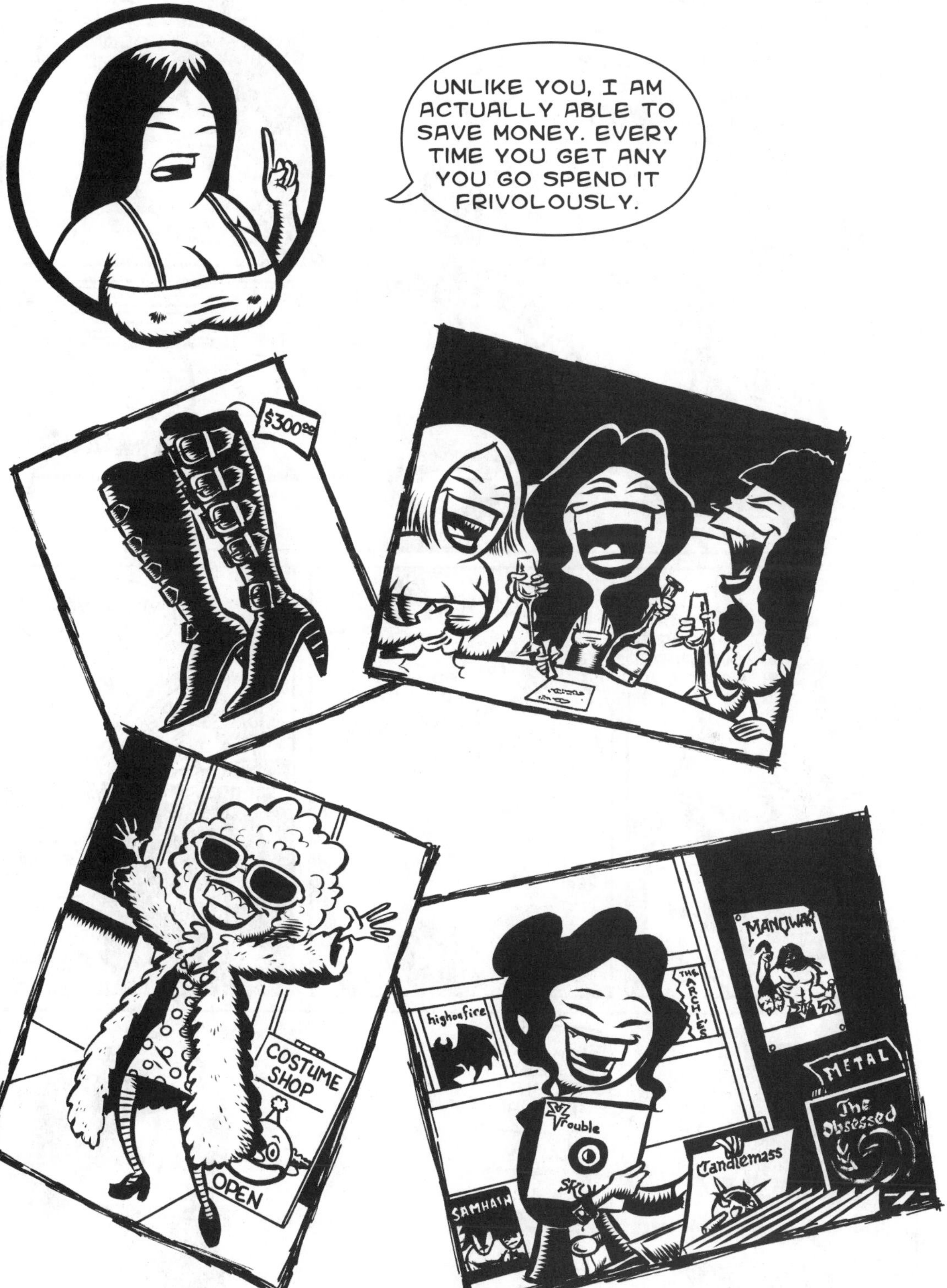
UNLIKE YOU, I AM ACTUALLY ABLE TO SAVE MONEY. EVERY TIME YOU GET ANY YOU GO SPEND IT FRIVOLOUSLY.
$300.00
COSTUME SHOP
OPEN
MANOWAR
THE ARCHIE'S
highonfire
METAL
The Obsessed
Trouble
Candlemass
SAMHAIN

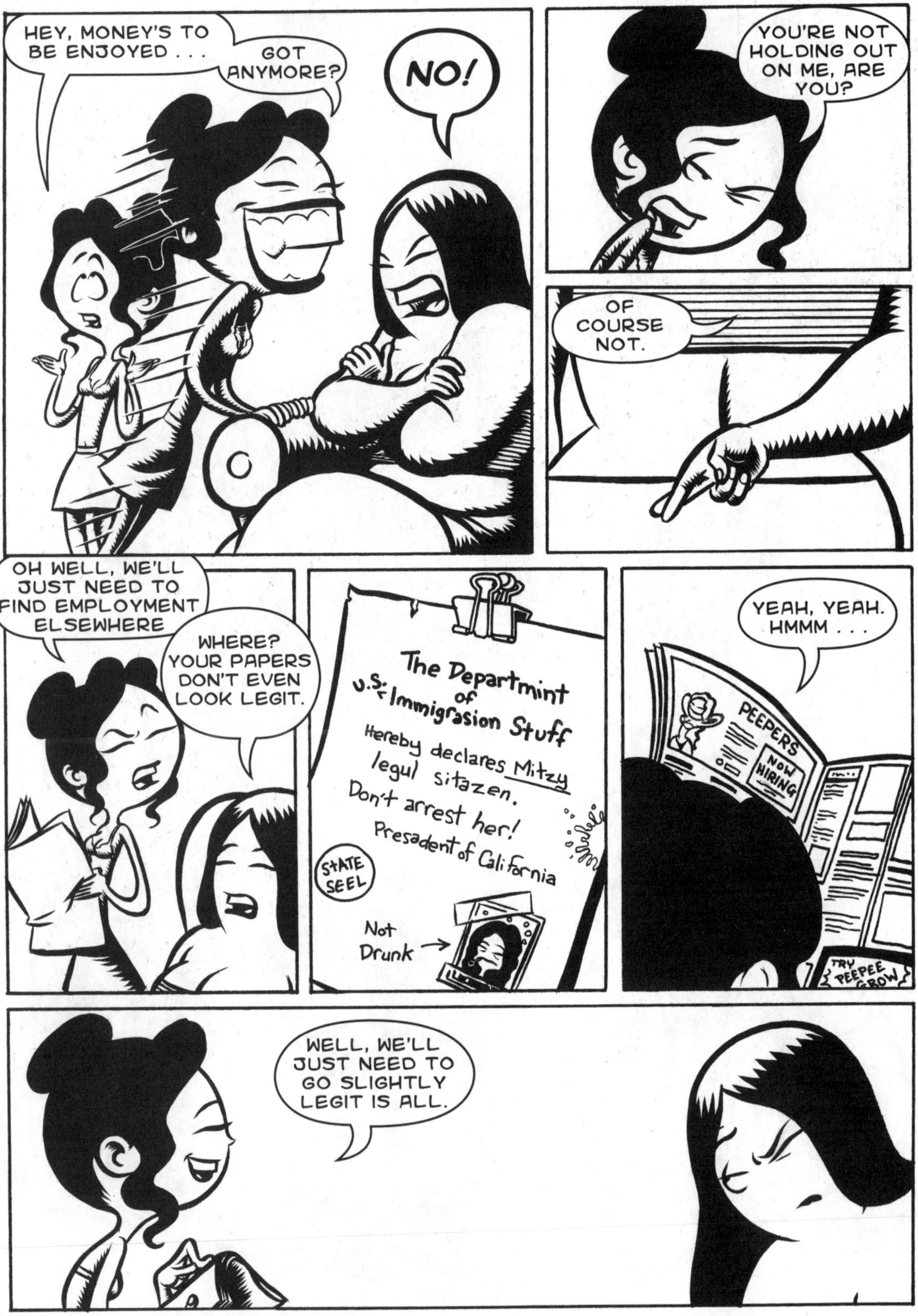
HEY, MONEY'S TO BE ENJOYED . . .
GOT ANYMORE?
NO!
YOU'RE NOT HOLDING OUT ON ME, ARE YOU?
OF COURSE NOT.
OH WELL, WE'LL JUST NEED TO FIND EMPLOYMENT ELSEWHERE
WHERE? YOUR PAPERS DON'T EVEN LOOK LEGIT.
The Departmint of U.S. & Immigrasion Stuff
Hereby declares Mitzy legul sitazen.
Don't arrest her!
Presadent of California
STATE SEEL
Not Drunk
YEAH, YEAH. HMMM . . .
PEEPERS
NOW HIRING
TRY PEEPEE GROW
WELL, WE'LL JUST NEED TO GO SLIGHTLY LEGIT IS ALL.

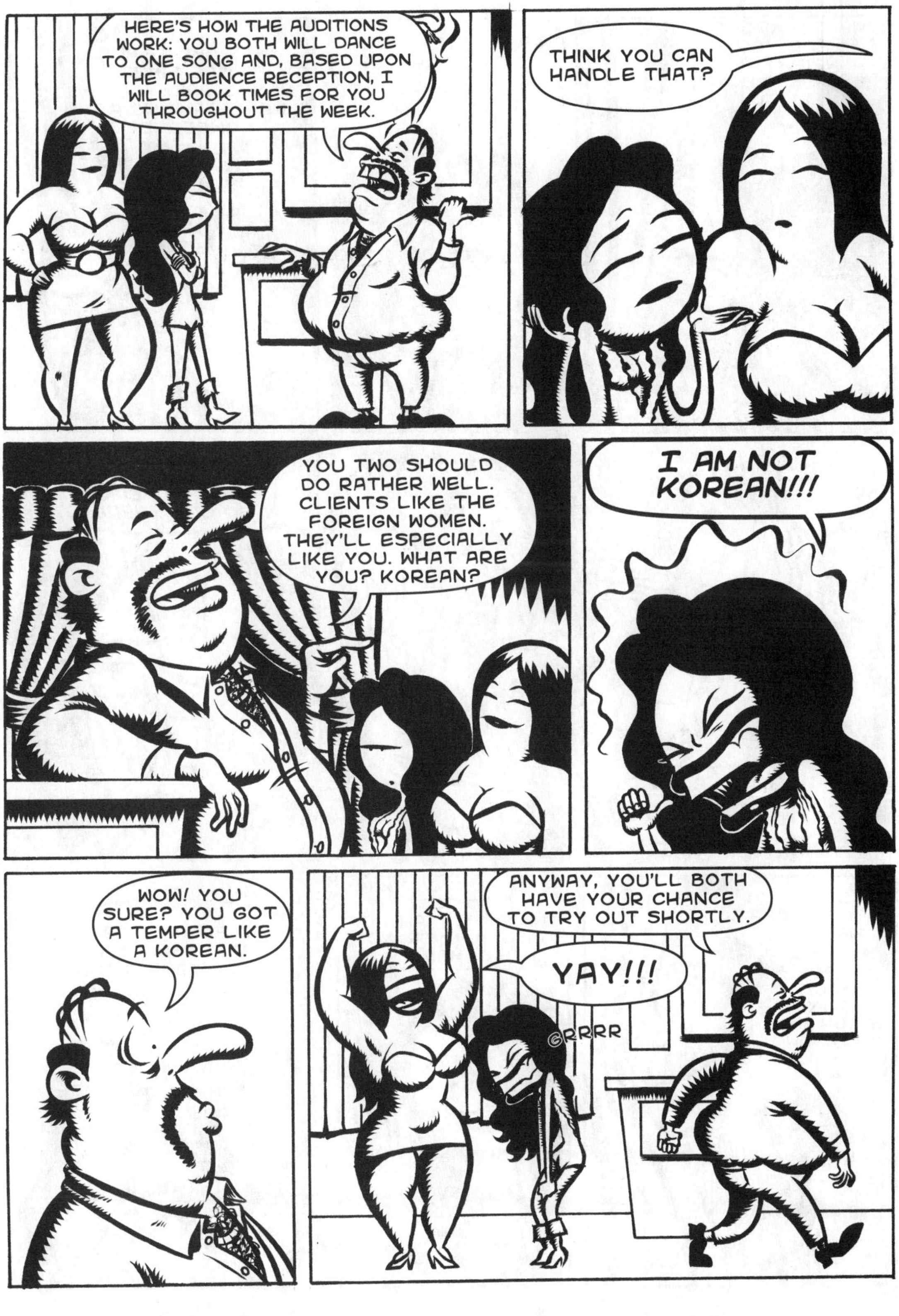
HERE'S HOW THE AUDITIONS WORK: YOU BOTH WILL DANCE TO ONE SONG AND, BASED UPON THE AUDIENCE RECEPTION, I WILL BOOK TIMES FOR YOU THROUGHOUT THE WEEK.
THINK YOU CAN HANDLE THAT?
YOU TWO SHOULD DO RATHER WELL. CLIENTS LIKE THE FOREIGN WOMEN. THEY'LL ESPECIALLY LIKE YOU. WHAT ARE YOU? KOREAN?
I AM NOT KOREAN!!!
WOW! YOU SURE? YOU GOT A TEMPER LIKE A KOREAN.
ANYWAY, YOU'LL BOTH HAVE YOUR CHANCE TO TRY OUT SHORTLY.
YAY!!!
GRRRR

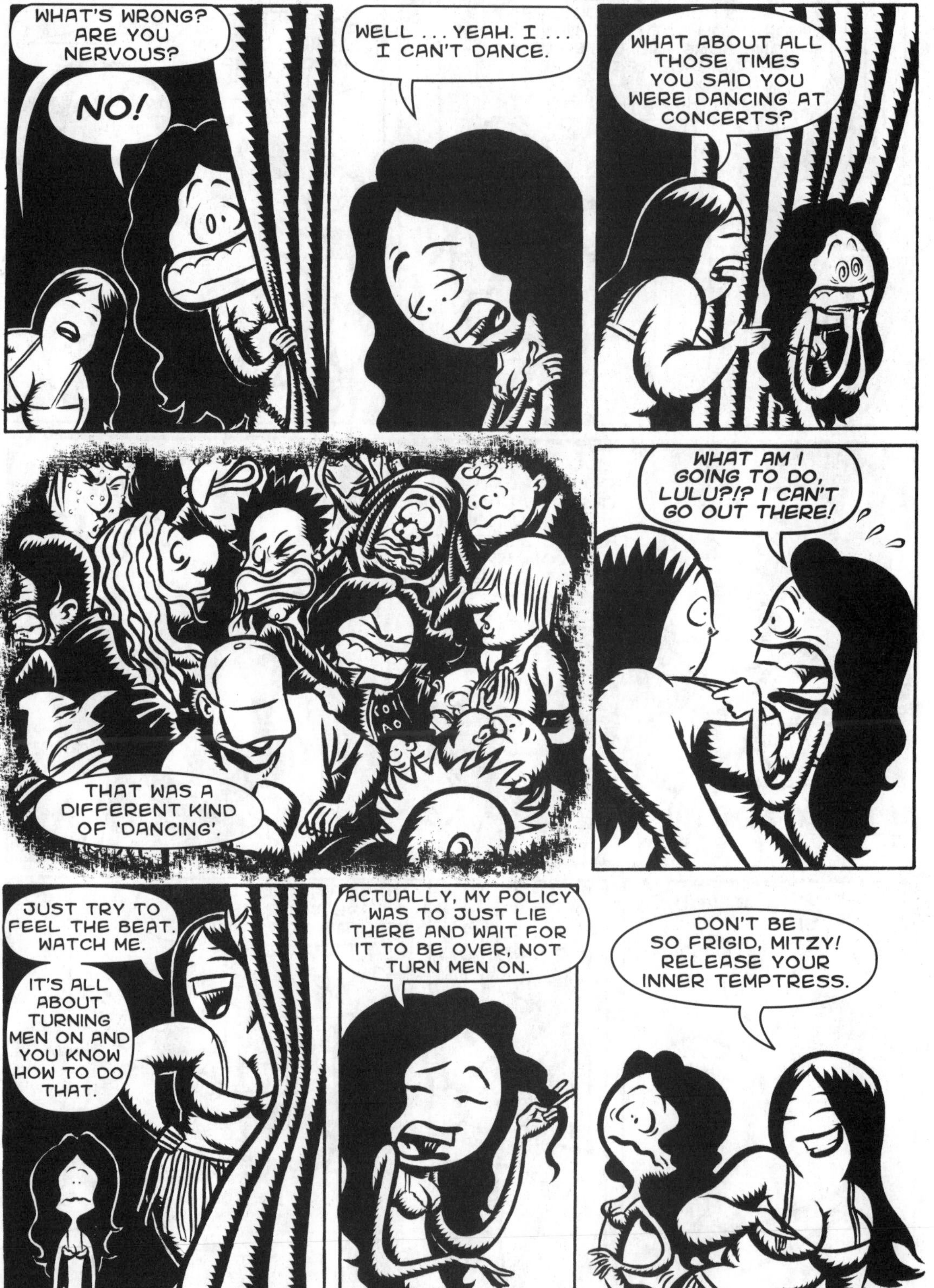
WHAT'S WRONG? ARE YOU NERVOUS?
NO!
WELL . . . YEAH. I . . . I CAN'T DANCE.
WHAT ABOUT ALL THOSE TIMES YOU SAID YOU WERE DANCING AT CONCERTS?
THAT WAS A DIFFERENT KIND OF 'DANCING'.
WHAT AM I GOING TO DO, LULU?!? I CAN'T GO OUT THERE!
JUST TRY TO FEEL THE BEAT. WATCH ME.
IT'S ALL ABOUT TURNING MEN ON AND YOU KNOW HOW TO DO THAT.
ACTUALLY, MY POLICY WAS TO JUST LIE THERE AND WAIT FOR IT TO BE OVER, NOT TURN MEN ON.
DON'T BE SO FRIGID, MITZY! RELEASE YOUR INNER TEMPTRESS.

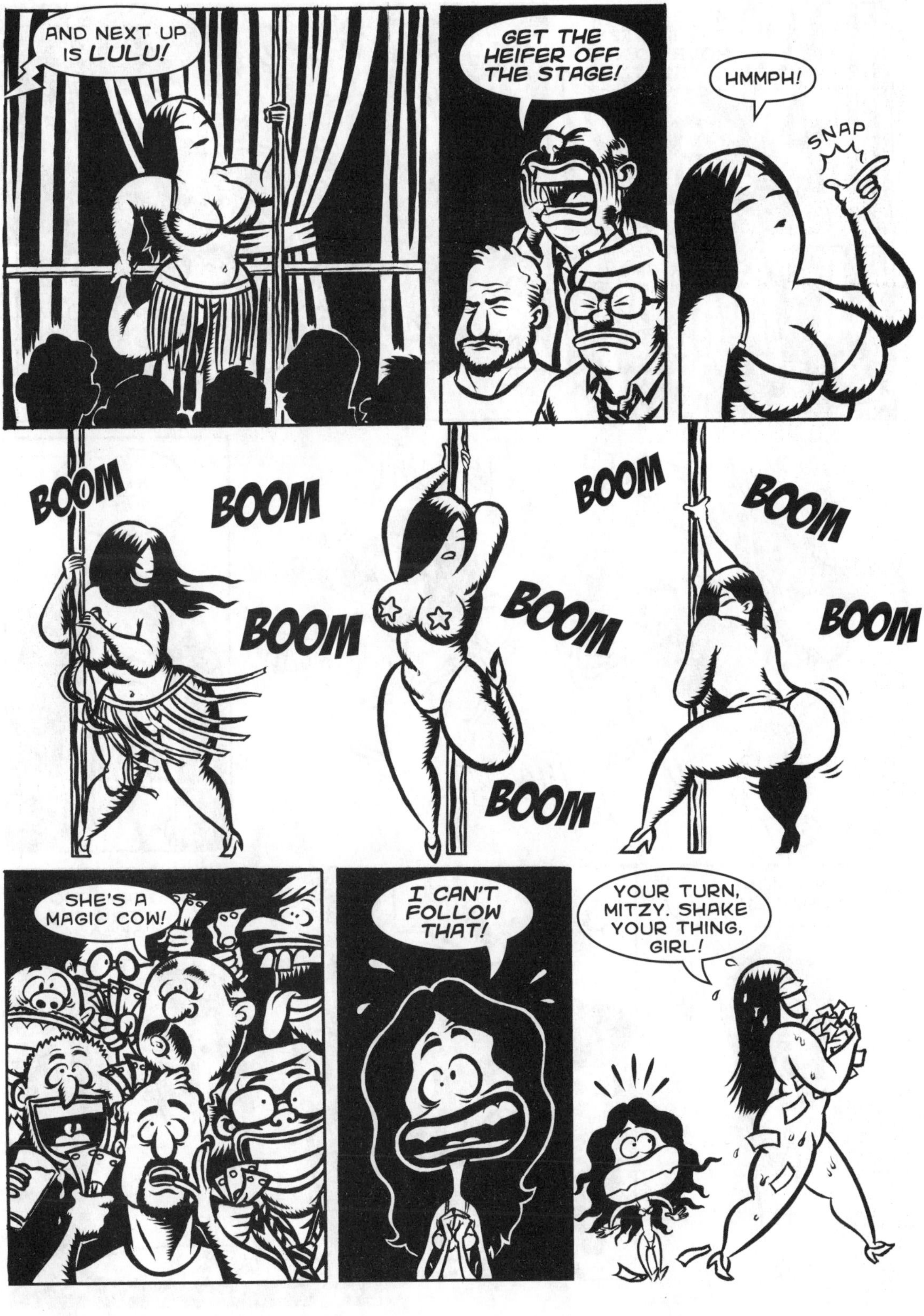
AND NEXT UP IS LULU!
GET THE HEIFER OFF THE STAGE!
HMMPH!
SNAP
BOOM
BOOM
BOOM
BOOM
BOOM
BOOM
BOOM
BOOM
SHE'S A MAGIC COW!
I CAN'T FOLLOW THAT!
YOUR TURN, MITZY. SHAKE YOUR THING, GIRL!

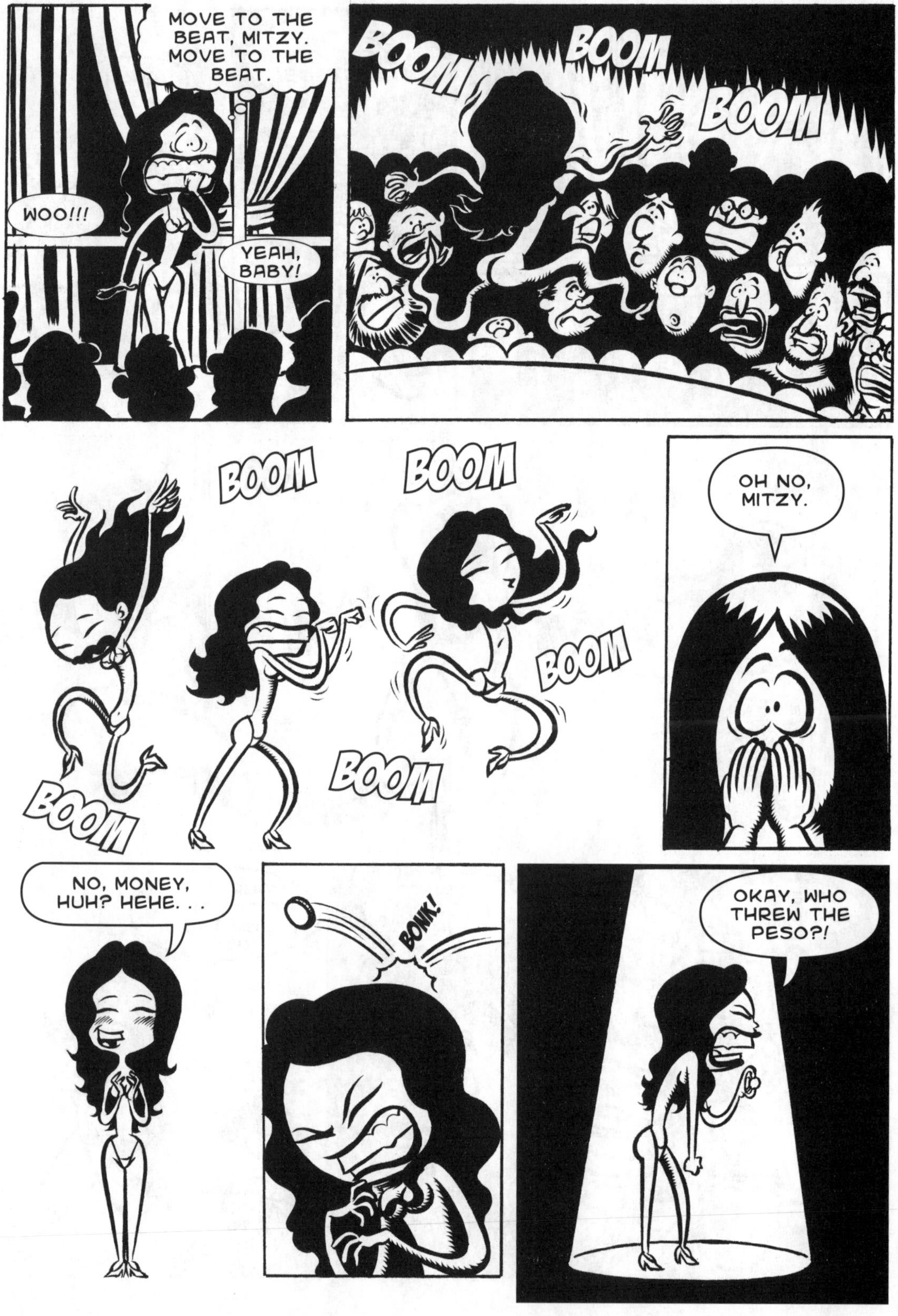
MOVE TO THE BEAT, MITZY. MOVE TO THE BEAT.
WOO!!!
YEAH, BABY!
BOOM
BOOM
BOOM
BOOM
BOOM
BOOM
BOOM
BOOM
OH NO, MITZY.
NO, MONEY, HUH? HEHE. . .
BONK!
OKAY, WHO THREW THE PESO?!

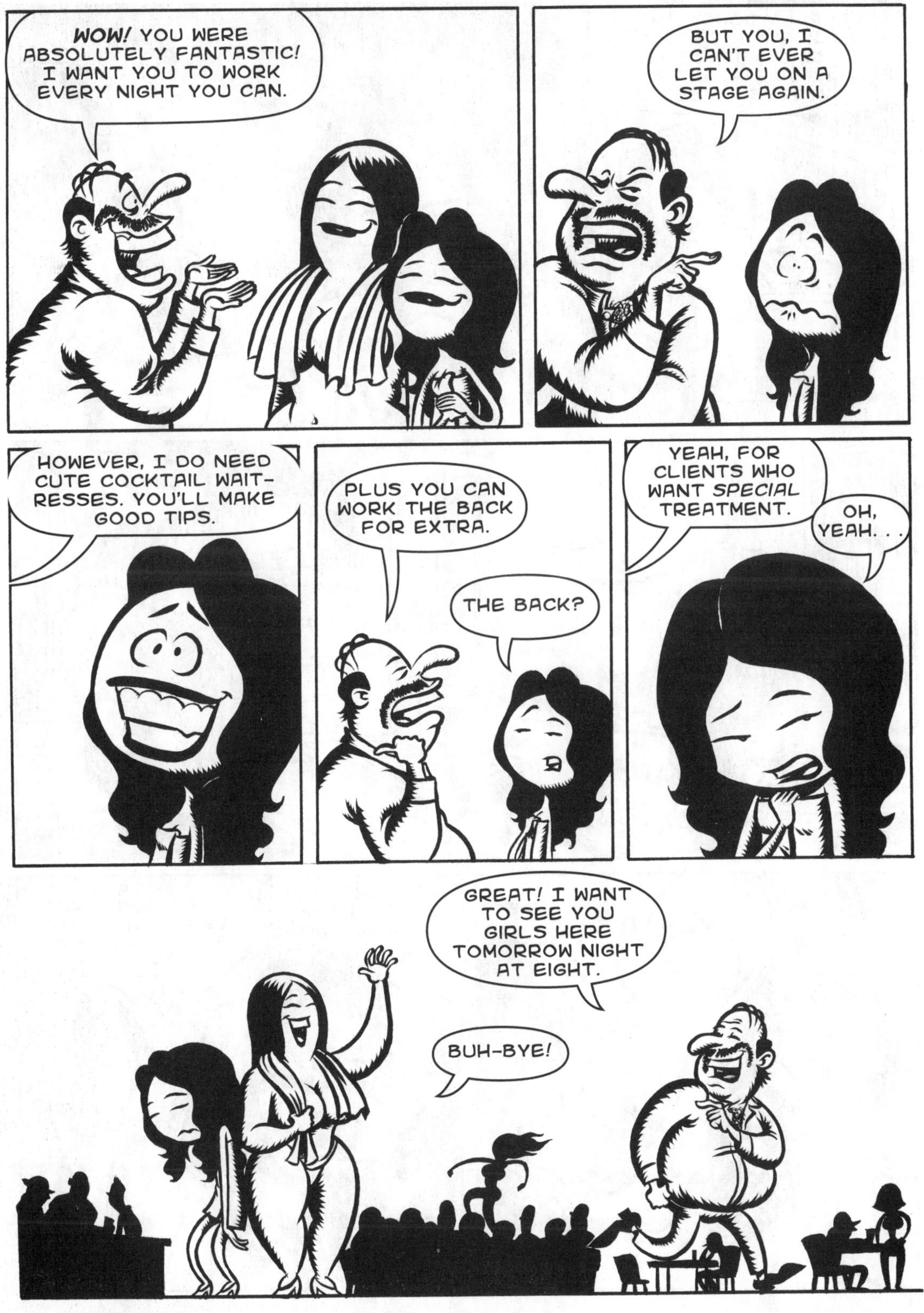
WOW! YOU WERE ABSOLUTELY FANTASTIC! I WANT YOU TO WORK EVERY NIGHT YOU CAN.
BUT YOU, I CAN'T EVER LET YOU ON A STAGE AGAIN.
HOWEVER, I DO NEED CUTE COCKTAIL WAIT-RESSES. YOU'LL MAKE GOOD TIPS.
PLUS YOU CAN WORK THE BACK FOR EXTRA.
THE BACK?
YEAH, FOR CLIENTS WHO WANT SPECIAL TREATMENT.
OH, YEAH. . .
GREAT! I WANT TO SEE YOU GIRLS HERE TOMORROW NIGHT AT EIGHT.
BUH-BYE!

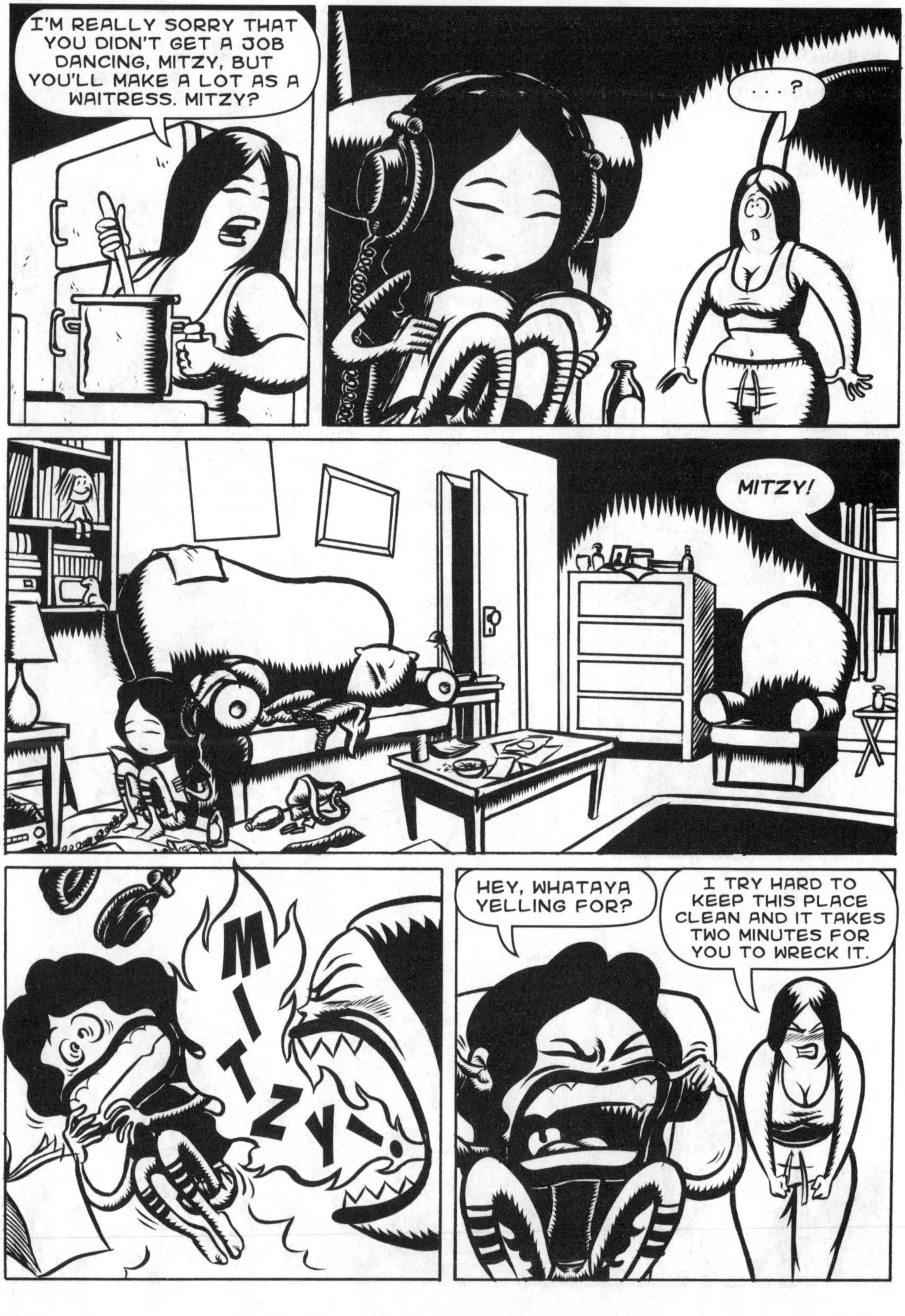
I'M REALLY SORRY THAT YOU DIDN'T GET A JOB DANCING, MITZY, BUT YOU'LL MAKE A LOT AS A WAITRESS. MITZY?
. . . ?
MITZY!
MITZY!
HEY, WHATAYA YELLING FOR?
I TRY HARD TO KEEP THIS PLACE CLEAN AND IT TAKES TWO MINUTES FOR YOU TO WRECK IT.

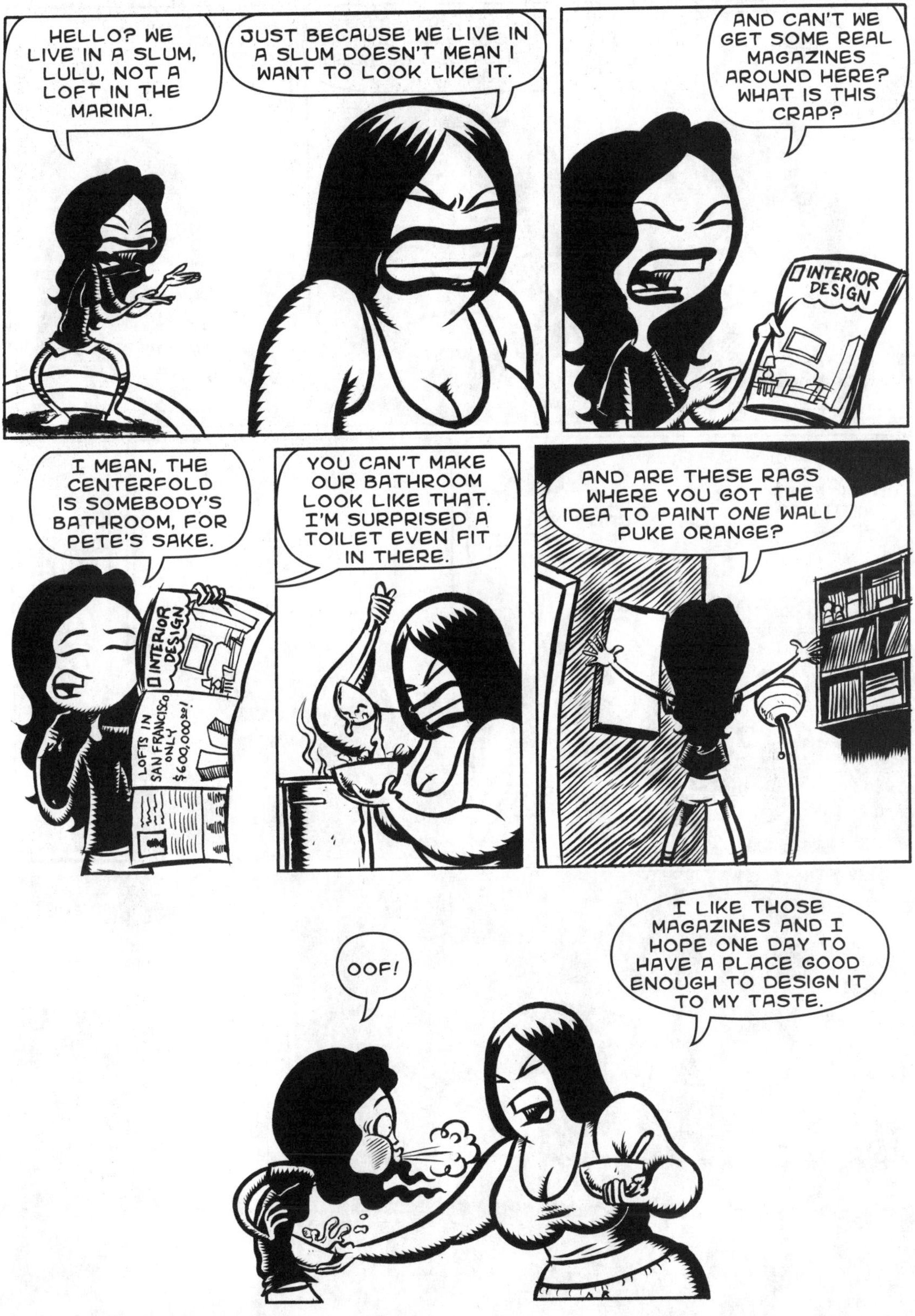
HELLO? WE LIVE IN A SLUM, LULU, NOT A LOFT IN THE MARINA.
JUST BECAUSE WE LIVE IN A SLUM DOESN'T MEAN I WANT TO LOOK LIKE IT.
AND CAN'T WE GET SOME REAL MAGAZINES AROUND HERE? WHAT IS THIS CRAP?
INTERIOR DESIGN
I MEAN, THE CENTERFOLD IS SOMEBODY'S BATHROOM, FOR PETE'S SAKE.
INTERIOR DESIGN
LOFTS IN SAN FRANCISCO ONLY $600,000.00!
YOU CAN'T MAKE OUR BATHROOM LOOK LIKE THAT. I'M SURPRISED A TOILET EVEN FIT IN THERE.
AND ARE THESE RAGS WHERE YOU GOT THE IDEA TO PAINT ONE WALL PUKE ORANGE?
I LIKE THOSE MAGAZINES AND I HOPE ONE DAY TO HAVE A PLACE GOOD ENOUGH TO DESIGN IT TO MY TASTE.
OOF!

SPEAKING OF TASTE. . .

WOULD IT KILL YOU TO COOK WITH SOME OTHER SPICES BESIDES GARLIC?

ALL I'M SAYIN' IS, YA KNOW, MAYBE NOT COOK EVERYTHING WITH GARLIC. . .

CAN'T YOU APPRECIATE ME JUST ONCE?

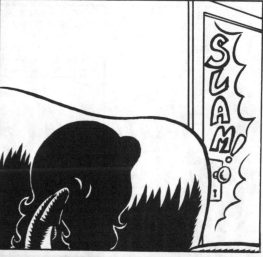

SLAM!

SIGH

UM. . . LULU? I HAVE TO USE THE BATHROOM.

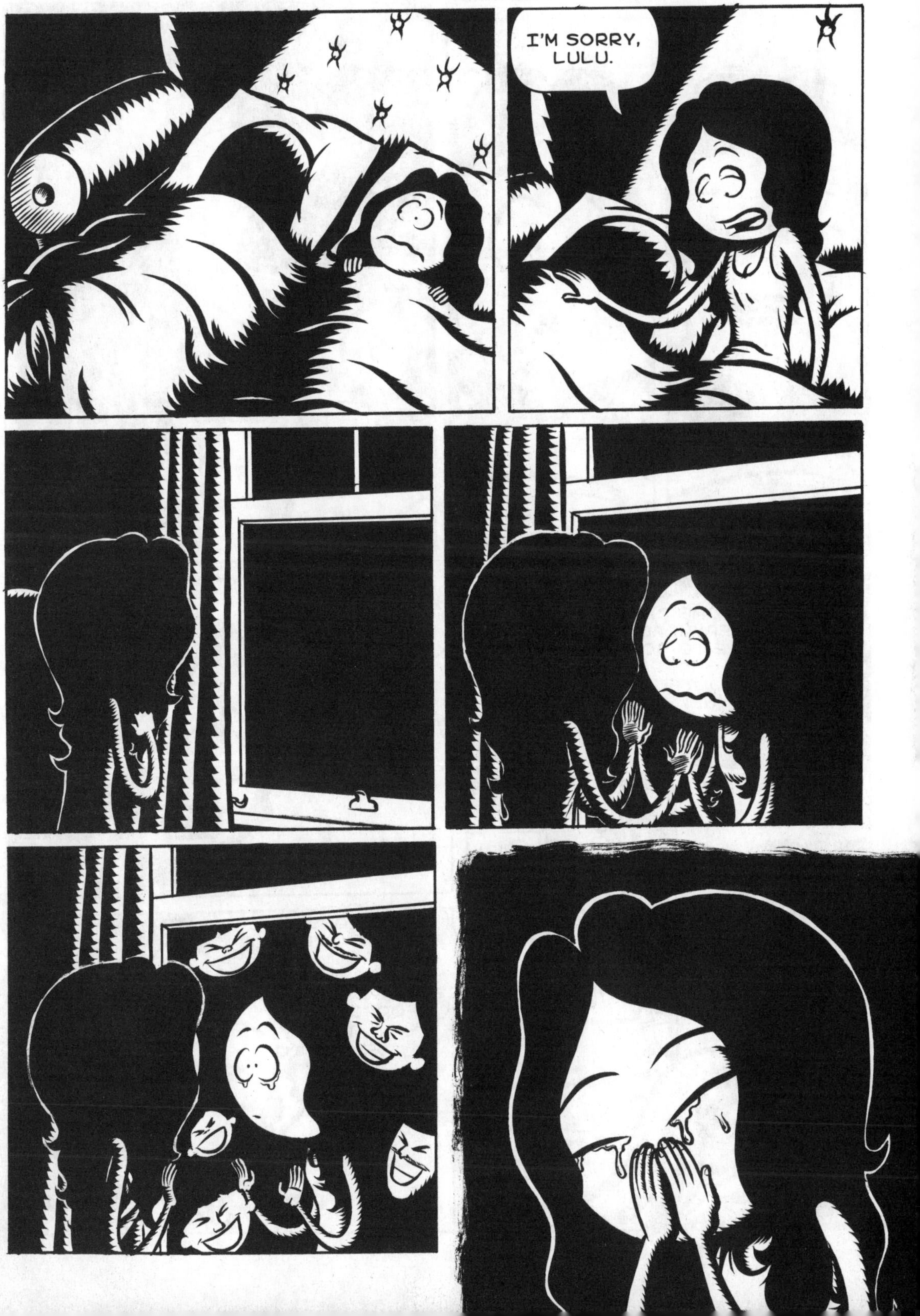
I'M SORRY, LULU.

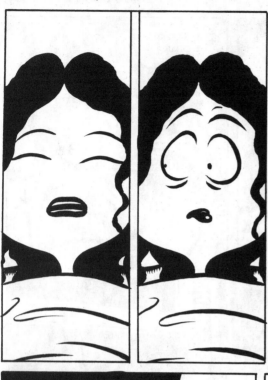

LULU?

COME ON, SLEEPYHEAD, WE HAVE TO GO DO SOME SHOPPING. I NEED OUTFITS FOR MY NEW JOB.

HUH? . . . OH, YEAH, SURE.

THAT'S ONE THING I LIKE ABOUT LULU, SHE EASILY FORGIVES AND FORGETS.

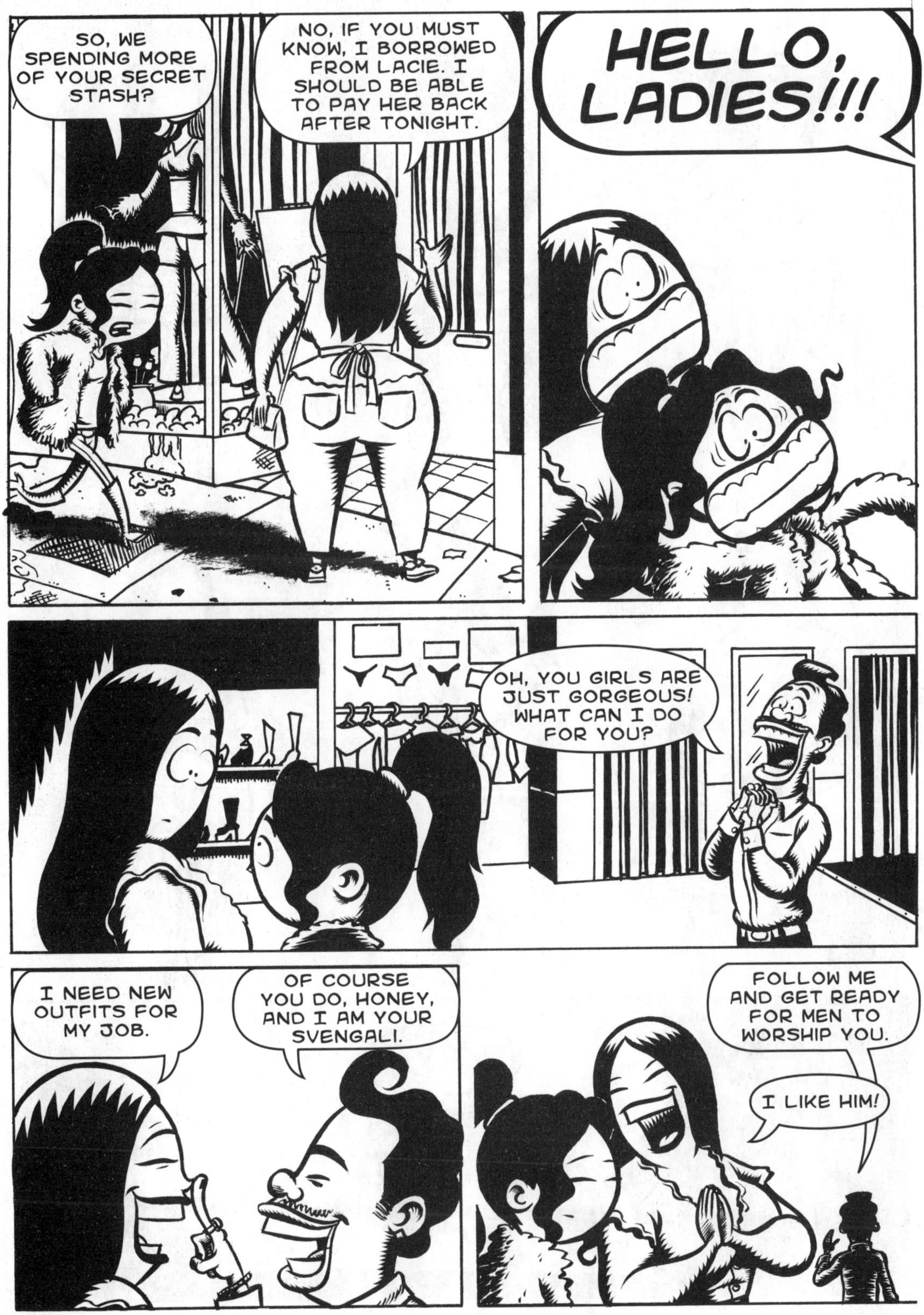
SO, WE SPENDING MORE OF YOUR SECRET STASH?
NO, IF YOU MUST KNOW, I BORROWED FROM LACIE. I SHOULD BE ABLE TO PAY HER BACK AFTER TONIGHT.
HELLO, LADIES!!!
OH, YOU GIRLS ARE JUST GORGEOUS! WHAT CAN I DO FOR YOU?
I NEED NEW OUTFITS FOR MY JOB.
OF COURSE YOU DO, HONEY, AND I AM YOUR SVENGALI.
FOLLOW ME AND GET READY FOR MEN TO WORSHIP YOU.
I LIKE HIM!

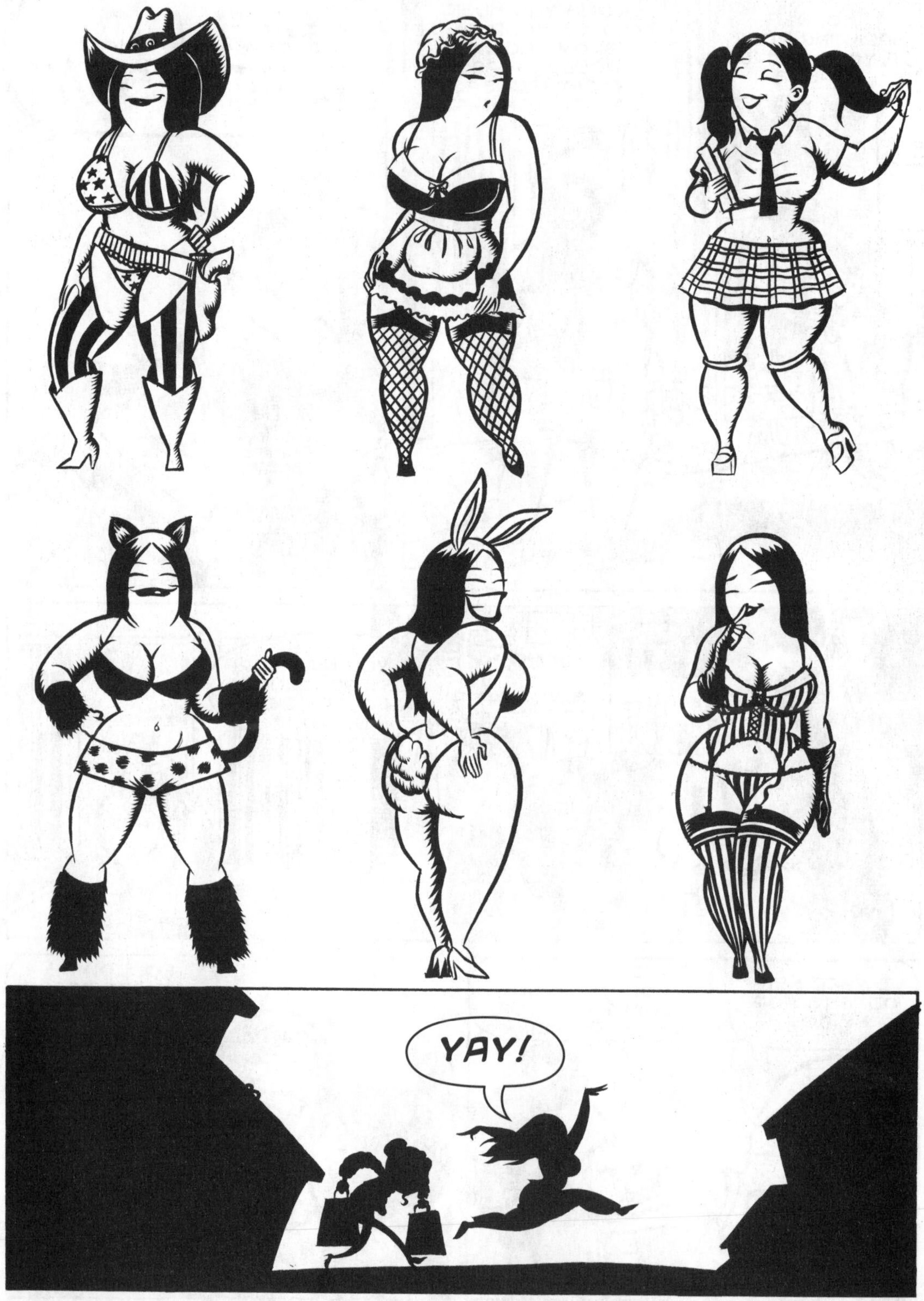
YAY!

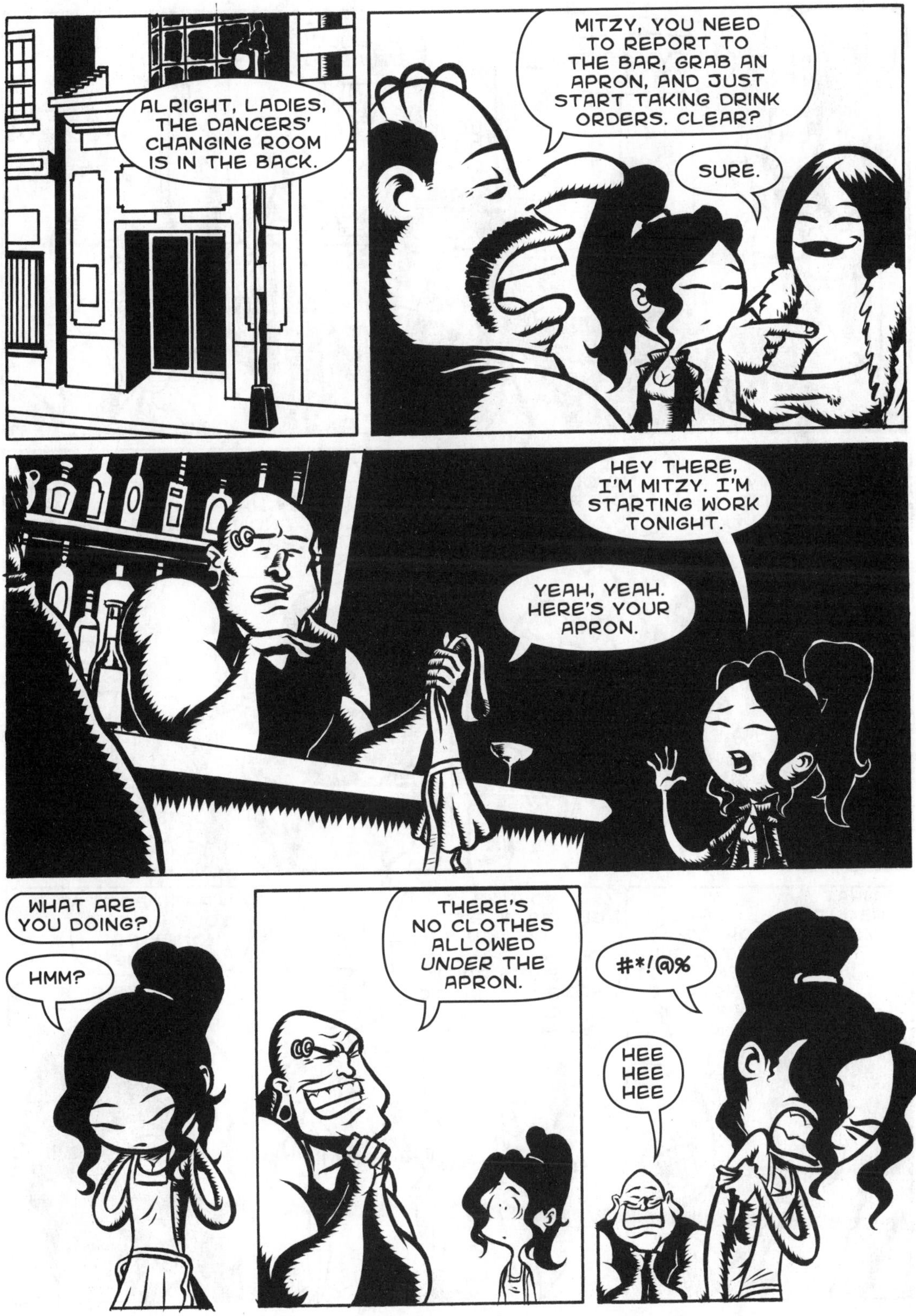
ALRIGHT, LADIES, THE DANCERS' CHANGING ROOM IS IN THE BACK.
MITZY, YOU NEED TO REPORT TO THE BAR, GRAB AN APRON, AND JUST START TAKING DRINK ORDERS. CLEAR?
SURE.
HEY THERE, I'M MITZY. I'M STARTING WORK TONIGHT.
YEAH, YEAH. HERE'S YOUR APRON.
WHAT ARE YOU DOING?
HMM?
THERE'S NO CLOTHES ALLOWED *UNDER* THE APRON.
#*!@%
HEE HEE HEE

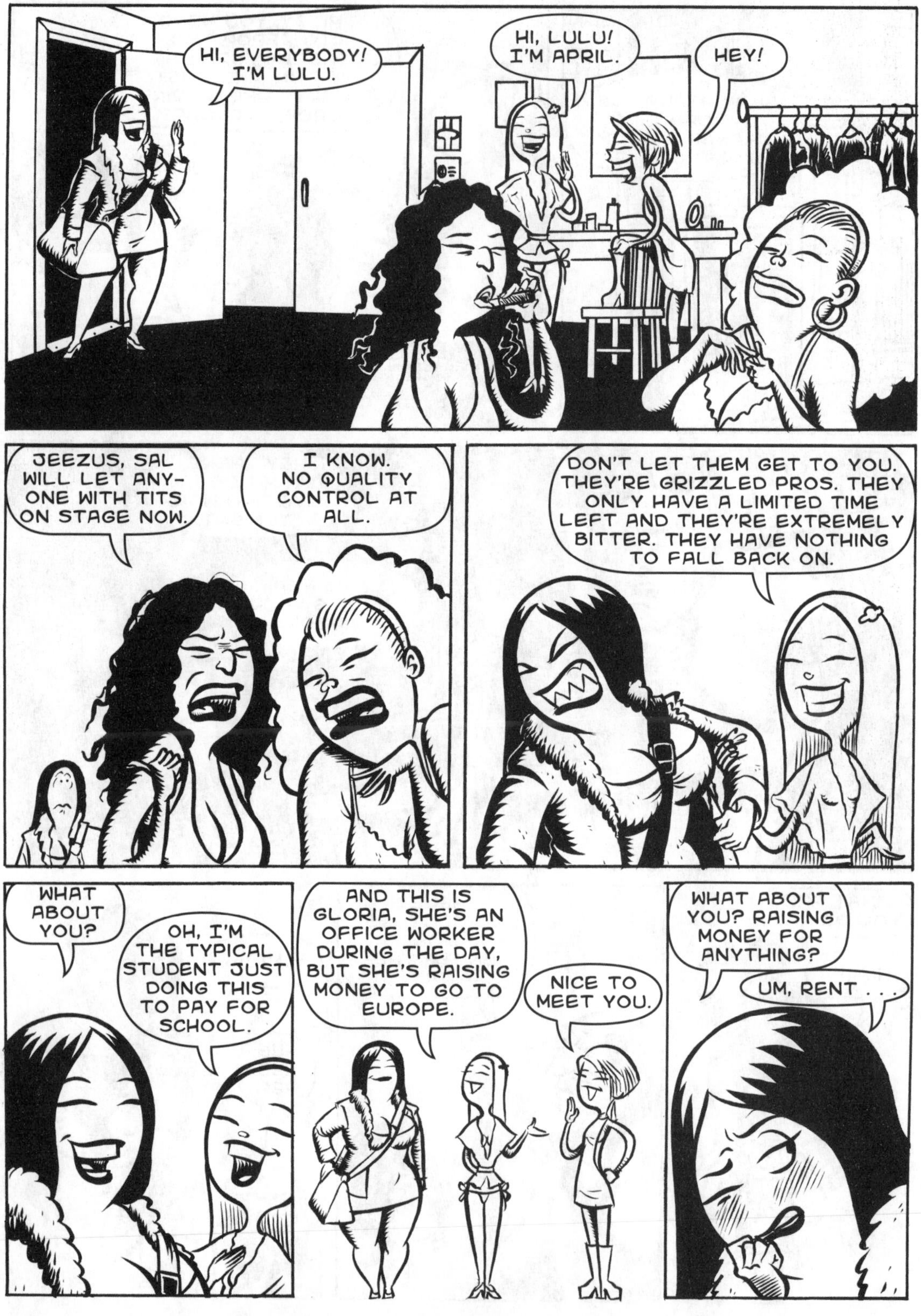
HI, EVERYBODY! I'M LULU.
HI, LULU! I'M APRIL.
HEY!
JEEZUS, SAL WILL LET ANY-ONE WITH TITS ON STAGE NOW.
I KNOW. NO QUALITY CONTROL AT ALL.
DON'T LET THEM GET TO YOU. THEY'RE GRIZZLED PROS. THEY ONLY HAVE A LIMITED TIME LEFT AND THEY'RE EXTREMELY BITTER. THEY HAVE NOTHING TO FALL BACK ON.
WHAT ABOUT YOU?
OH, I'M THE TYPICAL STUDENT JUST DOING THIS TO PAY FOR SCHOOL.
AND THIS IS GLORIA, SHE'S AN OFFICE WORKER DURING THE DAY, BUT SHE'S RAISING MONEY TO GO TO EUROPE.
NICE TO MEET YOU.
WHAT ABOUT YOU? RAISING MONEY FOR ANYTHING?
UM, RENT . . .

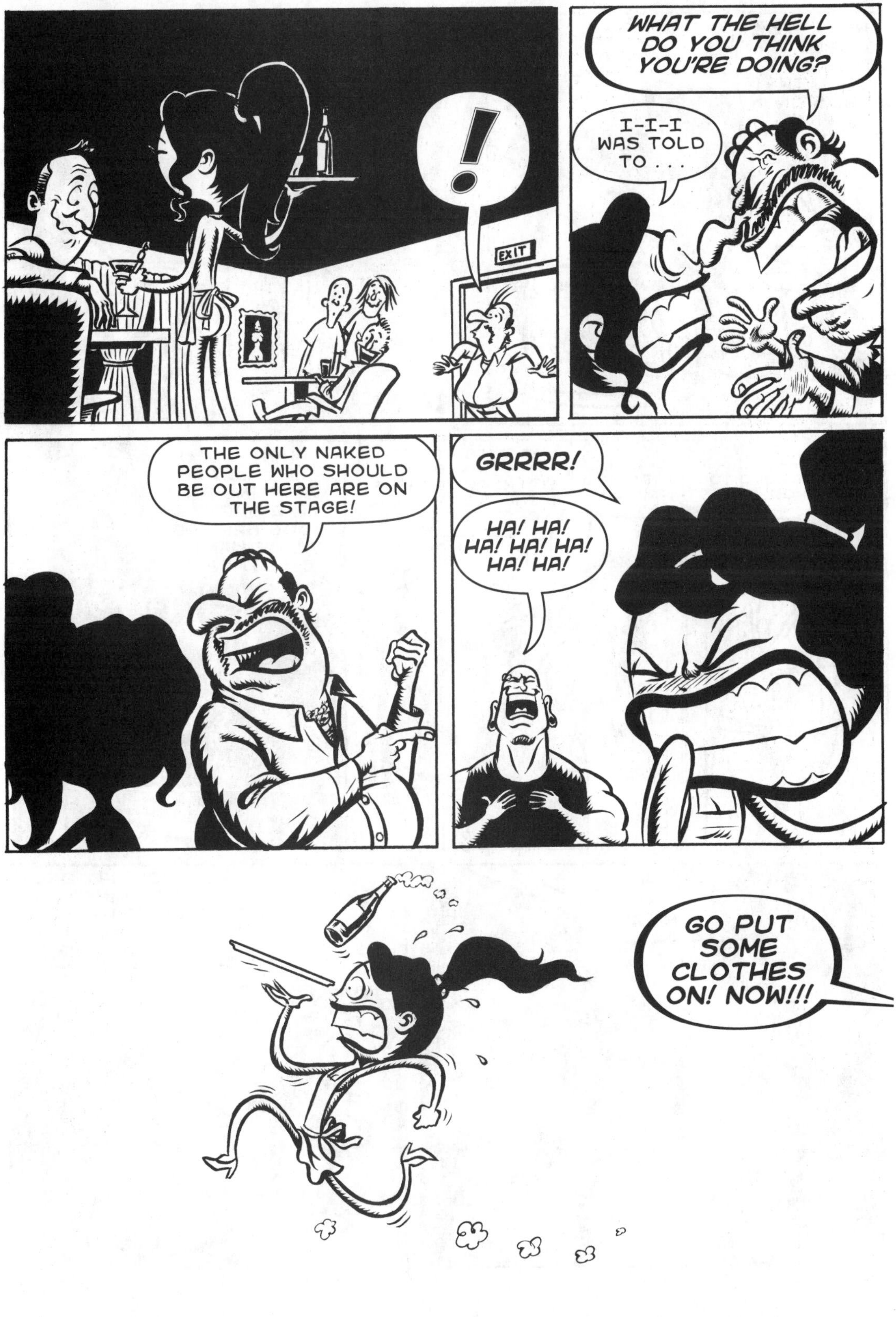
!
EXIT
WHAT THE HELL DO YOU THINK YOU'RE DOING?
I-I-I WAS TOLD TO . . .
THE ONLY NAKED PEOPLE WHO SHOULD BE OUT HERE ARE ON THE STAGE!
GRRRR!
HA! HA! HA! HA! HA! HA! HA!
GO PUT SOME CLOTHES ON! NOW!!!

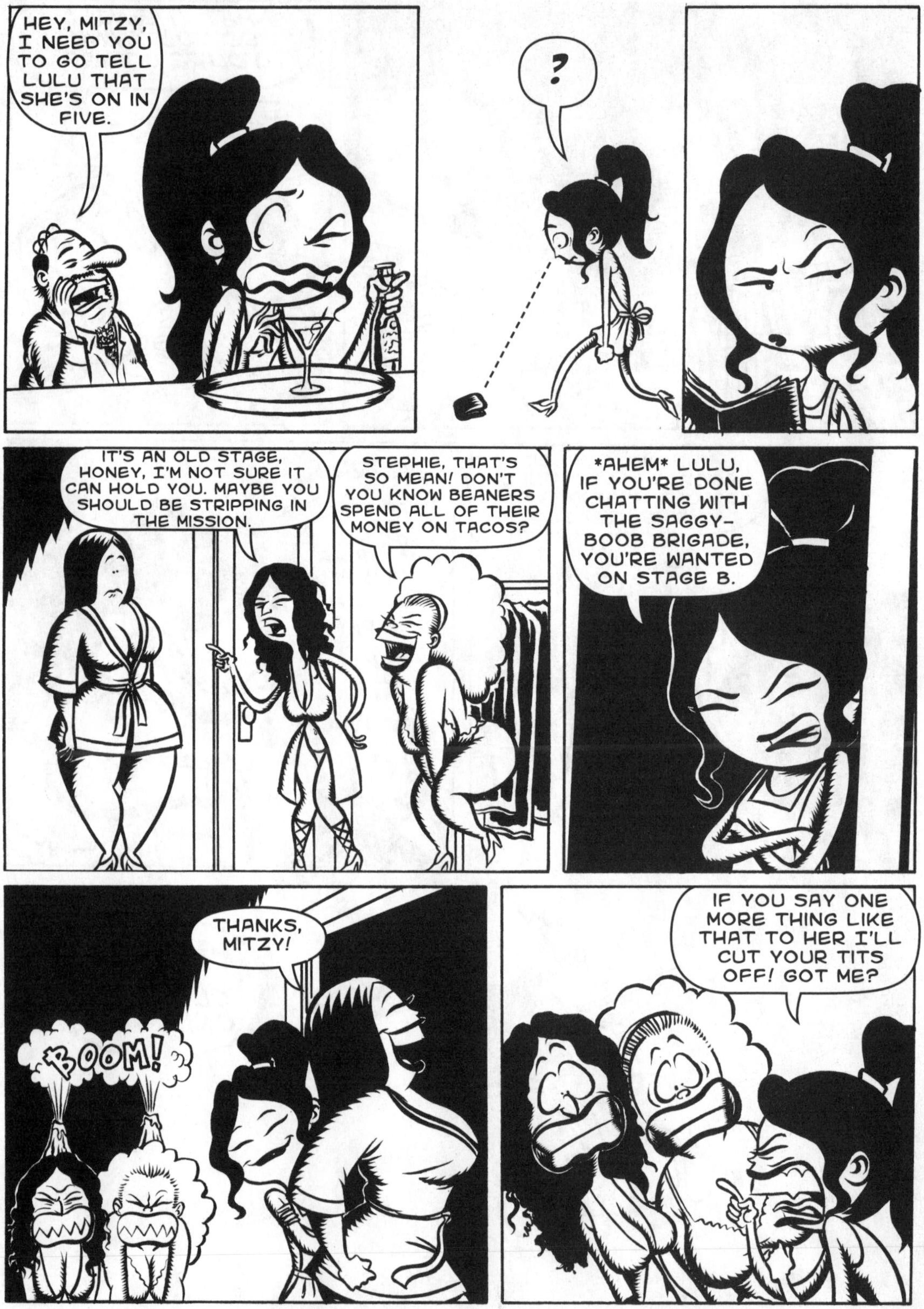
HEY, MITZY, I NEED YOU TO GO TELL LULU THAT SHE'S ON IN FIVE.
?
IT'S AN OLD STAGE, HONEY, I'M NOT SURE IT CAN HOLD YOU. MAYBE YOU SHOULD BE STRIPPING IN THE MISSION.
STEPHIE, THAT'S SO MEAN! DON'T YOU KNOW BEANERS SPEND ALL OF THEIR MONEY ON TACOS?
AHEM LULU, IF YOU'RE DONE CHATTING WITH THE SAGGY-BOOB BRIGADE, YOU'RE WANTED ON STAGE B.
THANKS, MITZY!
BOOM!
IF YOU SAY ONE MORE THING LIKE THAT TO HER I'LL CUT YOUR TITS OFF! GOT ME?

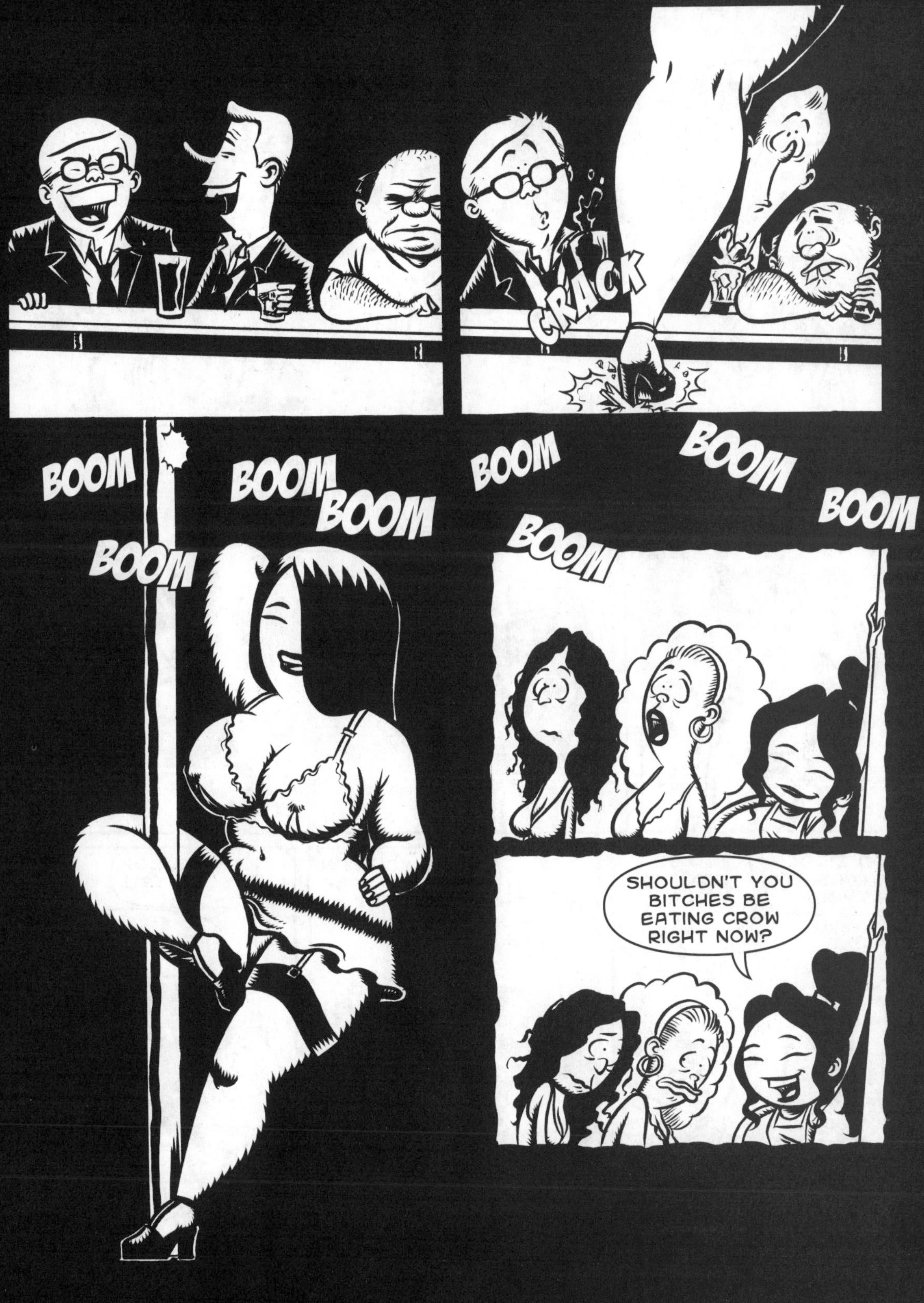
CRACK
BOOM
BOOM
BOOM
BOOM
BOOM
BOOM
BOOM
BOOM
SHOULDN'T YOU BITCHES BE EATING CROW RIGHT NOW?

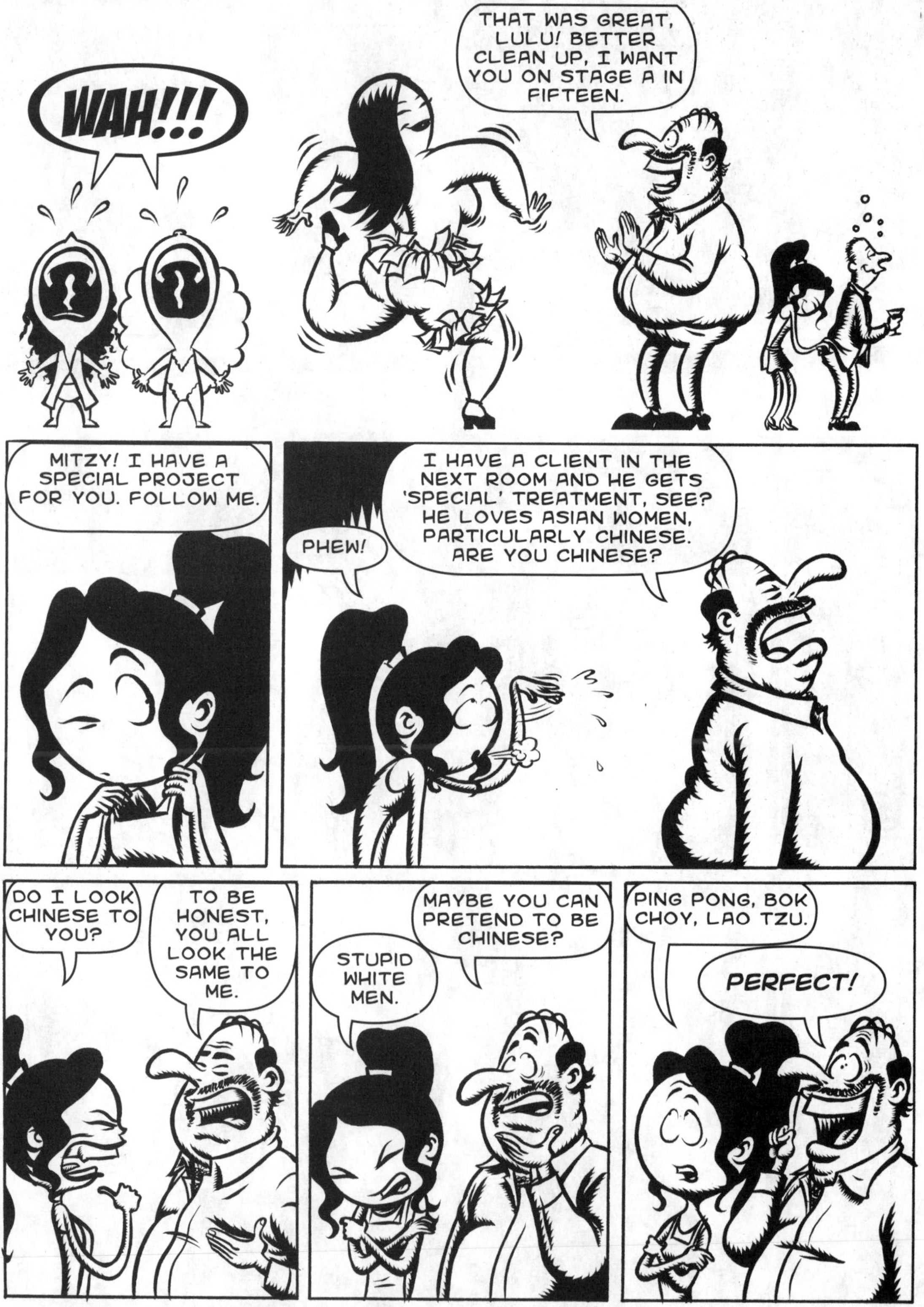
WAH!!!
THAT WAS GREAT, LULU! BETTER CLEAN UP, I WANT YOU ON STAGE A IN FIFTEEN.
MITZY! I HAVE A SPECIAL PROJECT FOR YOU. FOLLOW ME.
I HAVE A CLIENT IN THE NEXT ROOM AND HE GETS 'SPECIAL' TREATMENT, SEE? HE LOVES ASIAN WOMEN, PARTICULARLY CHINESE. ARE YOU CHINESE?
PHEW!
DO I LOOK CHINESE TO YOU?
TO BE HONEST, YOU ALL LOOK THE SAME TO ME.
MAYBE YOU CAN PRETEND TO BE CHINESE?
STUPID WHITE MEN.
PING PONG, BOK CHOY, LAO TZU.
PERFECT!

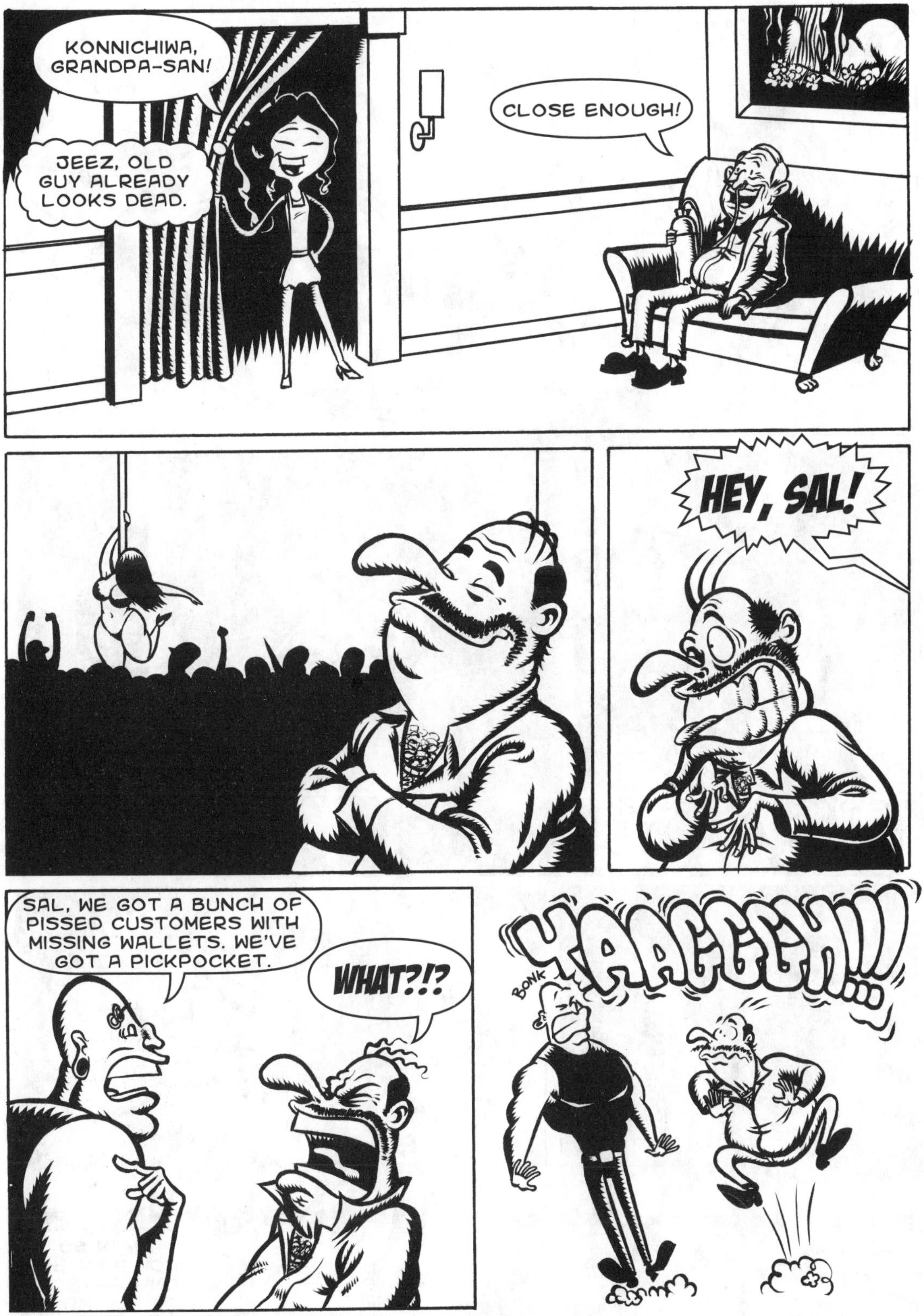
KONNICHIWA, GRANDPA-SAN!
JEEZ, OLD GUY ALREADY LOOKS DEAD.
CLOSE ENOUGH!
HEY, SAL!
SAL, WE GOT A BUNCH OF PISSED CUSTOMERS WITH MISSING WALLETS. WE'VE GOT A PICKPOCKET.
WHAT?!?
BONK
YAAGGGH!!!

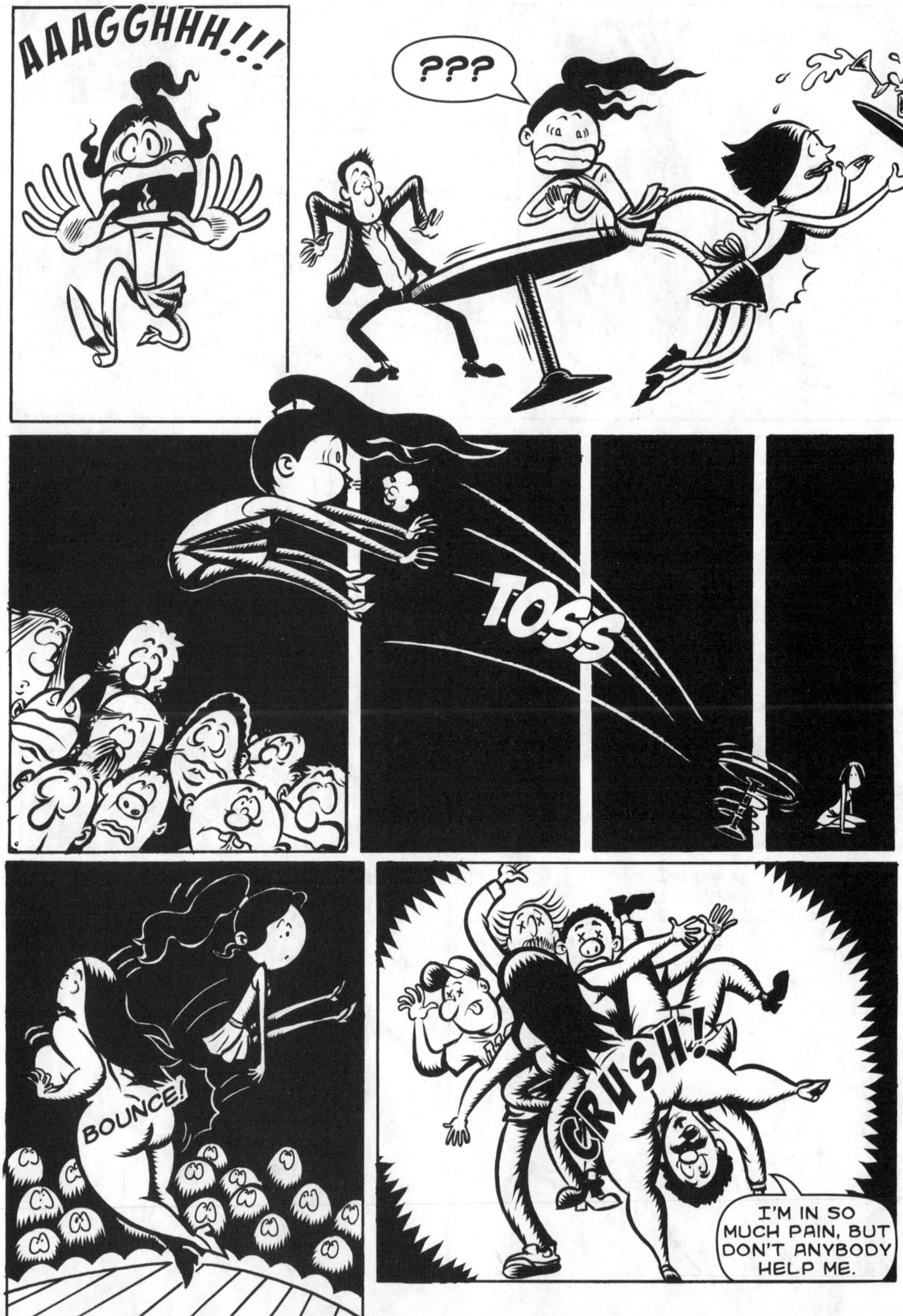
AAAGGHHH!!!
???
TOSS
BOUNCE!
CRUSH!
I'M IN SO MUCH PAIN, BUT DON'T ANYBODY HELP ME.

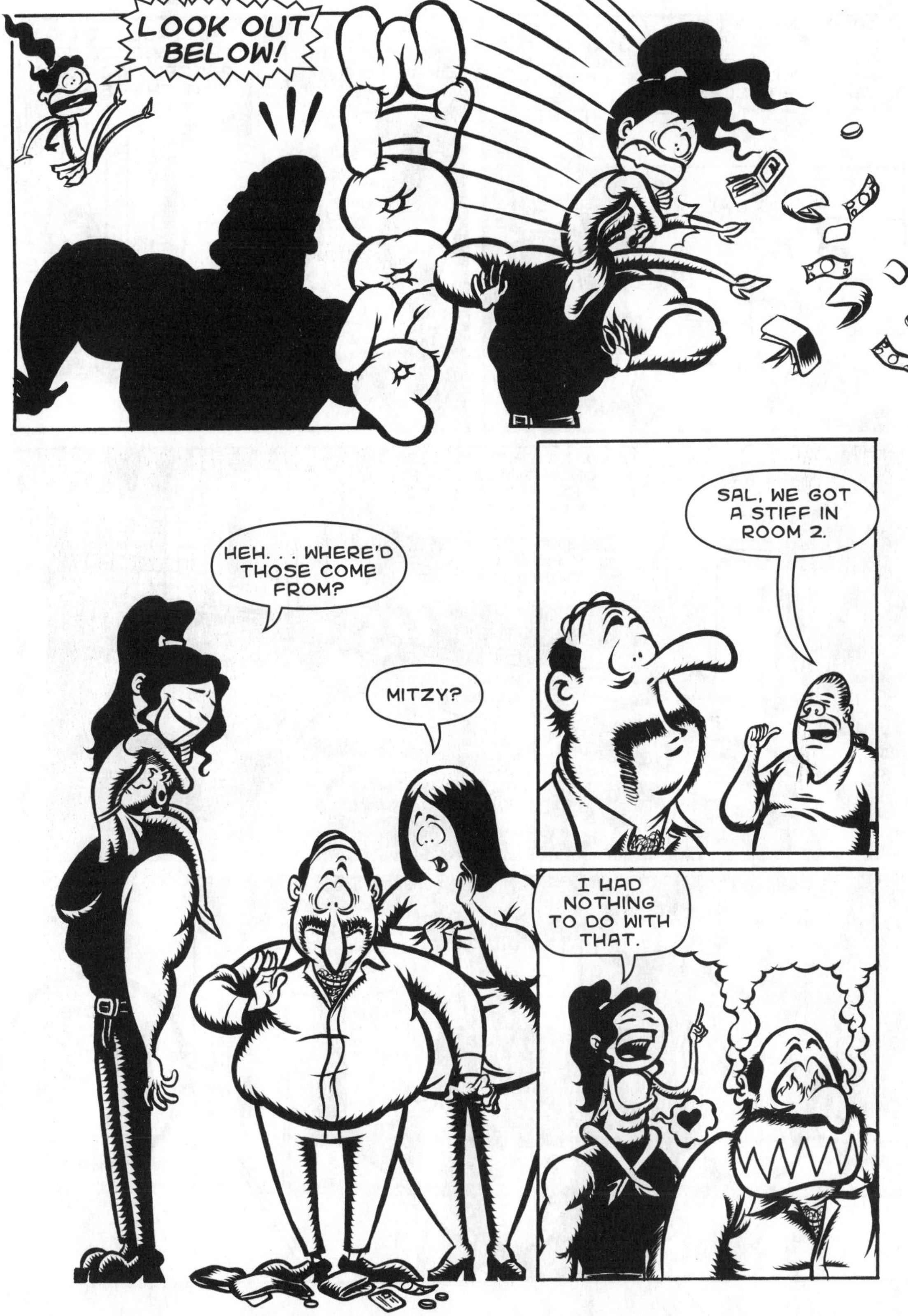
LOOK OUT BELOW!
HEH. . . WHERE'D THOSE COME FROM?
MITZY?
SAL, WE GOT A STIFF IN ROOM 2.
I HAD NOTHING TO DO WITH THAT.

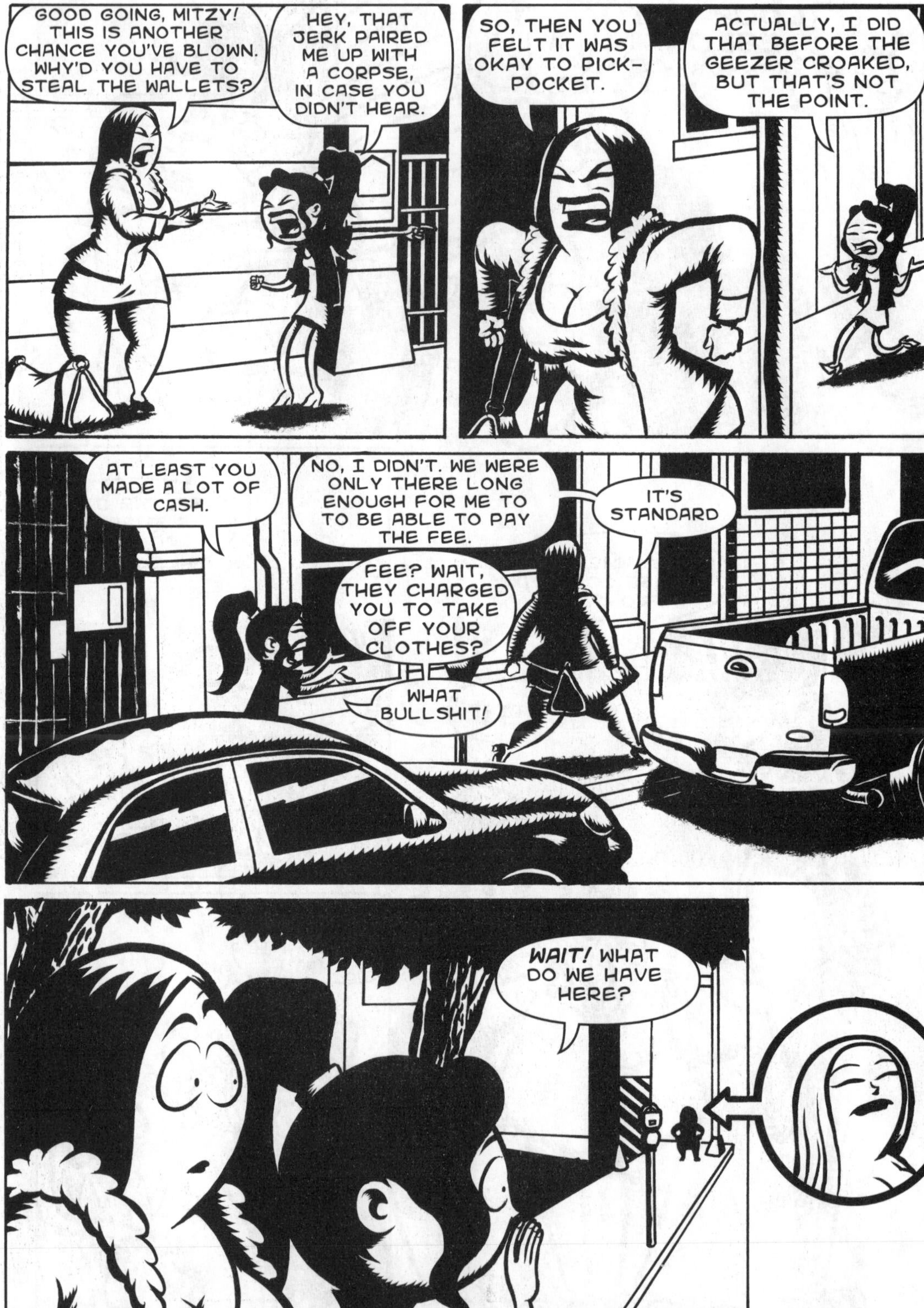
GOOD GOING, MITZY! THIS IS ANOTHER CHANCE YOU'VE BLOWN. WHY'D YOU HAVE TO STEAL THE WALLETS?
HEY, THAT JERK PAIRED ME UP WITH A CORPSE, IN CASE YOU DIDN'T HEAR.
SO, THEN YOU FELT IT WAS OKAY TO PICK-POCKET.
ACTUALLY, I DID THAT BEFORE THE GEEZER CROAKED, BUT THAT'S NOT THE POINT.
AT LEAST YOU MADE A LOT OF CASH.
NO, I DIDN'T. WE WERE ONLY THERE LONG ENOUGH FOR ME TO TO BE ABLE TO PAY THE FEE.
IT'S STANDARD
FEE? WAIT, THEY CHARGED YOU TO TAKE OFF YOUR CLOTHES?
WHAT BULLSHIT!
WAIT! WHAT DO WE HAVE HERE?

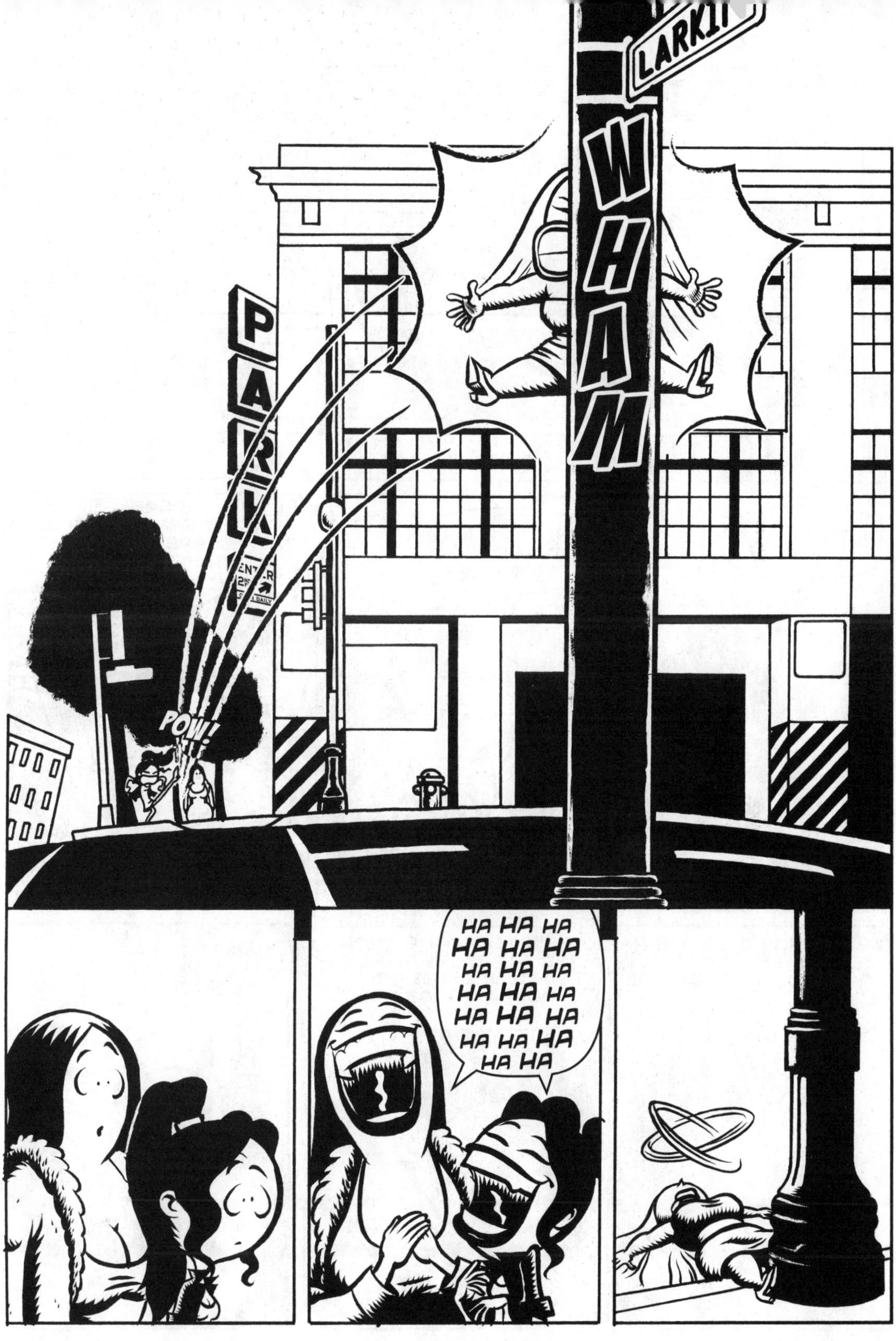

LARKIN
WHAM
PARK
POW!
HA HA HA
HA HA HA
HA HA HA
HA HA HA
HA HA HA
HA HA HA
HA HA

SHOULD WE BE EATING OUT WHEN WE DON'T HAVE ANY MONEY OR JOB PROSPECTS?

IT'S A $4 CONTINENTAL BREAKFAST, LULU. COME ON.

BESIDES, I GOT IT COVERED.

WAIT. . . WHERE DID YOU KEEP THAT ONE?

I DON'T UNDERSTAND HOW WHORES CAN ADVERTISE IN THE PAPER. ISN'T THAT SUSPICIOUS?

WINK, WINK! KNOW WHAT I'M SAYING?

MY WEBSITE HAS BOOBS. BLUR MY FACE

CALL SHEBA! 555-2319

TRACI 555 4593

LONELY? UGLY? CALL 555

FREE STD! FIRST TIME

WELL, THEY CALL THEM-SELVES 'ESCORTS' AND THEY DON'T ADVERTISE SEX.

SHE'S WEARING A THONG AND STARS! WHAT ELSE COULD SHE BE ADVERTISING? BAD WEAVES?

NO, SILLY. THEY STATE THAT THEY ARE PAID FOR THEIR TIME AND NOT SEX. AVOIDS ILLEGAL TALK.

SLURP

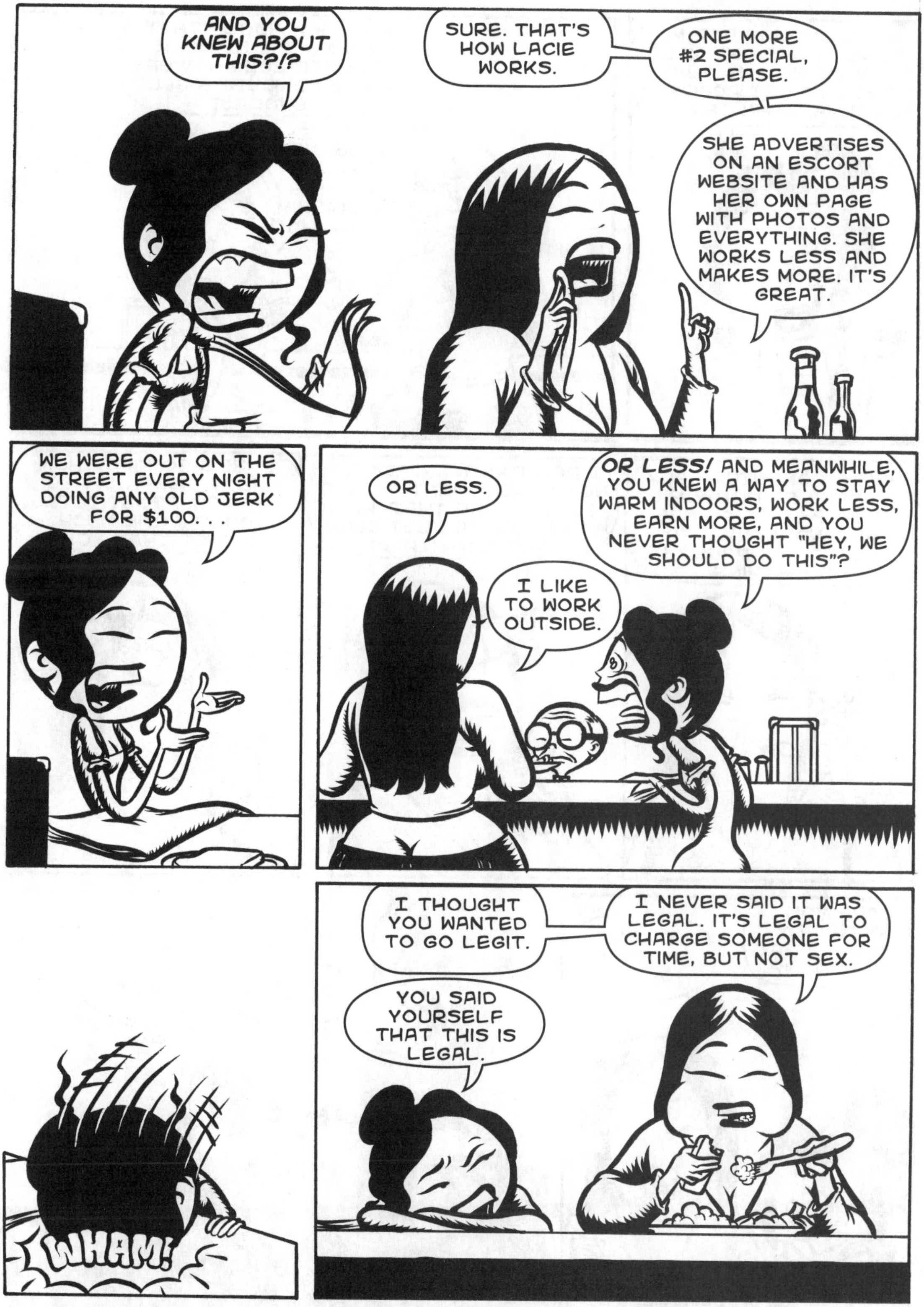
AND YOU KNEW ABOUT THIS?!?
SURE. THAT'S HOW LACIE WORKS.
ONE MORE #2 SPECIAL, PLEASE.
SHE ADVERTISES ON AN ESCORT WEBSITE AND HAS HER OWN PAGE WITH PHOTOS AND EVERYTHING. SHE WORKS LESS AND MAKES MORE. IT'S GREAT.
WE WERE OUT ON THE STREET EVERY NIGHT DOING ANY OLD JERK FOR $100. . .
OR LESS.
OR LESS! AND MEANWHILE, YOU KNEW A WAY TO STAY WARM INDOORS, WORK LESS, EARN MORE, AND YOU NEVER THOUGHT "HEY, WE SHOULD DO THIS"?
I LIKE TO WORK OUTSIDE.
I THOUGHT YOU WANTED TO GO LEGIT.
I NEVER SAID IT WAS LEGAL. IT'S LEGAL TO CHARGE SOMEONE FOR TIME, BUT NOT SEX.
YOU SAID YOURSELF THAT THIS IS LEGAL.
WHAM!

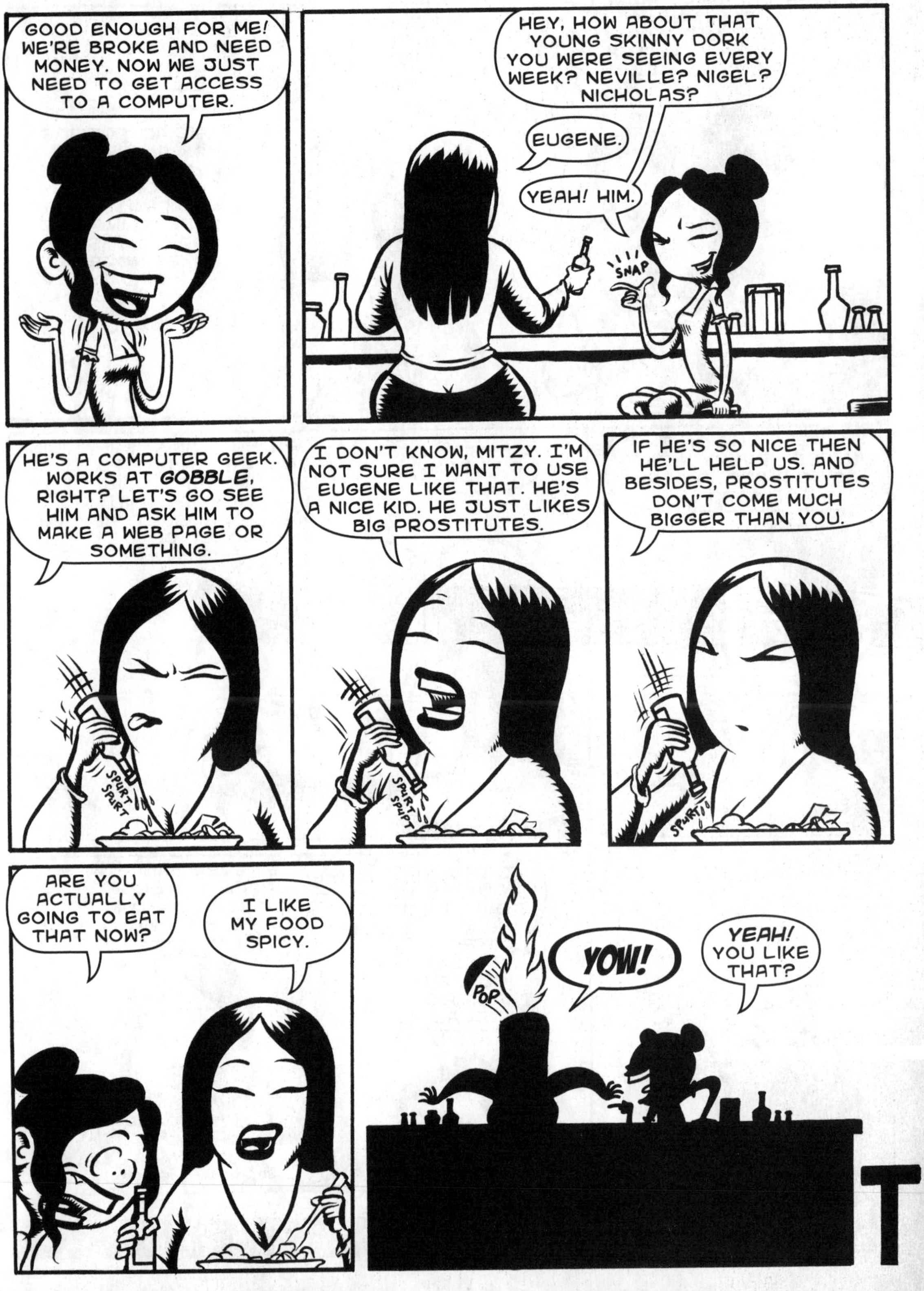
GOOD ENOUGH FOR ME! WE'RE BROKE AND NEED MONEY. NOW WE JUST NEED TO GET ACCESS TO A COMPUTER.
HEY, HOW ABOUT THAT YOUNG SKINNY DORK YOU WERE SEEING EVERY WEEK? NEVILLE? NIGEL? NICHOLAS?
EUGENE.
YEAH! HIM.
SNAP
HE'S A COMPUTER GEEK. WORKS AT GOBBLE, RIGHT? LET'S GO SEE HIM AND ASK HIM TO MAKE A WEB PAGE OR SOMETHING.
SPURT SPURT
I DON'T KNOW, MITZY. I'M NOT SURE I WANT TO USE EUGENE LIKE THAT. HE'S A NICE KID. HE JUST LIKES BIG PROSTITUTES.
SPURT SPURT
IF HE'S SO NICE THEN HE'LL HELP US. AND BESIDES, PROSTITUTES DON'T COME MUCH BIGGER THAN YOU.
SPURT
ARE YOU ACTUALLY GOING TO EAT THAT NOW?
I LIKE MY FOOD SPICY.
POP
YOW!
YEAH! YOU LIKE THAT?

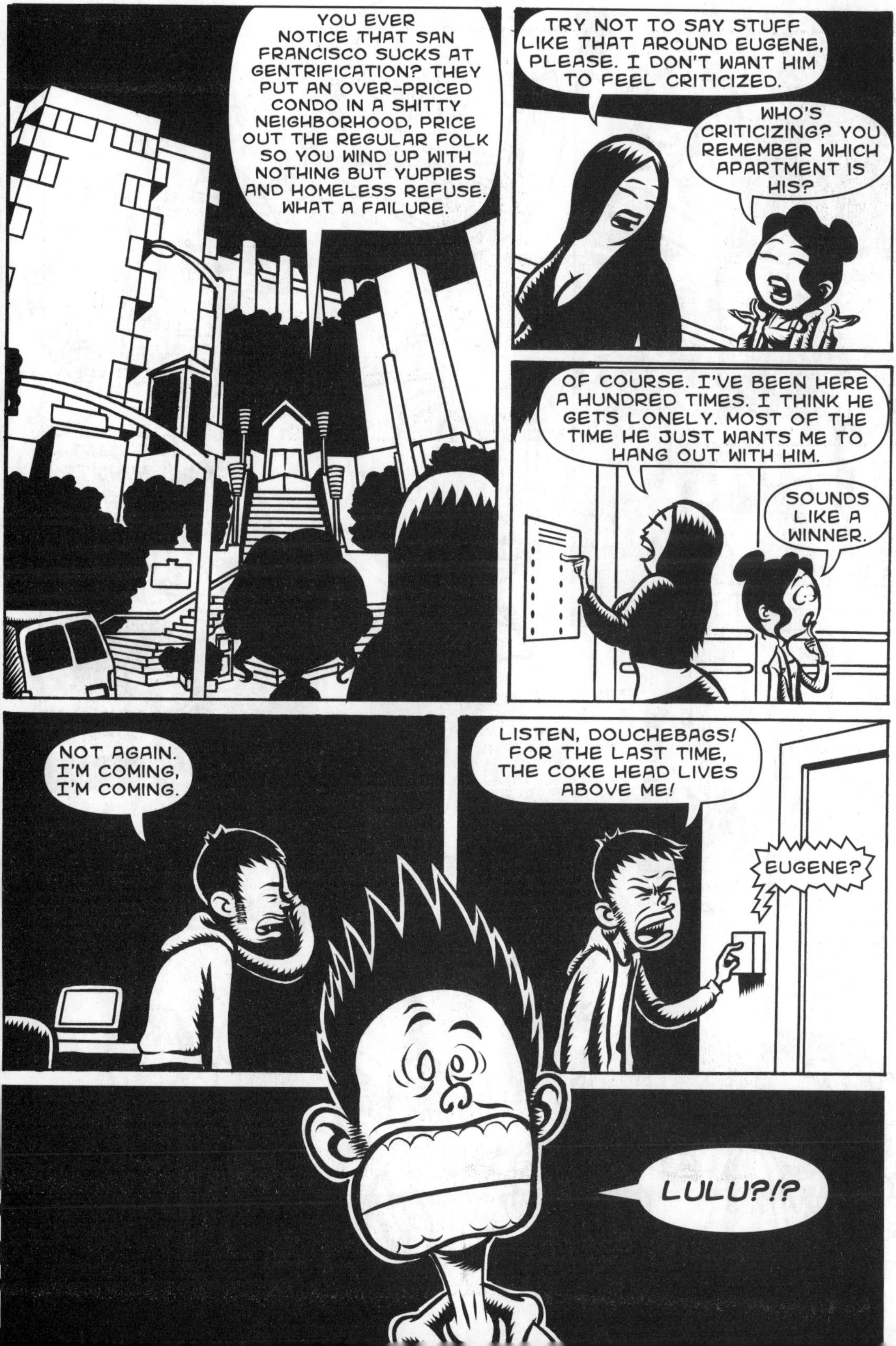
YOU EVER NOTICE THAT SAN FRANCISCO SUCKS AT GENTRIFICATION? THEY PUT AN OVER-PRICED CONDO IN A SHITTY NEIGHBORHOOD, PRICE OUT THE REGULAR FOLK SO YOU WIND UP WITH NOTHING BUT YUPPIES AND HOMELESS REFUSE. WHAT A FAILURE.
TRY NOT TO SAY STUFF LIKE THAT AROUND EUGENE, PLEASE. I DON'T WANT HIM TO FEEL CRITICIZED.
WHO'S CRITICIZING? YOU REMEMBER WHICH APARTMENT IS HIS?
OF COURSE. I'VE BEEN HERE A HUNDRED TIMES. I THINK HE GETS LONELY. MOST OF THE TIME HE JUST WANTS ME TO HANG OUT WITH HIM.
SOUNDS LIKE A WINNER.
NOT AGAIN. I'M COMING, I'M COMING.
LISTEN, DOUCHEBAGS! FOR THE LAST TIME, THE COKE HEAD LIVES ABOVE ME!
EUGENE?
LULU?!?

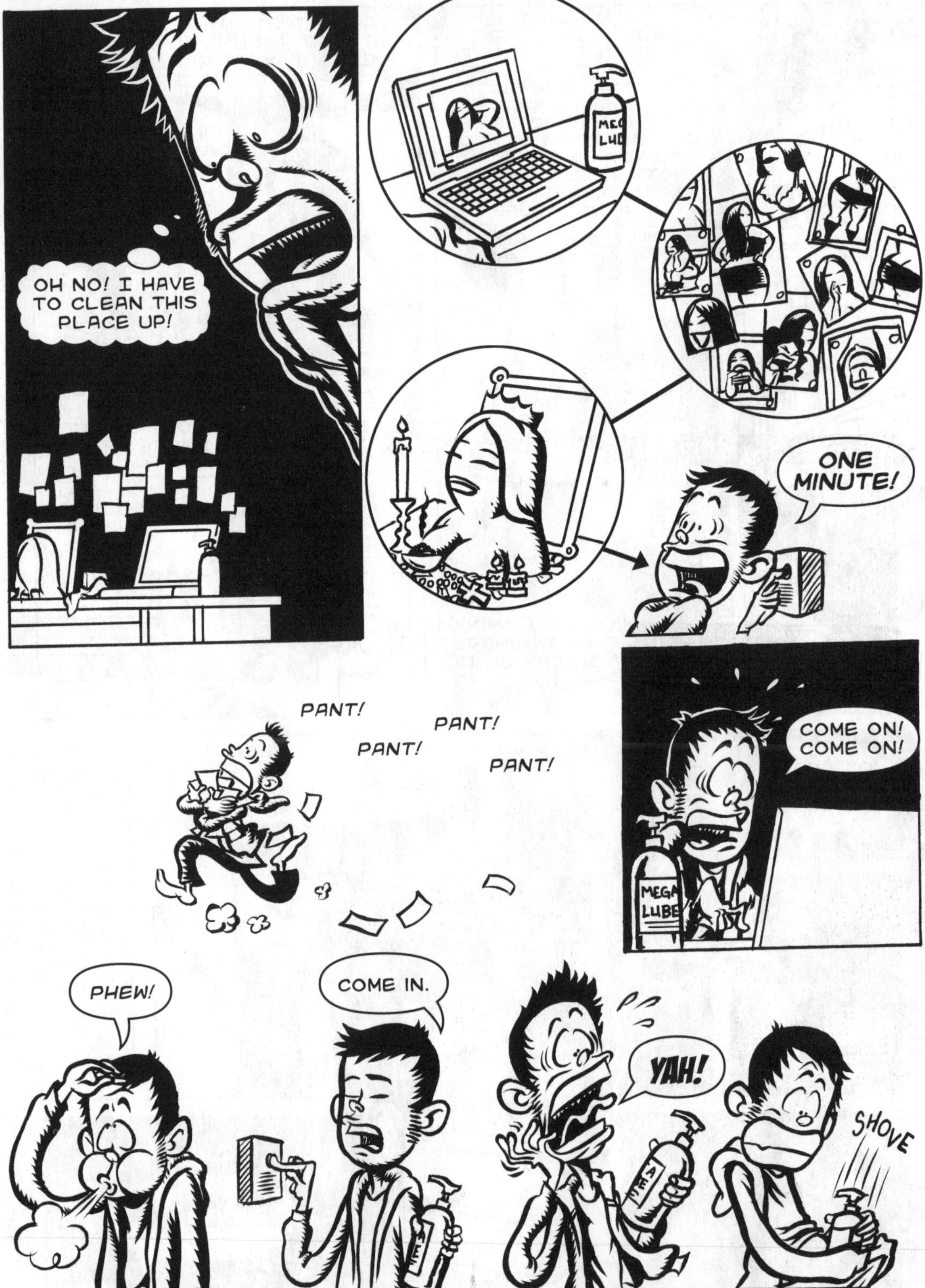
OH NO! I HAVE TO CLEAN THIS PLACE UP!
MEG LUB
ONE MINUTE!
PANT!
PANT!
PANT!
PANT!
COME ON! COME ON!
MEGA LUBE
PHEW!
COME IN.
YAH!
SHOVE

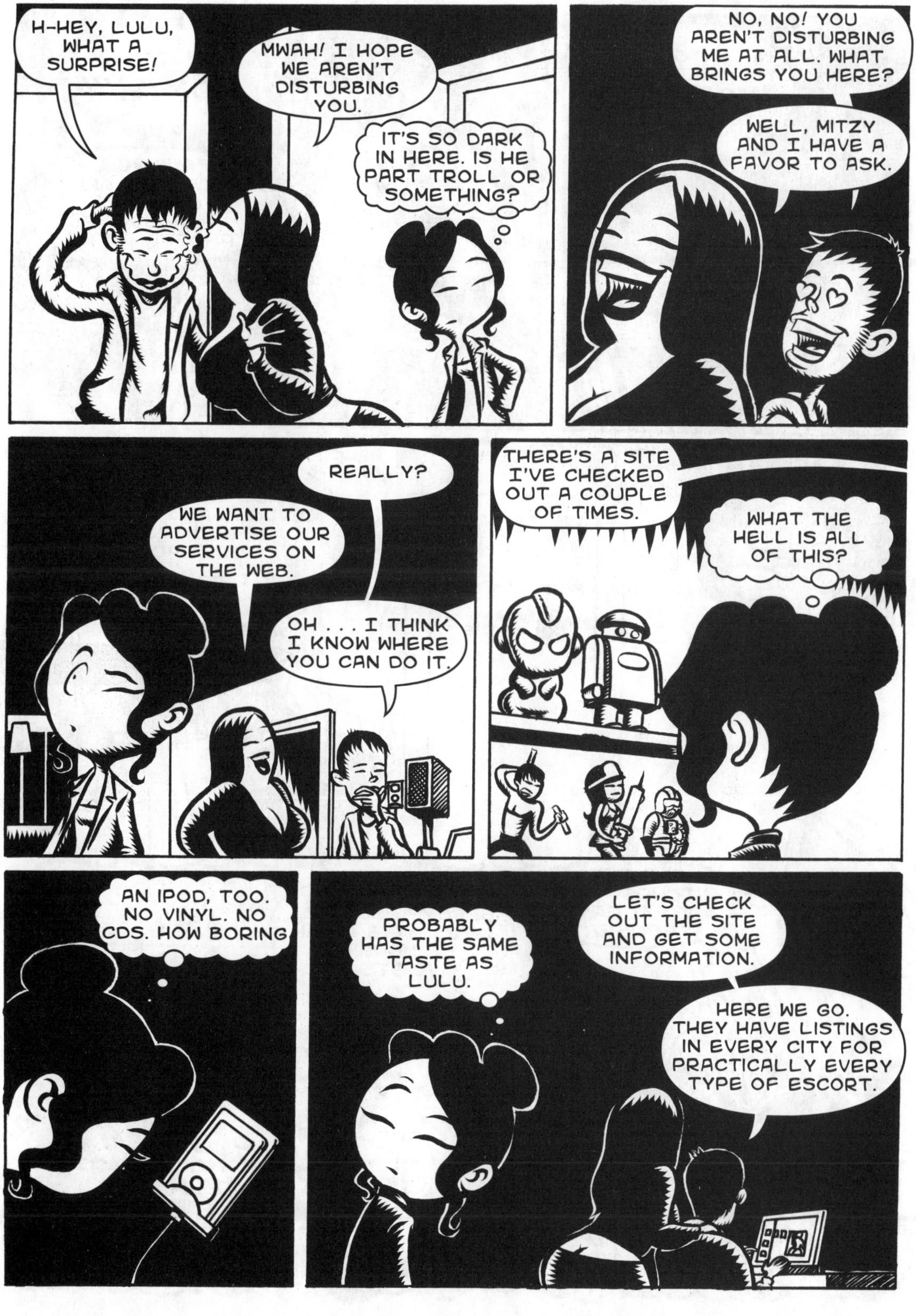
H-HEY, LULU, WHAT A SURPRISE!
MWAH! I HOPE WE AREN'T DISTURBING YOU.
IT'S SO DARK IN HERE. IS HE PART TROLL OR SOMETHING?
NO, NO! YOU AREN'T DISTURBING ME AT ALL. WHAT BRINGS YOU HERE?
WELL, MITZY AND I HAVE A FAVOR TO ASK.
REALLY?
WE WANT TO ADVERTISE OUR SERVICES ON THE WEB.
OH . . . I THINK I KNOW WHERE YOU CAN DO IT.
THERE'S A SITE I'VE CHECKED OUT A COUPLE OF TIMES.
WHAT THE HELL IS ALL OF THIS?
AN IPOD, TOO. NO VINYL. NO CDS. HOW BORING
PROBABLY HAS THE SAME TASTE AS LULU.
LET'S CHECK OUT THE SITE AND GET SOME INFORMATION.
HERE WE GO. THEY HAVE LISTINGS IN EVERY CITY FOR PRACTICALLY EVERY TYPE OF ESCORT.

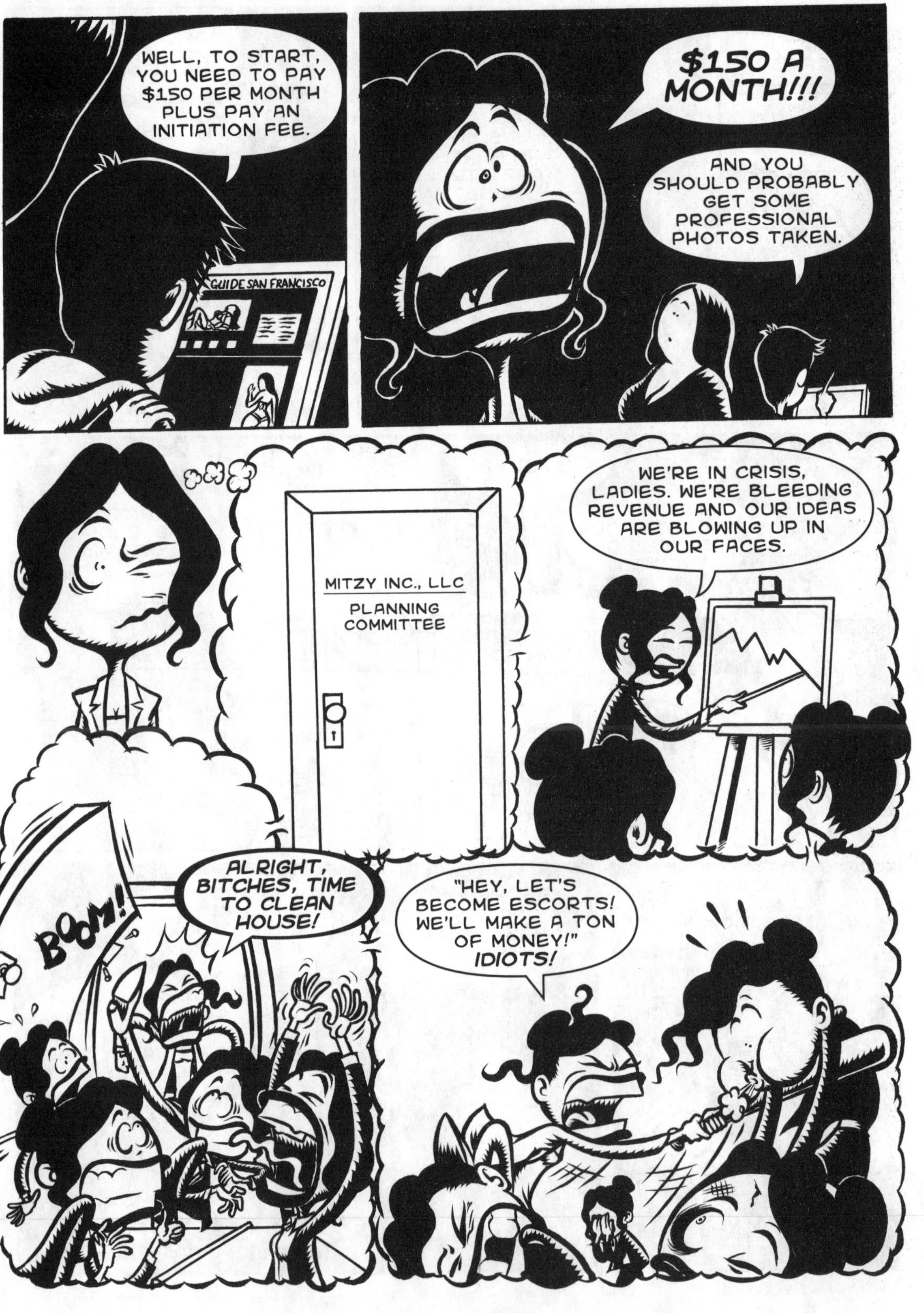
WELL, TO START, YOU NEED TO PAY $150 PER MONTH PLUS PAY AN INITIATION FEE.
GUIDE SAN FRANCISCO
$150 A MONTH!!!
AND YOU SHOULD PROBABLY GET SOME PROFESSIONAL PHOTOS TAKEN.
MITZY INC., LLC
PLANNING COMMITTEE
WE'RE IN CRISIS, LADIES. WE'RE BLEEDING REVENUE AND OUR IDEAS ARE BLOWING UP IN OUR FACES.
BOOM!
ALRIGHT, BITCHES, TIME TO CLEAN HOUSE!
"HEY, LET'S BECOME ESCORTS! WE'LL MAKE A TON OF MONEY!" IDIOTS!

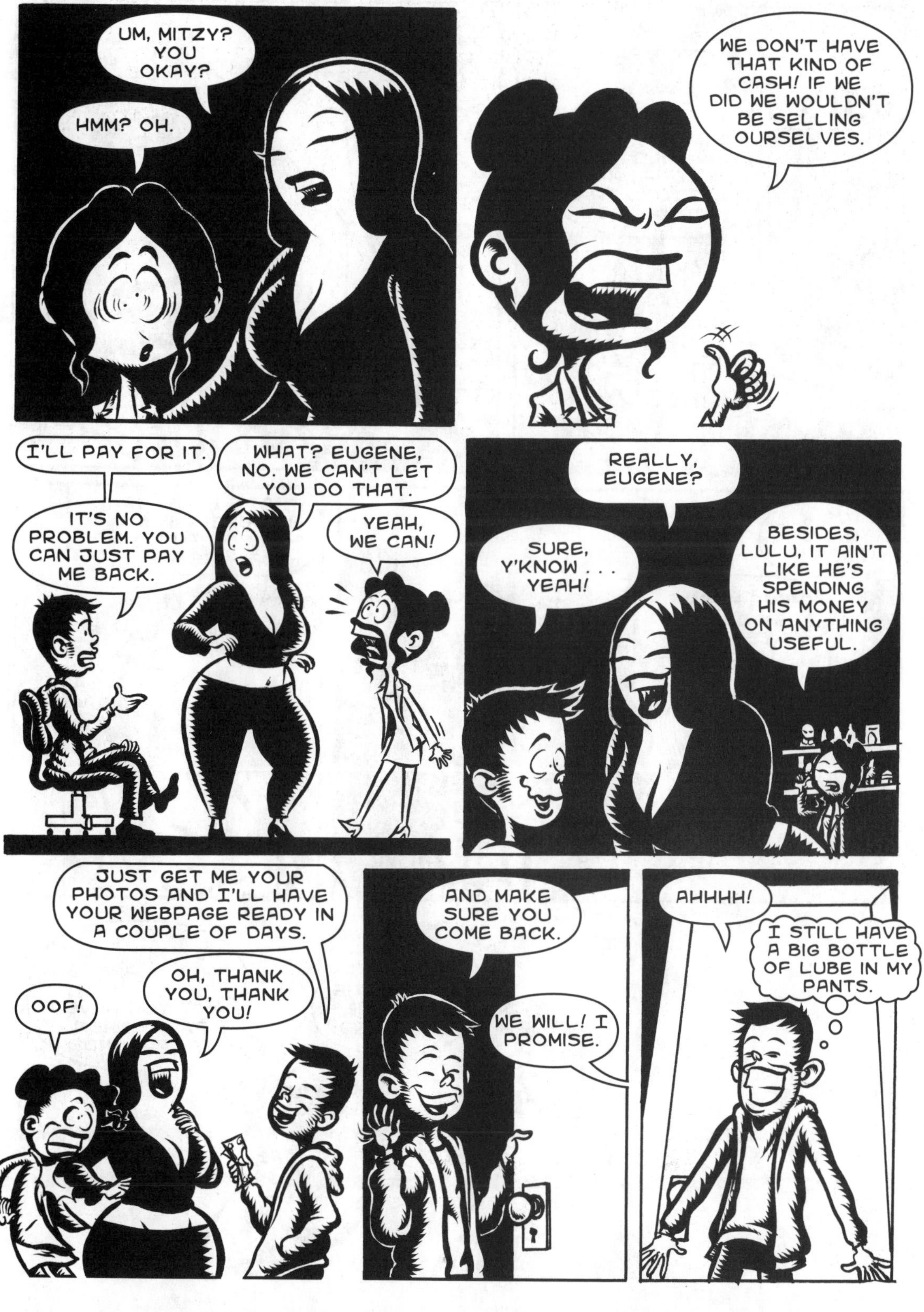
UM, MITZY? YOU OKAY?
HMM? OH.
WE DON'T HAVE THAT KIND OF CASH! IF WE DID WE WOULDN'T BE SELLING OURSELVES.
I'LL PAY FOR IT.
IT'S NO PROBLEM. YOU CAN JUST PAY ME BACK.
WHAT? EUGENE, NO. WE CAN'T LET YOU DO THAT.
YEAH, WE CAN!
REALLY, EUGENE?
SURE, Y'KNOW . . . YEAH!
BESIDES, LULU, IT AIN'T LIKE HE'S SPENDING HIS MONEY ON ANYTHING USEFUL.
JUST GET ME YOUR PHOTOS AND I'LL HAVE YOUR WEBPAGE READY IN A COUPLE OF DAYS.
OOF!
OH, THANK YOU, THANK YOU!
AND MAKE SURE YOU COME BACK.
WE WILL! I PROMISE.
AHHHH!
I STILL HAVE A BIG BOTTLE OF LUBE IN MY PANTS.

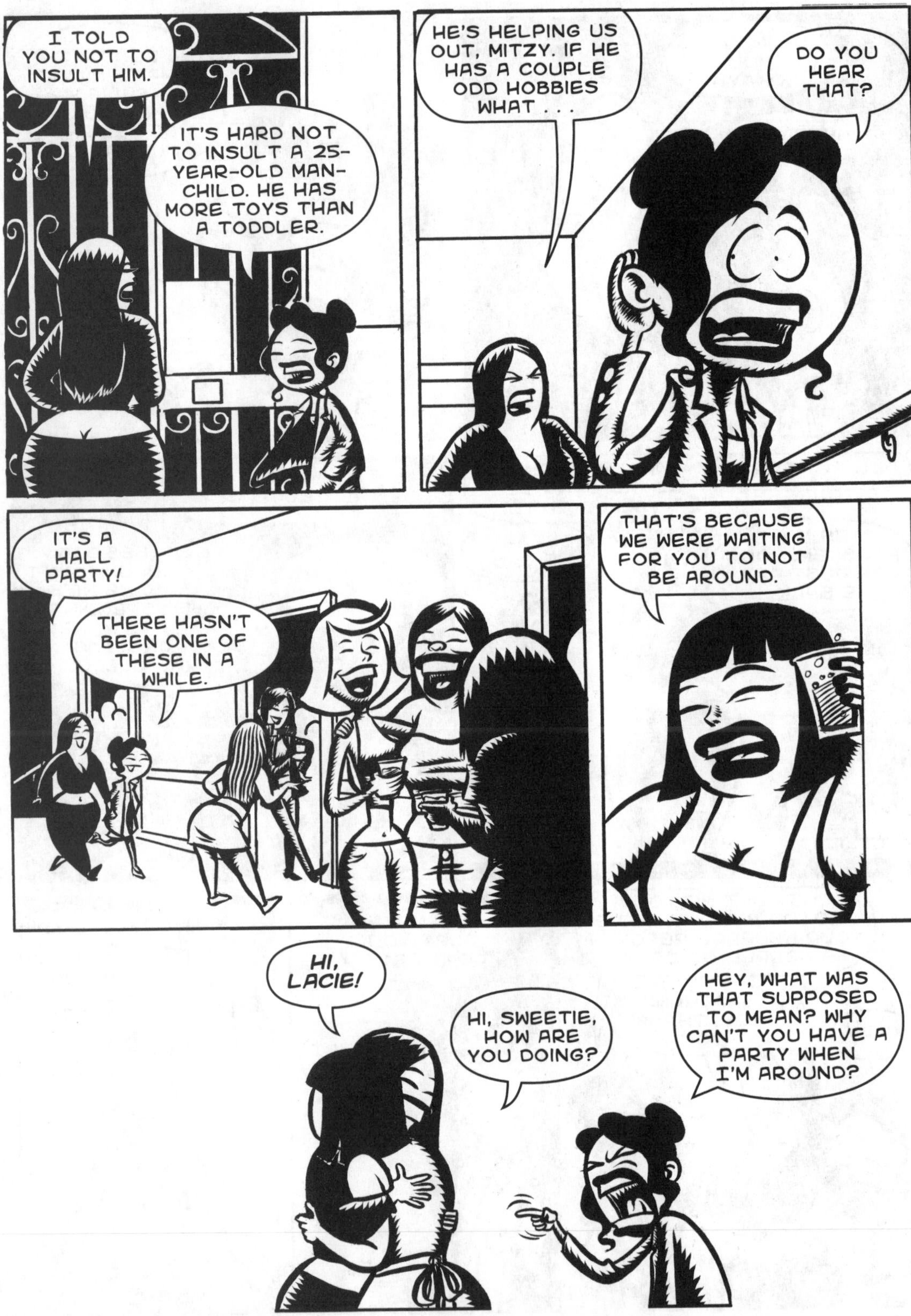
I TOLD YOU NOT TO INSULT HIM.
IT'S HARD NOT TO INSULT A 25-YEAR-OLD MAN-CHILD. HE HAS MORE TOYS THAN A TODDLER.
HE'S HELPING US OUT, MITZY. IF HE HAS A COUPLE ODD HOBBIES WHAT . . .
DO YOU HEAR THAT?
IT'S A HALL PARTY!
THERE HASN'T BEEN ONE OF THESE IN A WHILE.
THAT'S BECAUSE WE WERE WAITING FOR YOU TO NOT BE AROUND.
HI, LACIE!
HI, SWEETIE, HOW ARE YOU DOING?
HEY, WHAT WAS THAT SUPPOSED TO MEAN? WHY CAN'T YOU HAVE A PARTY WHEN I'M AROUND?

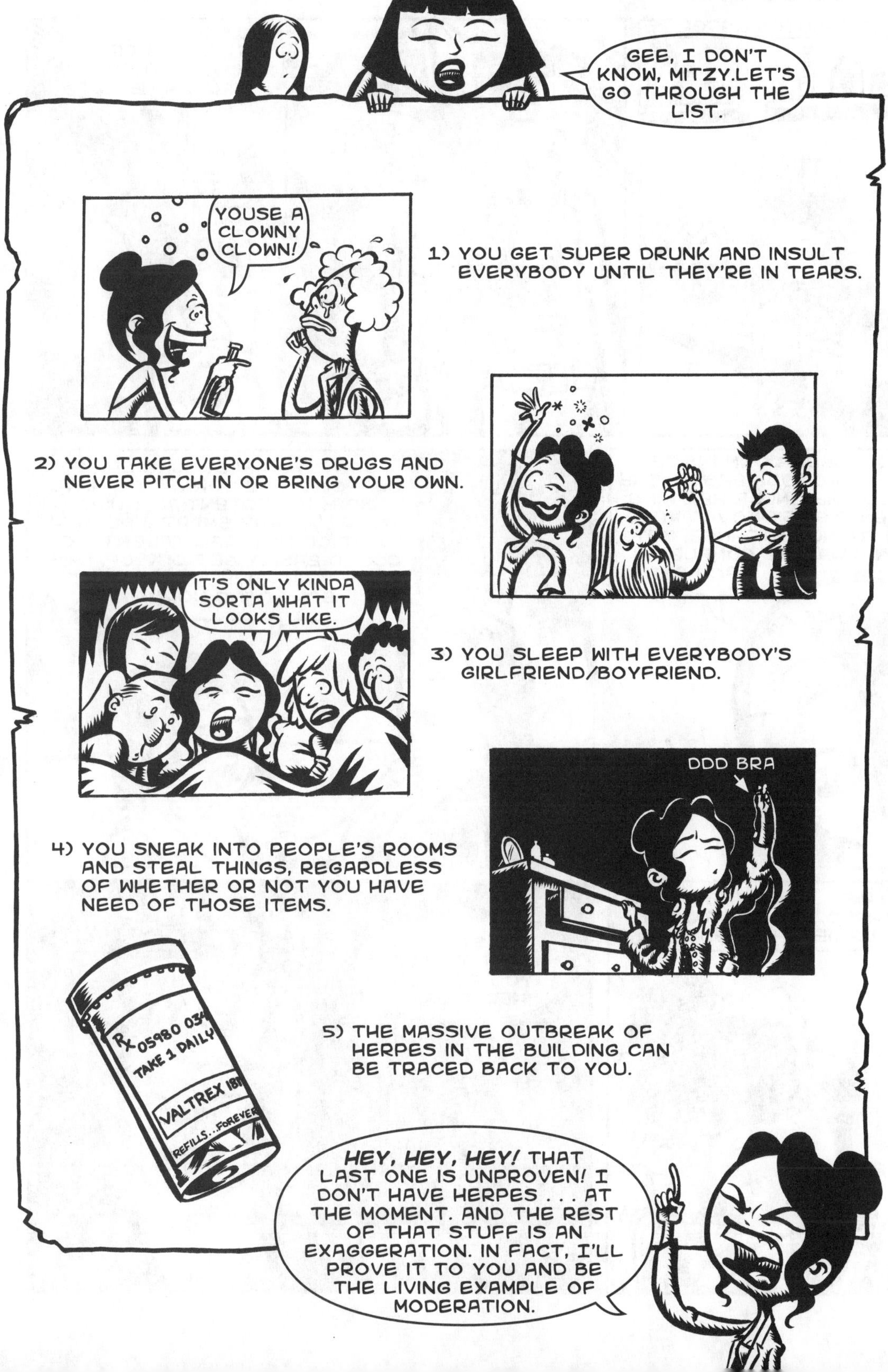
GEE, I DON'T KNOW, MITZY. LET'S GO THROUGH THE LIST.
YOUSE A CLOWNY CLOWN!
1) YOU GET SUPER DRUNK AND INSULT EVERYBODY UNTIL THEY'RE IN TEARS.
2) YOU TAKE EVERYONE'S DRUGS AND NEVER PITCH IN OR BRING YOUR OWN.
IT'S ONLY KINDA SORTA WHAT IT LOOKS LIKE.
3) YOU SLEEP WITH EVERYBODY'S GIRLFRIEND/BOYFRIEND.
DDD BRA
4) YOU SNEAK INTO PEOPLE'S ROOMS AND STEAL THINGS, REGARDLESS OF WHETHER OR NOT YOU HAVE NEED OF THOSE ITEMS.
Rx 05980 034
TAKE 1 DAILY
VALTREX
REFILLS...FOREVER
5) THE MASSIVE OUTBREAK OF HERPES IN THE BUILDING CAN BE TRACED BACK TO YOU.
HEY, HEY, HEY! THAT LAST ONE IS UNPROVEN! I DON'T HAVE HERPES . . . AT THE MOMENT. AND THE REST OF THAT STUFF IS AN EXAGGERATION. IN FACT, I'LL PROVE IT TO YOU AND BE THE LIVING EXAMPLE OF MODERATION.

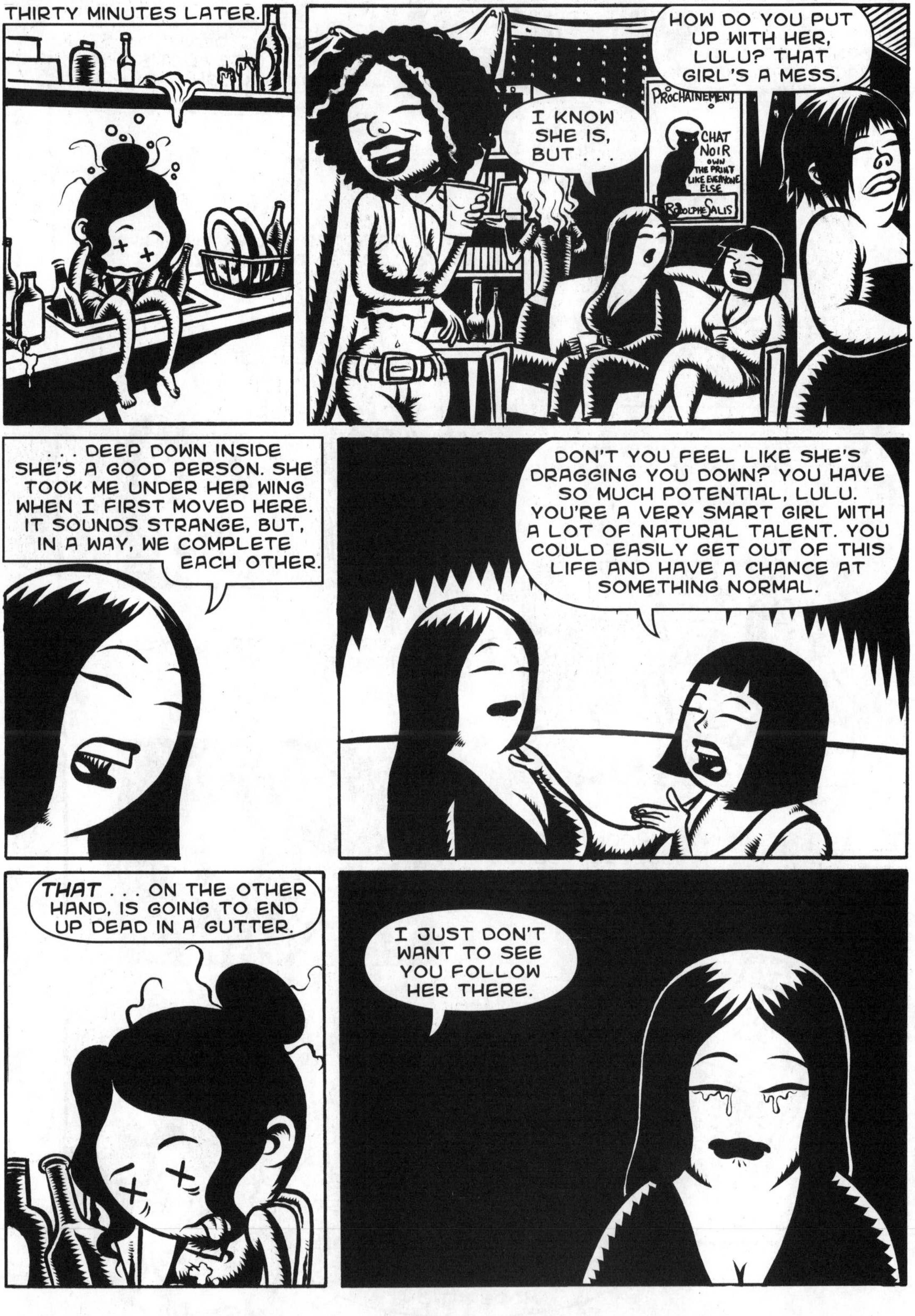
THIRTY MINUTES LATER.
HOW DO YOU PUT UP WITH HER, LULU? THAT GIRL'S A MESS.
I KNOW SHE IS, BUT . . .
PROCHAINEMENT
CHAT NOIR
OWN THE PRINT LIKE EVERYONE ELSE
RODOLPHE SALIS
. . . DEEP DOWN INSIDE SHE'S A GOOD PERSON. SHE TOOK ME UNDER HER WING WHEN I FIRST MOVED HERE. IT SOUNDS STRANGE, BUT, IN A WAY, WE COMPLETE EACH OTHER.
DON'T YOU FEEL LIKE SHE'S DRAGGING YOU DOWN? YOU HAVE SO MUCH POTENTIAL, LULU. YOU'RE A VERY SMART GIRL WITH A LOT OF NATURAL TALENT. YOU COULD EASILY GET OUT OF THIS LIFE AND HAVE A CHANCE AT SOMETHING NORMAL.
THAT . . . ON THE OTHER HAND, IS GOING TO END UP DEAD IN A GUTTER.
I JUST DON'T WANT TO SEE YOU FOLLOW HER THERE.

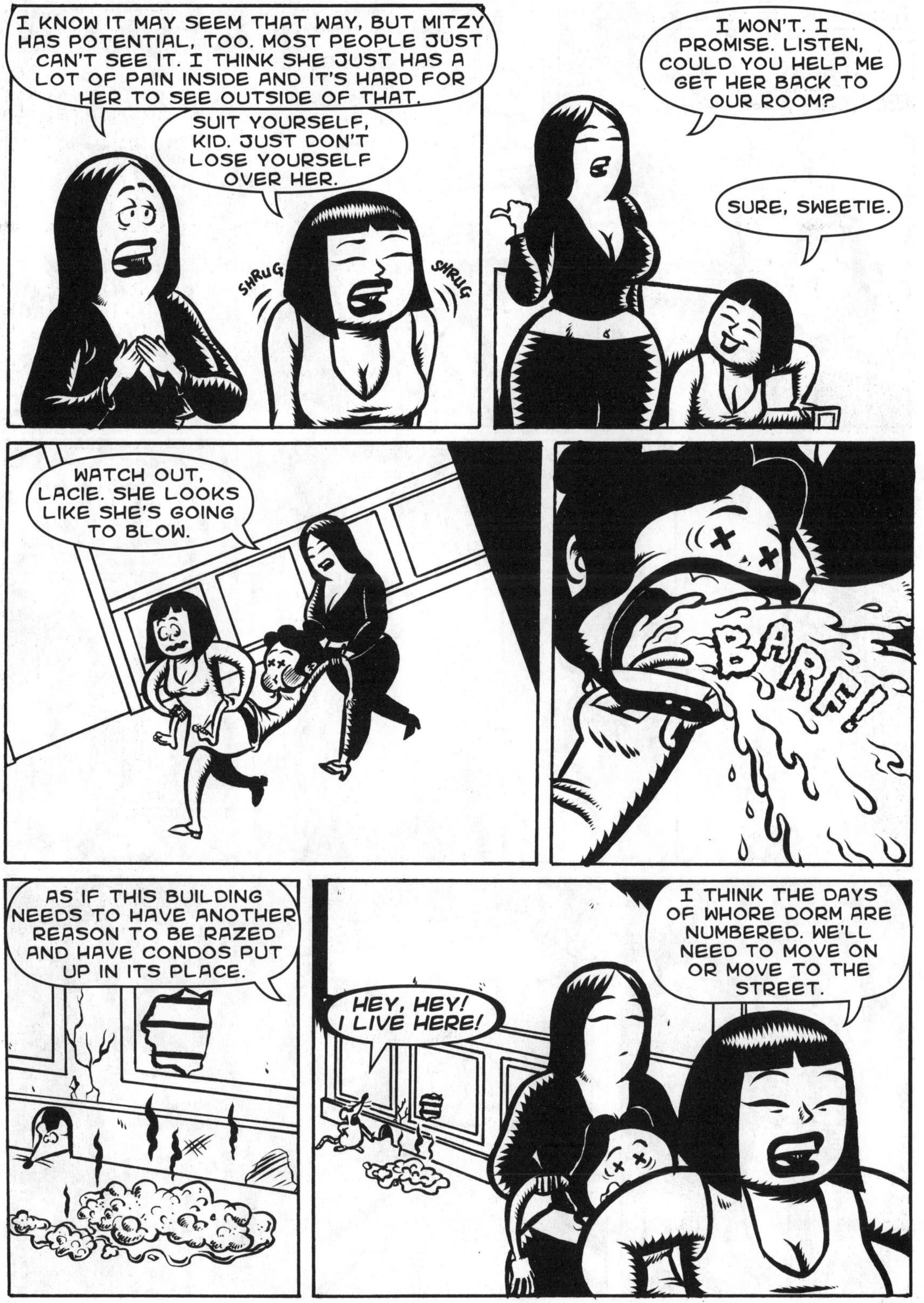
I KNOW IT MAY SEEM THAT WAY, BUT MITZY HAS POTENTIAL, TOO. MOST PEOPLE JUST CAN'T SEE IT. I THINK SHE JUST HAS A LOT OF PAIN INSIDE AND IT'S HARD FOR HER TO SEE OUTSIDE OF THAT.
SUIT YOURSELF, KID. JUST DON'T LOSE YOURSELF OVER HER.
SHRUG
SHRUG
I WON'T. I PROMISE. LISTEN, COULD YOU HELP ME GET HER BACK TO OUR ROOM?
SURE, SWEETIE.
WATCH OUT, LACIE. SHE LOOKS LIKE SHE'S GOING TO BLOW.
BARF!
AS IF THIS BUILDING NEEDS TO HAVE ANOTHER REASON TO BE RAZED AND HAVE CONDOS PUT UP IN ITS PLACE.
HEY, HEY! I LIVE HERE!
I THINK THE DAYS OF WHORE DORM ARE NUMBERED. WE'LL NEED TO MOVE ON OR MOVE TO THE STREET.

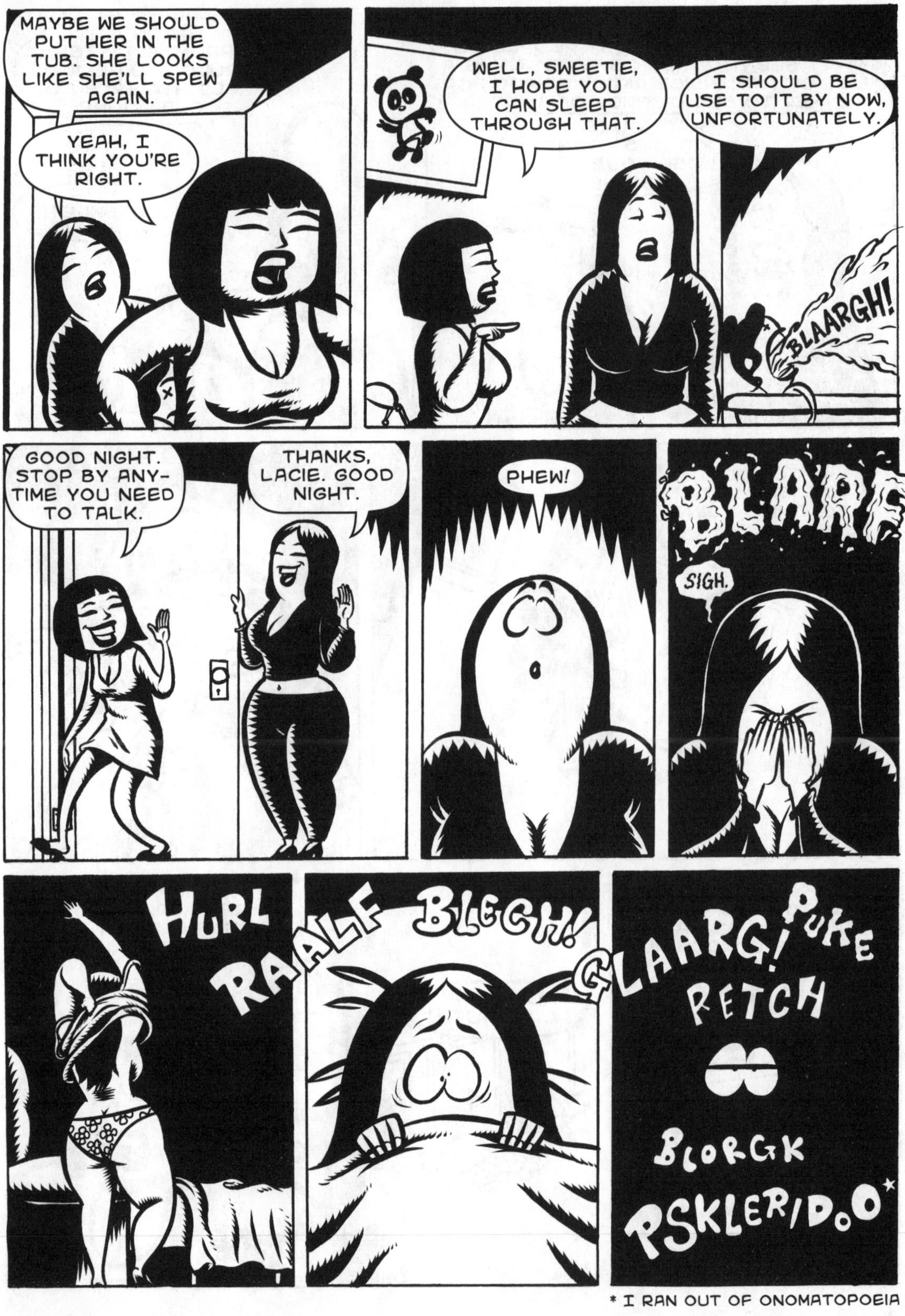
MAYBE WE SHOULD PUT HER IN THE TUB. SHE LOOKS LIKE SHE'LL SPEW AGAIN.
YEAH, I THINK YOU'RE RIGHT.
WELL, SWEETIE, I HOPE YOU CAN SLEEP THROUGH THAT.
I SHOULD BE USE TO IT BY NOW, UNFORTUNATELY.
BLAARGH!
GOOD NIGHT. STOP BY ANY-TIME YOU NEED TO TALK.
THANKS, LACIE. GOOD NIGHT.
PHEW!
BLARF
SIGH.
HURL
RAALF
BLECH!
GLAARG!
PUKE
RETCH
BLORGK
PSKLERIDOO*

* I RAN OUT OF ONOMATOPOEIA

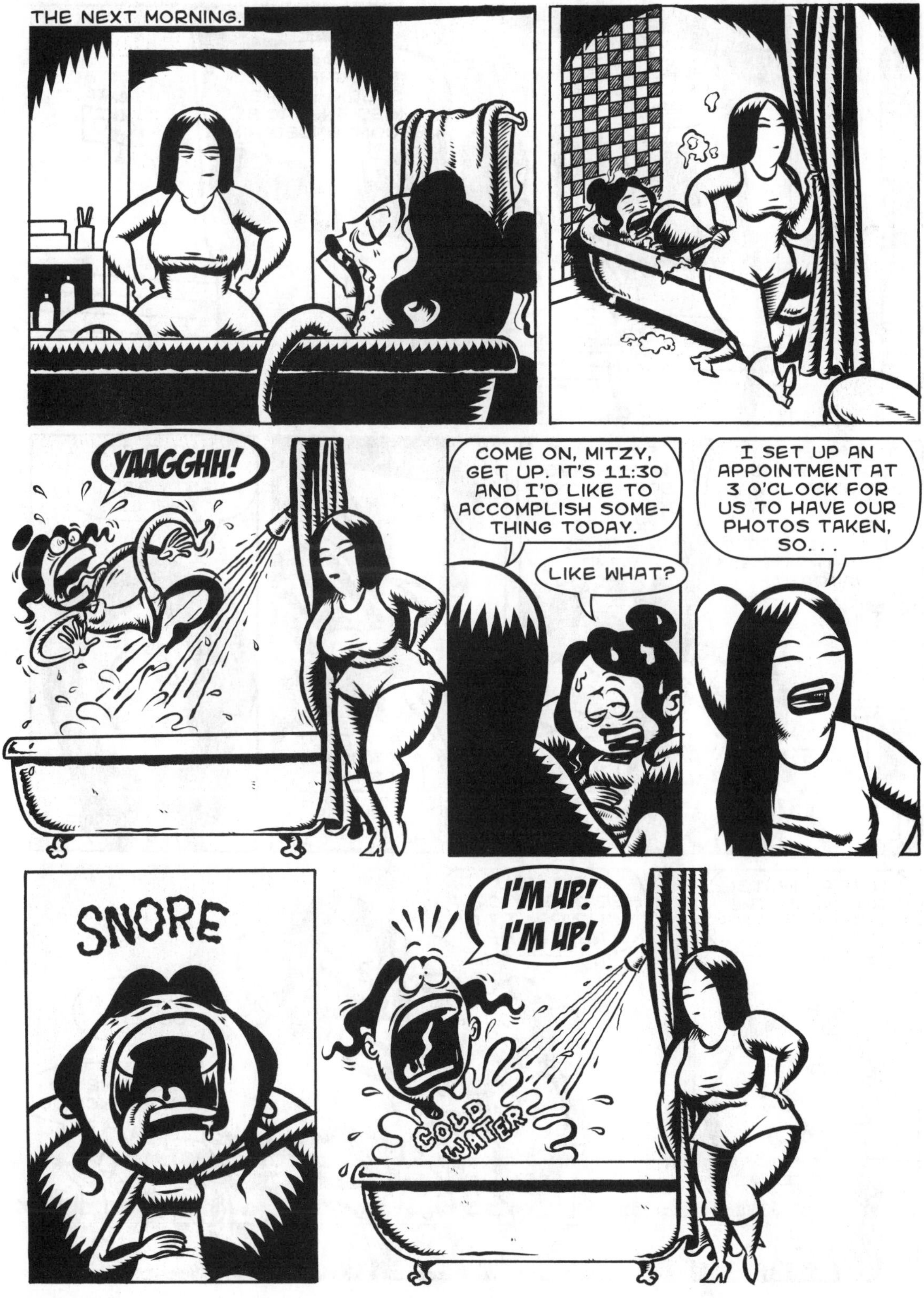
THE NEXT MORNING.
YAAGGHH!
COME ON, MITZY, GET UP. IT'S 11:30 AND I'D LIKE TO ACCOMPLISH SOMETHING TODAY.
LIKE WHAT?
I SET UP AN APPOINTMENT AT 3 O'CLOCK FOR US TO HAVE OUR PHOTOS TAKEN, SO. . .
SNORE
I'M UP! I'M UP!
COLD WATER

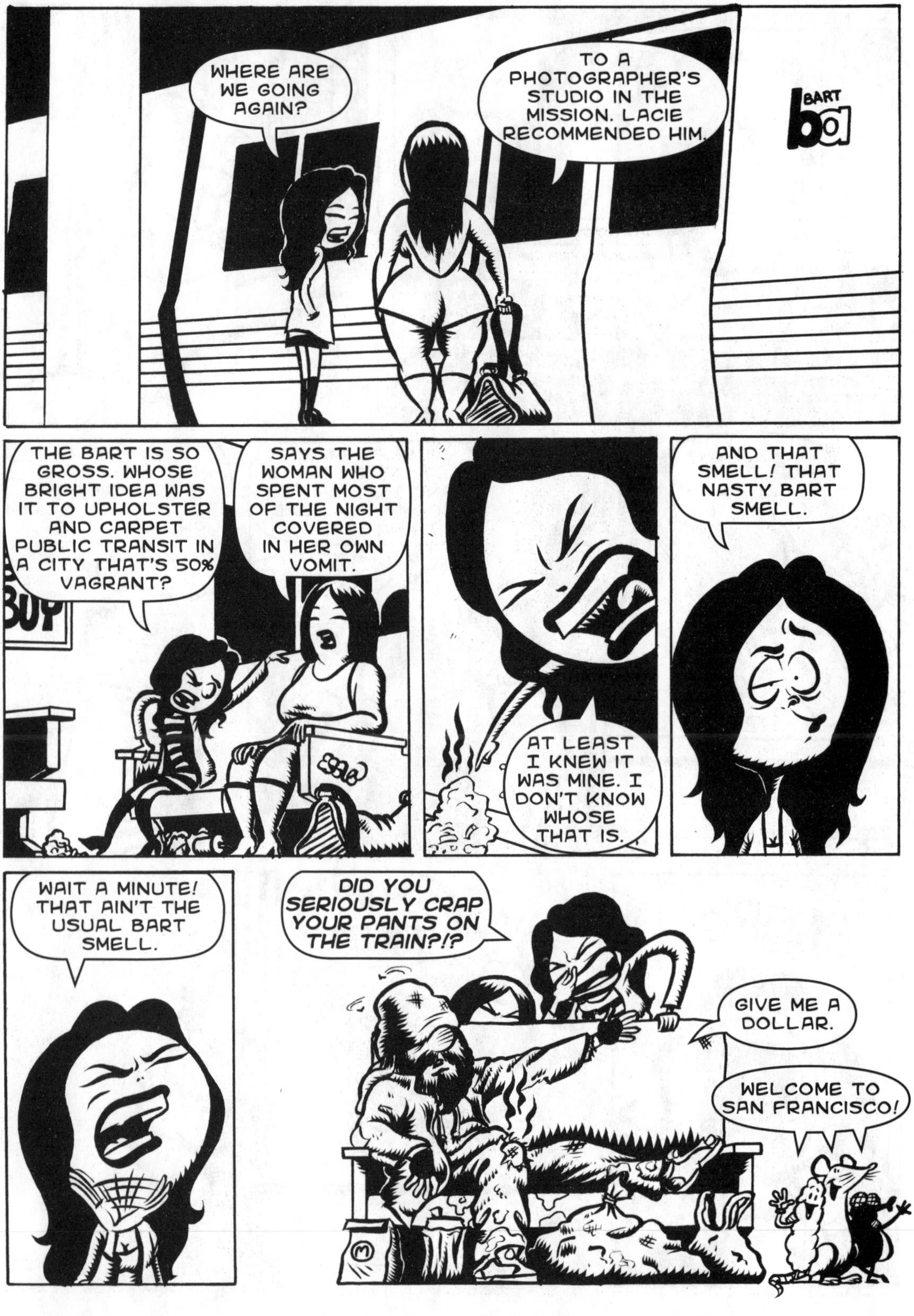
WHERE ARE WE GOING AGAIN?
TO A PHOTOGRAPHER'S STUDIO IN THE MISSION. LACIE RECOMMENDED HIM.
BART
THE BART IS SO GROSS. WHOSE BRIGHT IDEA WAS IT TO UPHOLSTER AND CARPET PUBLIC TRANSIT IN A CITY THAT'S 50% VAGRANT?
SAYS THE WOMAN WHO SPENT MOST OF THE NIGHT COVERED IN HER OWN VOMIT.
AT LEAST I KNEW IT WAS MINE. I DON'T KNOW WHOSE THAT IS.
AND THAT SMELL! THAT NASTY BART SMELL.
WAIT A MINUTE! THAT AIN'T THE USUAL BART SMELL.
DID YOU SERIOUSLY CRAP YOUR PANTS ON THE TRAIN?!?
GIVE ME A DOLLAR.
WELCOME TO SAN FRANCISCO!

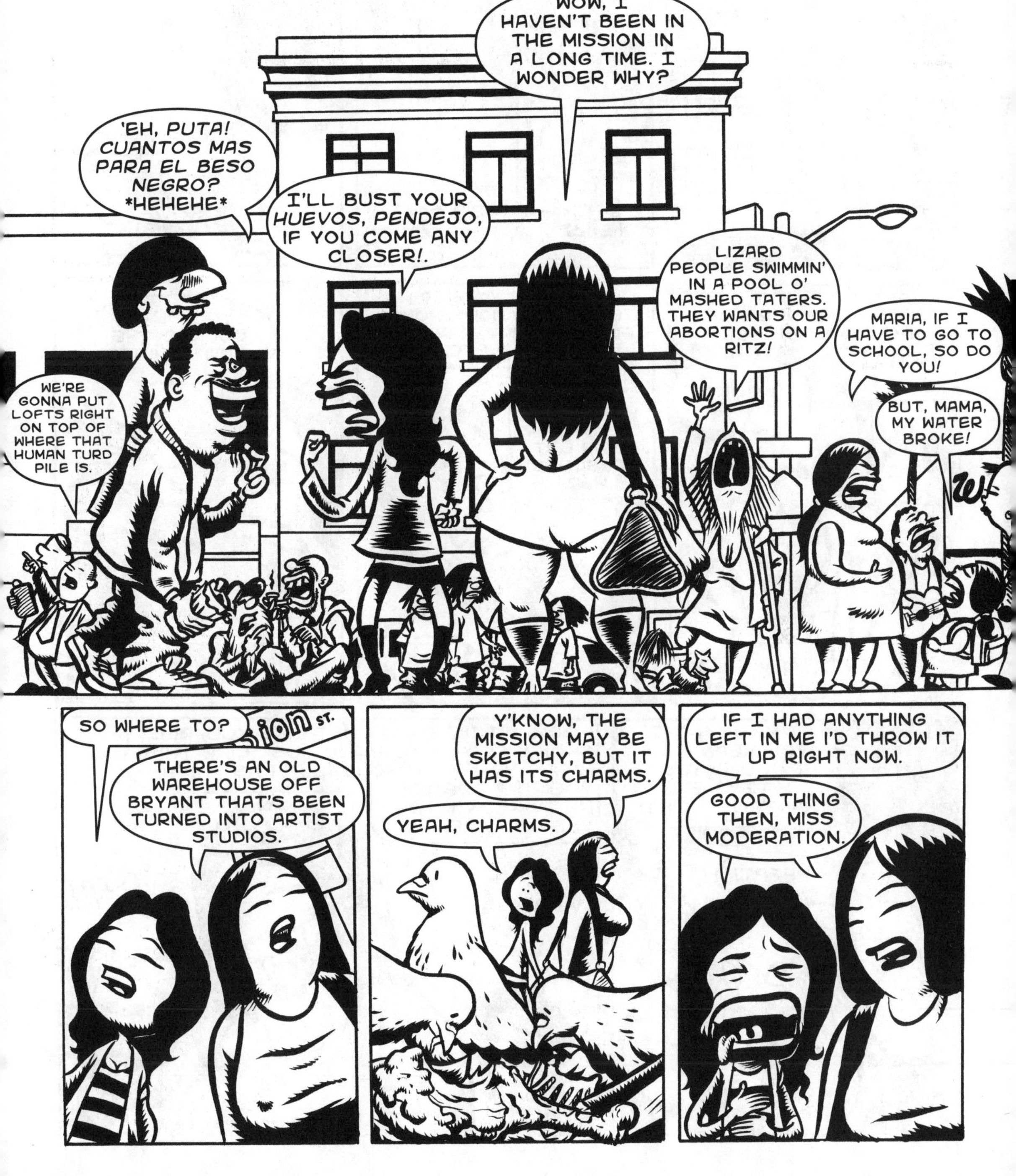
WOW, I HAVEN'T BEEN IN THE MISSION IN A LONG TIME. I WONDER WHY?
'EH, PUTA! CUANTOS MAS PARA EL BESO NEGRO? *HEHEHE*
I'LL BUST YOUR HUEVOS, PENDEJO, IF YOU COME ANY CLOSER!.
WE'RE GONNA PUT LOFTS RIGHT ON TOP OF WHERE THAT HUMAN TURD PILE IS.
LIZARD PEOPLE SWIMMIN' IN A POOL O' MASHED TATERS. THEY WANTS OUR ABORTIONS ON A RITZ!
MARIA, IF I HAVE TO GO TO SCHOOL, SO DO YOU!
BUT, MAMA, MY WATER BROKE!
SO WHERE TO?
THERE'S AN OLD WAREHOUSE OFF BRYANT THAT'S BEEN TURNED INTO ARTIST STUDIOS.
Y'KNOW, THE MISSION MAY BE SKETCHY, BUT IT HAS ITS CHARMS.
YEAH, CHARMS.
IF I HAD ANYTHING LEFT IN ME I'D THROW IT UP RIGHT NOW.
GOOD THING THEN, MISS MODERATION.

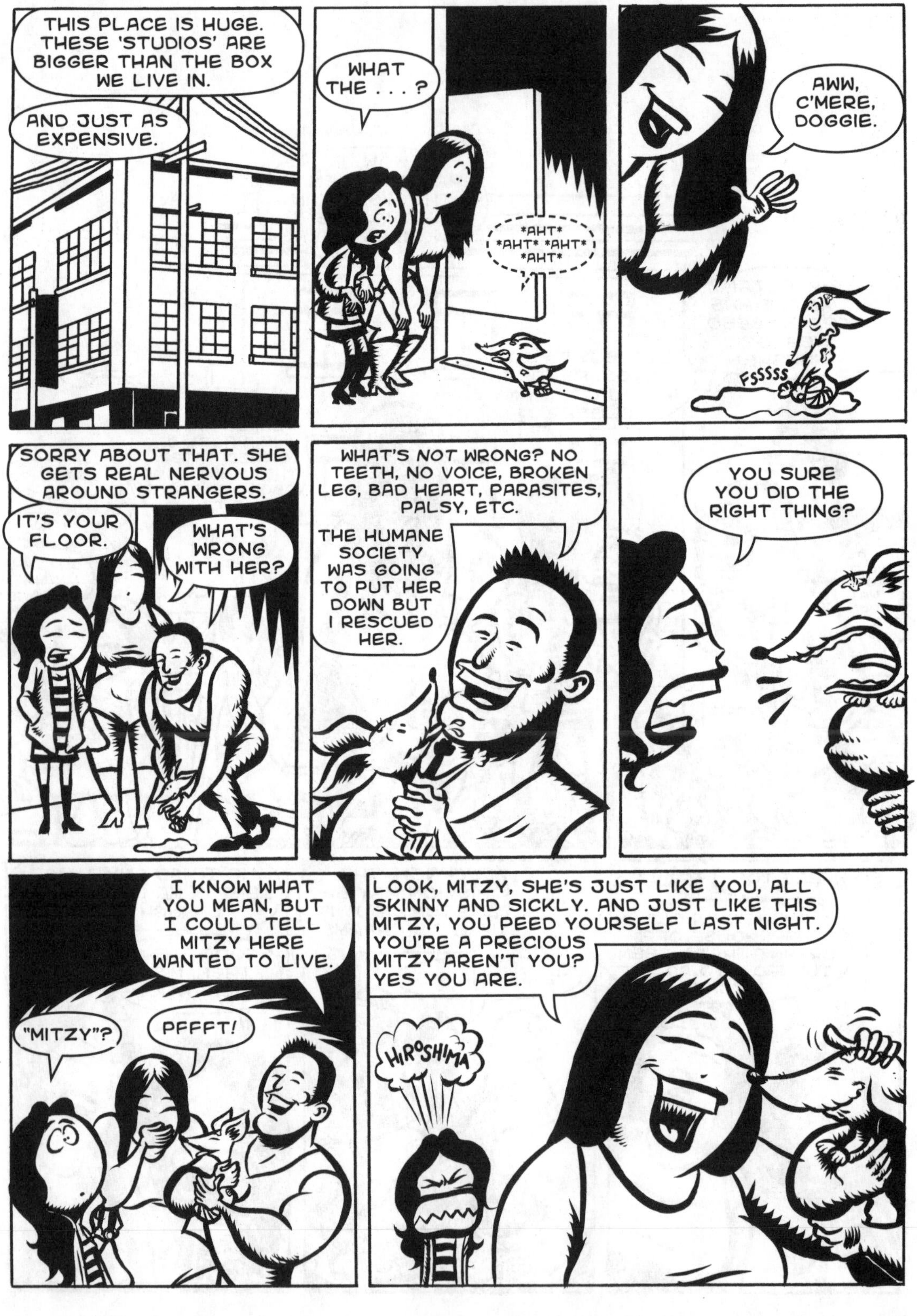
THIS PLACE IS HUGE. THESE 'STUDIOS' ARE BIGGER THAN THE BOX WE LIVE IN.
AND JUST AS EXPENSIVE.
WHAT THE . . . ?
AHT *AHT* *AHT* *AHT*
AWW, C'MERE, DOGGIE.
FSSSSS
SORRY ABOUT THAT. SHE GETS REAL NERVOUS AROUND STRANGERS.
IT'S YOUR FLOOR.
WHAT'S WRONG WITH HER?
WHAT'S NOT WRONG? NO TEETH, NO VOICE, BROKEN LEG, BAD HEART, PARASITES, PALSY, ETC.
THE HUMANE SOCIETY WAS GOING TO PUT HER DOWN BUT I RESCUED HER.
YOU SURE YOU DID THE RIGHT THING?
I KNOW WHAT YOU MEAN, BUT I COULD TELL MITZY HERE WANTED TO LIVE.
"MITZY"?
PFFFT!
LOOK, MITZY, SHE'S JUST LIKE YOU, ALL SKINNY AND SICKLY. AND JUST LIKE THIS MITZY, YOU PEED YOURSELF LAST NIGHT. YOU'RE A PRECIOUS MITZY AREN'T YOU? YES YOU ARE.
HIROSHIMA

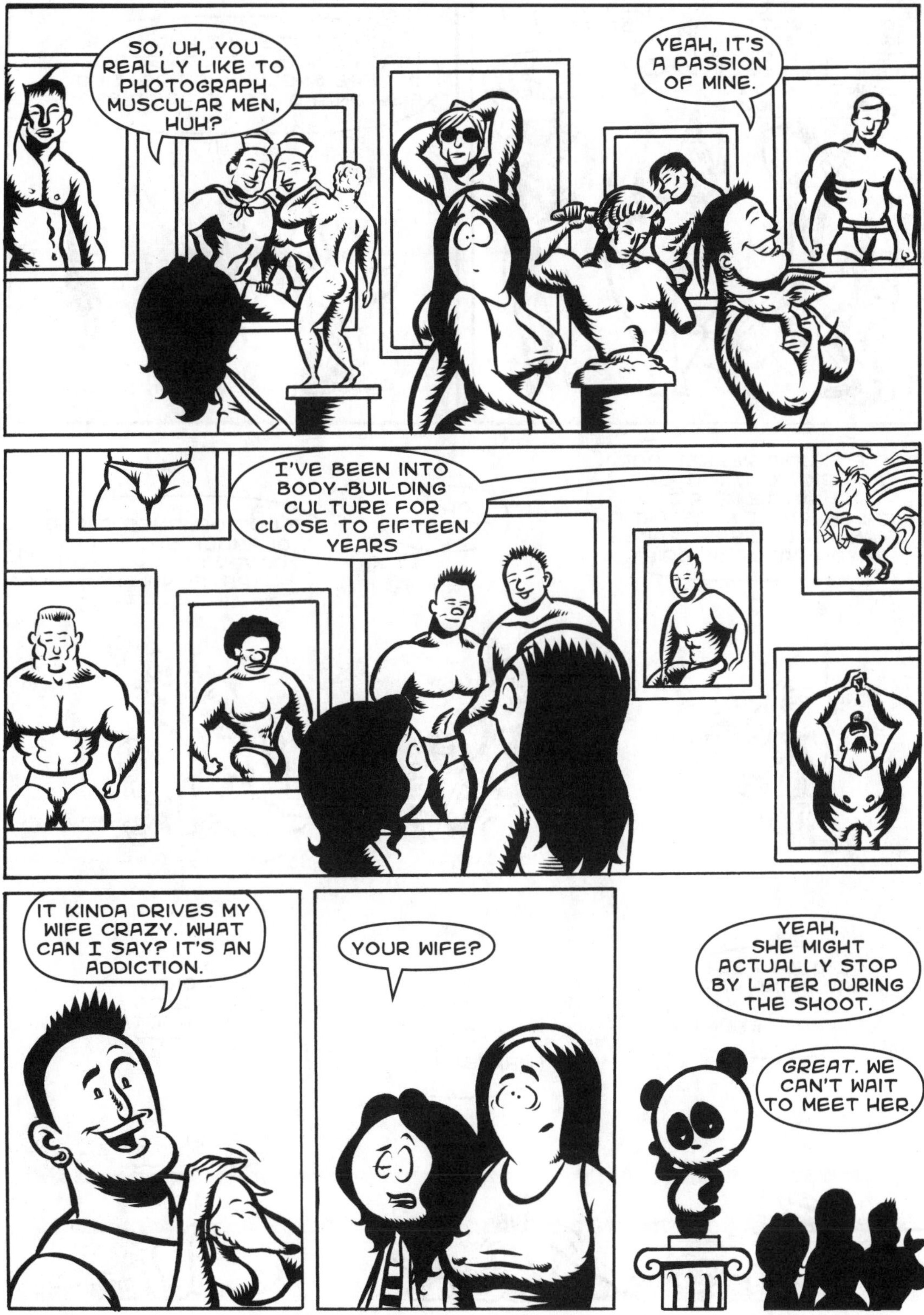
SO, UH, YOU REALLY LIKE TO PHOTOGRAPH MUSCULAR MEN, HUH?
YEAH, IT'S A PASSION OF MINE.
I'VE BEEN INTO BODY-BUILDING CULTURE FOR CLOSE TO FIFTEEN YEARS
IT KINDA DRIVES MY WIFE CRAZY. WHAT CAN I SAY? IT'S AN ADDICTION.
YOUR WIFE?
YEAH, SHE MIGHT ACTUALLY STOP BY LATER DURING THE SHOOT.
GREAT. WE CAN'T WAIT TO MEET HER.

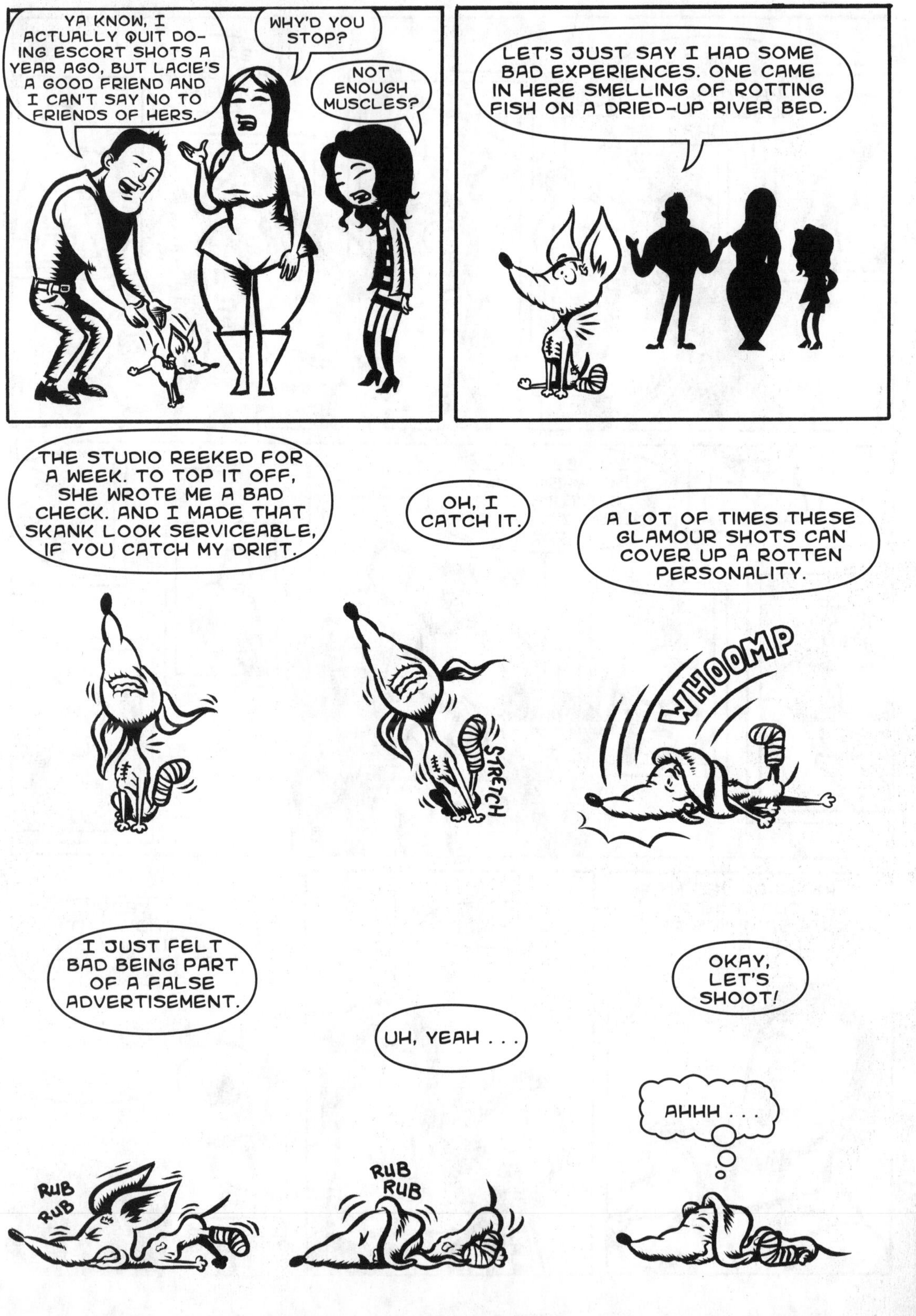
YA KNOW, I ACTUALLY QUIT DOING ESCORT SHOTS A YEAR AGO, BUT LACIE'S A GOOD FRIEND AND I CAN'T SAY NO TO FRIENDS OF HERS.
WHY'D YOU STOP?
NOT ENOUGH MUSCLES?
LET'S JUST SAY I HAD SOME BAD EXPERIENCES. ONE CAME IN HERE SMELLING OF ROTTING FISH ON A DRIED-UP RIVER BED.
THE STUDIO REEKED FOR A WEEK. TO TOP IT OFF, SHE WROTE ME A BAD CHECK. AND I MADE THAT SKANK LOOK SERVICEABLE, IF YOU CATCH MY DRIFT.
OH, I CATCH IT.
A LOT OF TIMES THESE GLAMOUR SHOTS CAN COVER UP A ROTTEN PERSONALITY.
STRETCH
WHOOMP
I JUST FELT BAD BEING PART OF A FALSE ADVERTISEMENT.
UH, YEAH . . .
OKAY, LET'S SHOOT!
AHHH . . .
RUB RUB
RUB RUB

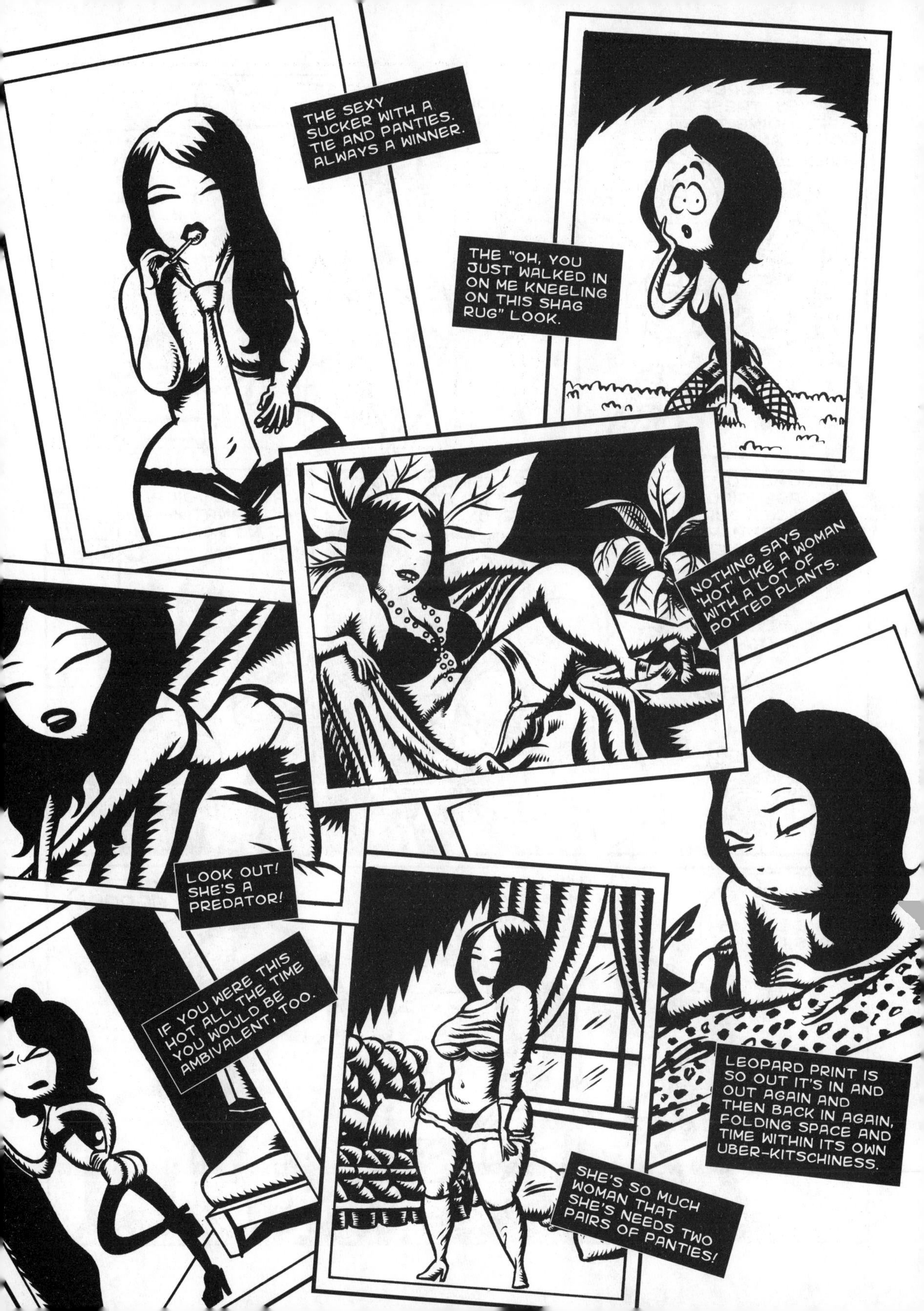
THE SEXY SUCKER WITH A TIE AND PANTIES. ALWAYS A WINNER.
THE "OH, YOU JUST WALKED IN ON ME KNEELING ON THIS SHAG RUG" LOOK.
NOTHING SAYS 'HOT' LIKE A WOMAN WITH A LOT OF POTTED PLANTS.
LOOK OUT! SHE'S A PREDATOR!
IF YOU WERE THIS HOT ALL THE TIME YOU WOULD BE AMBIVALENT, TOO.
LEOPARD PRINT IS SO OUT IT'S IN AND OUT AGAIN AND THEN BACK IN AGAIN, FOLDING SPACE AND TIME WITHIN ITS OWN UBER-KITSCHINESS.
SHE'S SO MUCH WOMAN THAT SHE'S NEEDS TWO PAIRS OF PANTIES!

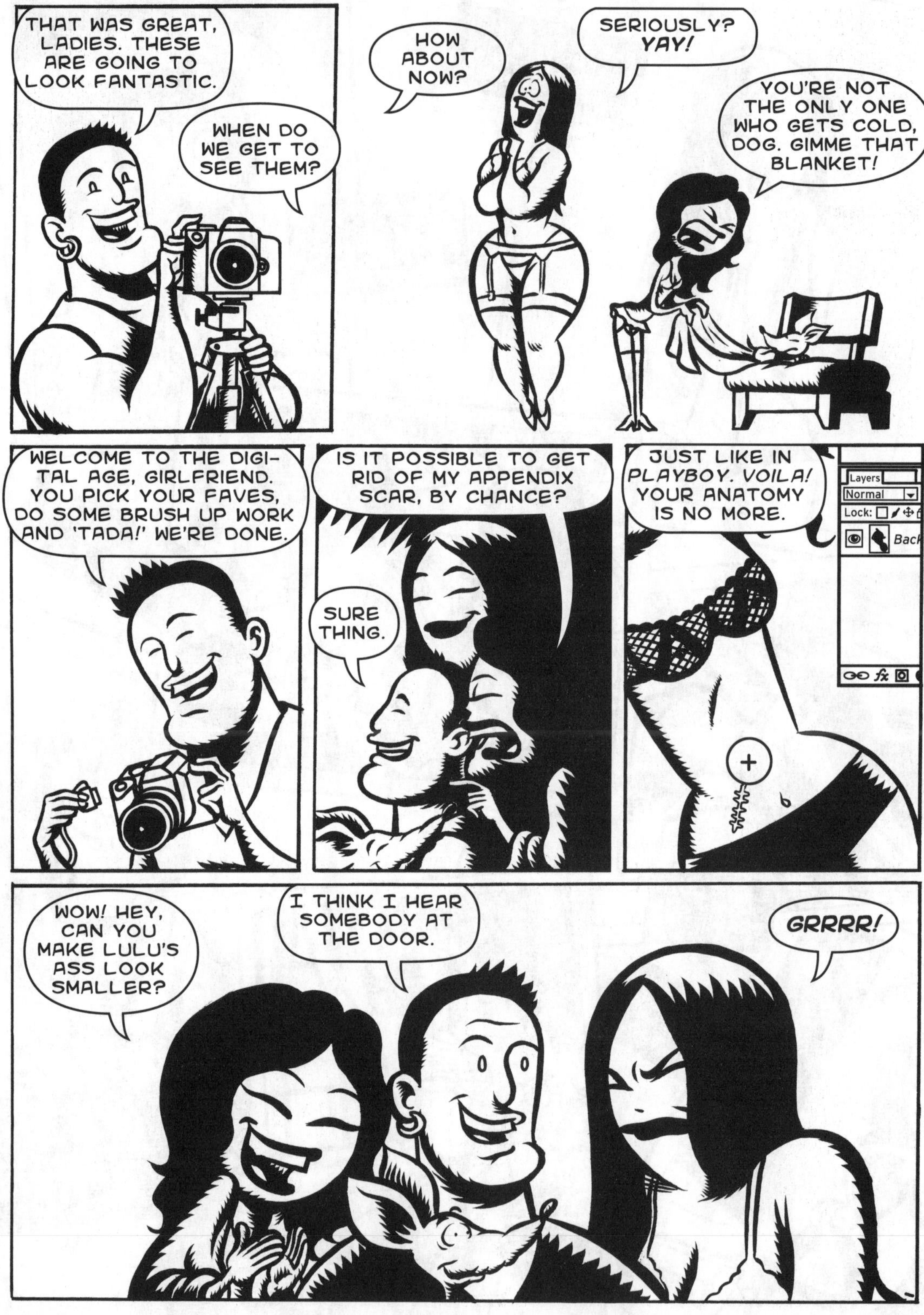
THAT WAS GREAT, LADIES. THESE ARE GOING TO LOOK FANTASTIC.
WHEN DO WE GET TO SEE THEM?
HOW ABOUT NOW?
SERIOUSLY? *YAY!*
YOU'RE NOT THE ONLY ONE WHO GETS COLD, DOG. GIMME THAT BLANKET!
WELCOME TO THE DIGITAL AGE, GIRLFRIEND. YOU PICK YOUR FAVES, DO SOME BRUSH UP WORK AND 'TADA!' WE'RE DONE.
IS IT POSSIBLE TO GET RID OF MY APPENDIX SCAR, BY CHANCE?
SURE THING.
JUST LIKE IN *PLAYBOY. VOILA!* YOUR ANATOMY IS NO MORE.
Layers
Normal
Lock:
Back
WOW! HEY, CAN YOU MAKE LULU'S ASS LOOK SMALLER?
I THINK I HEAR SOMEBODY AT THE DOOR.
GRRRR!

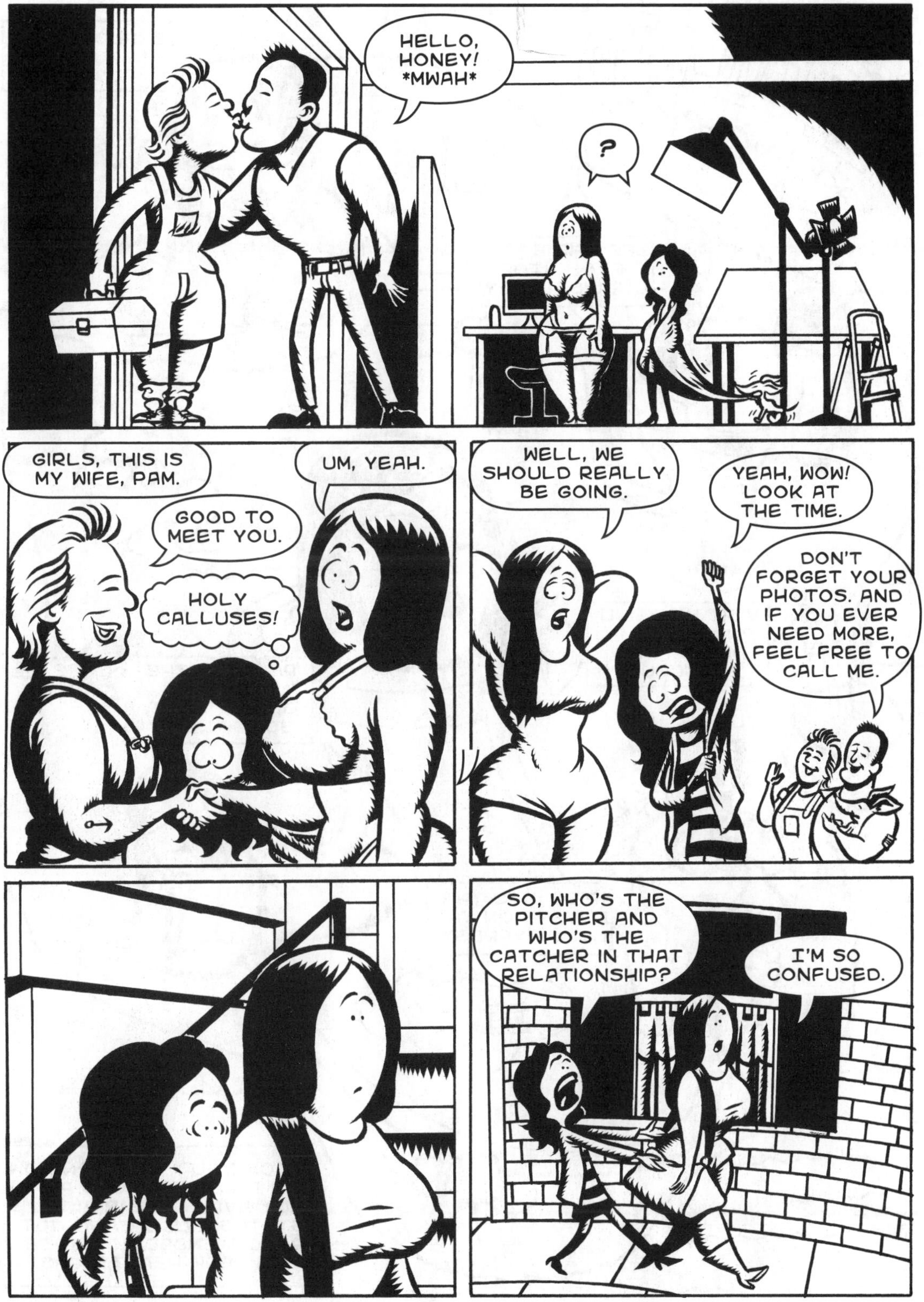
HELLO, HONEY! *MWAH*
?
GIRLS, THIS IS MY WIFE, PAM.
GOOD TO MEET YOU.
HOLY CALLUSES!
UM, YEAH.
WELL, WE SHOULD REALLY BE GOING.
YEAH, WOW! LOOK AT THE TIME.
DON'T FORGET YOUR PHOTOS. AND IF YOU EVER NEED MORE, FEEL FREE TO CALL ME.
SO, WHO'S THE PITCHER AND WHO'S THE CATCHER IN THAT RELATIONSHIP?
I'M SO CONFUSED.

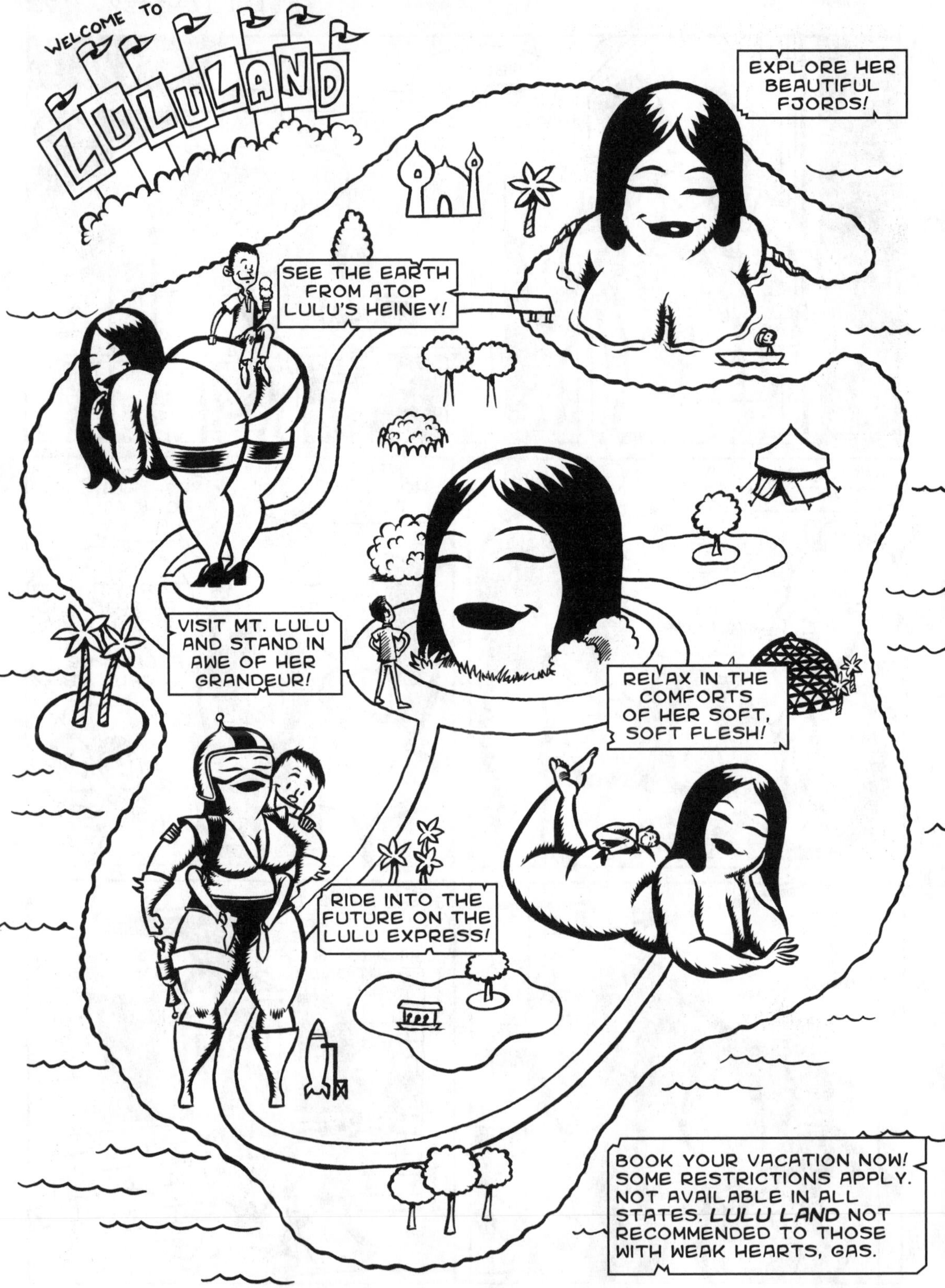
WELCOME TO
LULULAND
EXPLORE HER BEAUTIFUL FJORDS!
SEE THE EARTH FROM ATOP LULU'S HEINEY!
VISIT MT. LULU AND STAND IN AWE OF HER GRANDEUR!
RELAX IN THE COMFORTS OF HER SOFT, SOFT FLESH!
RIDE INTO THE FUTURE ON THE LULU EXPRESS!
BOOK YOUR VACATION NOW! SOME RESTRICTIONS APPLY. NOT AVAILABLE IN ALL STATES. LULU LAND NOT RECOMMENDED TO THOSE WITH WEAK HEARTS, GAS.

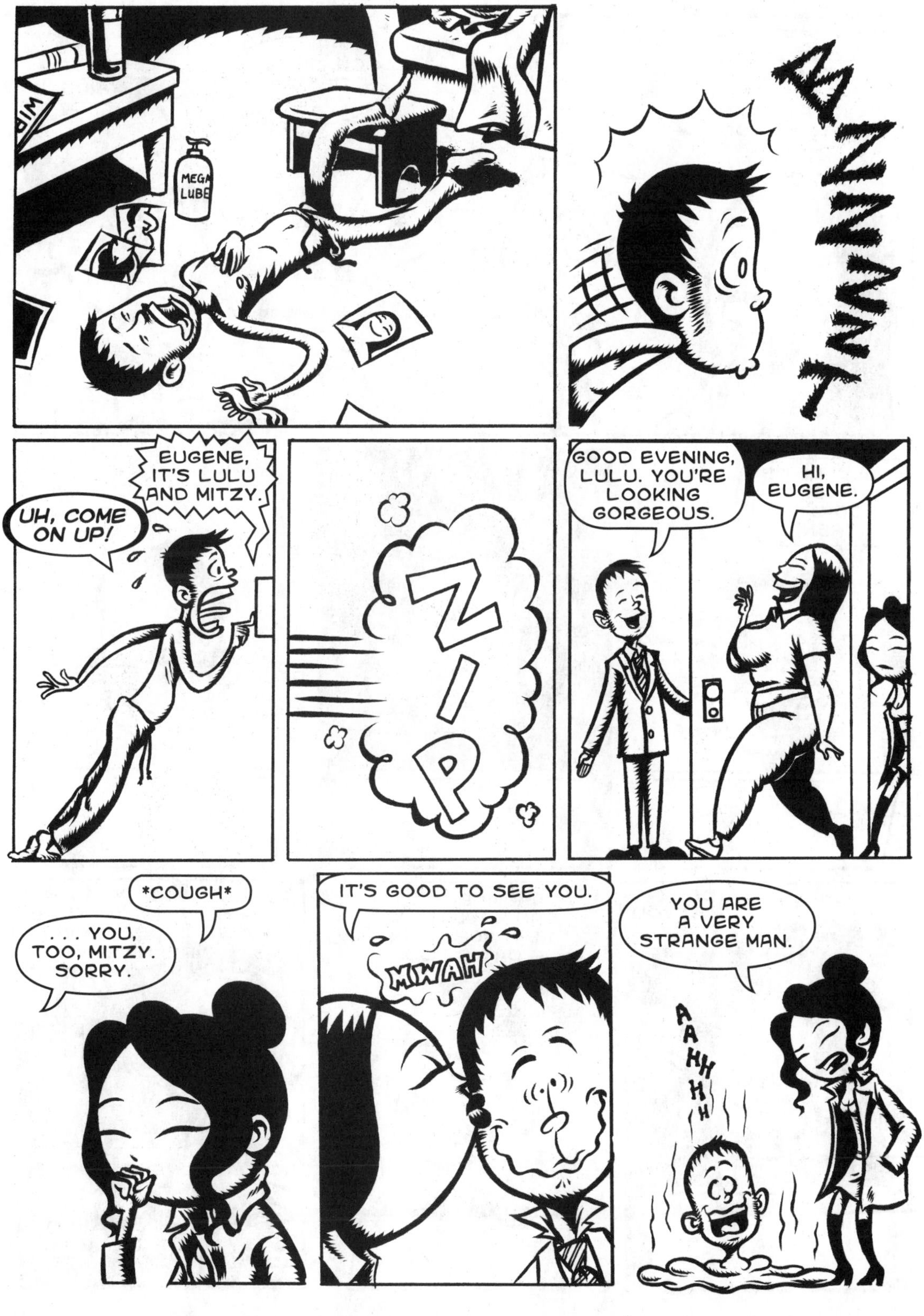
MEGA LUBE
BZZZZT
EUGENE, IT'S LULU AND MITZY.
UH, COME ON UP!
ZIP
GOOD EVENING, LULU. YOU'RE LOOKING GORGEOUS.
HI, EUGENE.
COUGH
. . . YOU, TOO, MITZY. SORRY.
IT'S GOOD TO SEE YOU.
MWAH
YOU ARE A VERY STRANGE MAN.
AAHHHH

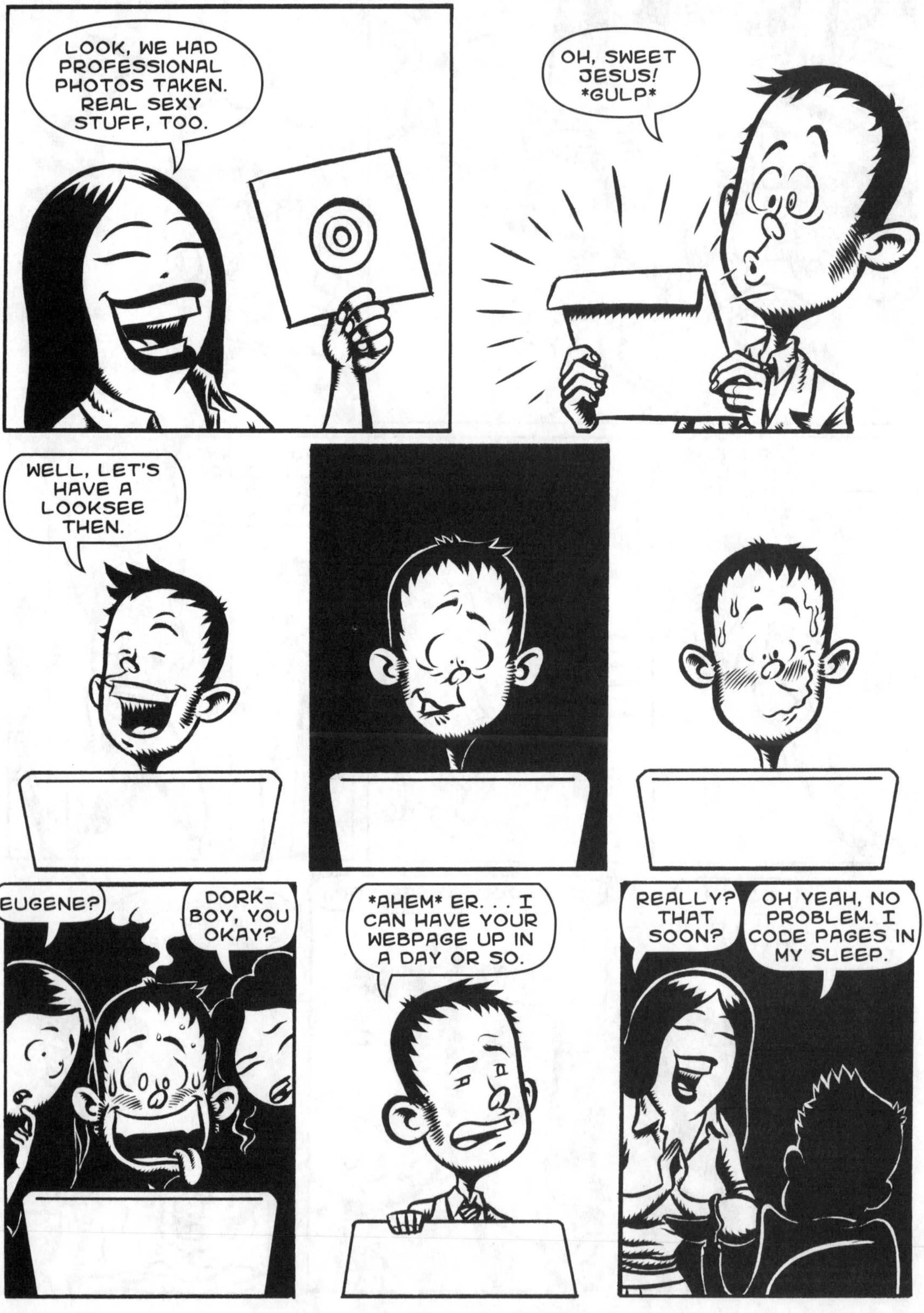
LOOK, WE HAD PROFESSIONAL PHOTOS TAKEN. REAL SEXY STUFF, TOO.
OH, SWEET JESUS! *GULP*
WELL, LET'S HAVE A LOOKSEE THEN.
EUGENE?
DORK-BOY, YOU OKAY?
AHEM ER. . . I CAN HAVE YOUR WEBPAGE UP IN A DAY OR SO.
REALLY? THAT SOON?
OH YEAH, NO PROBLEM. I CODE PAGES IN MY SLEEP.

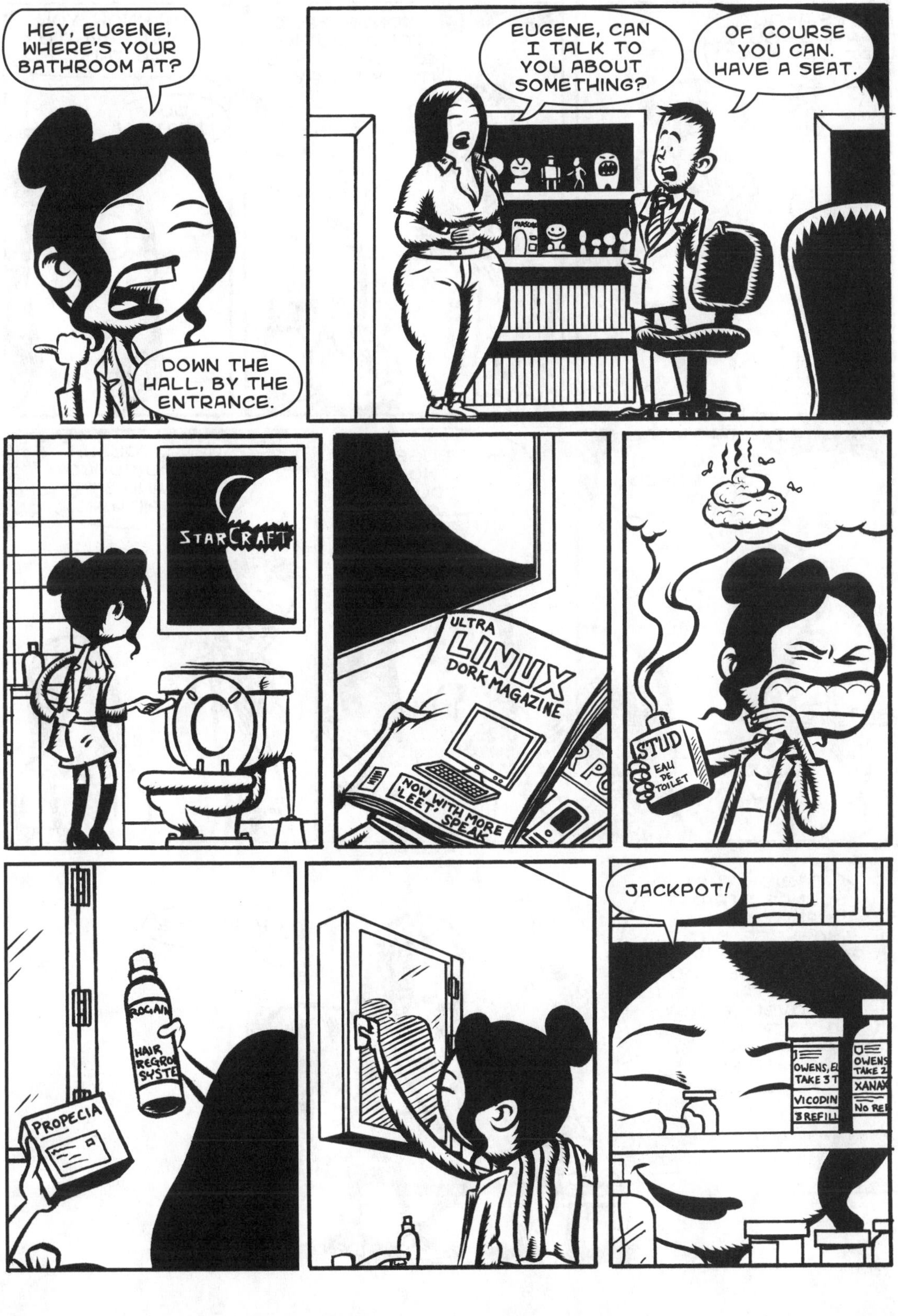
HEY, EUGENE, WHERE'S YOUR BATHROOM AT?
DOWN THE HALL, BY THE ENTRANCE.
EUGENE, CAN I TALK TO YOU ABOUT SOMETHING?
OF COURSE YOU CAN. HAVE A SEAT.
STARCRAFT
ULTRA LINUX DORK MAGAZINE
NOW WITH MORE 'LEET' SPEAK
STUD EAU DE TOILET
PROPECIA
HAIR
JACKPOT!
VICODIN
XANAX

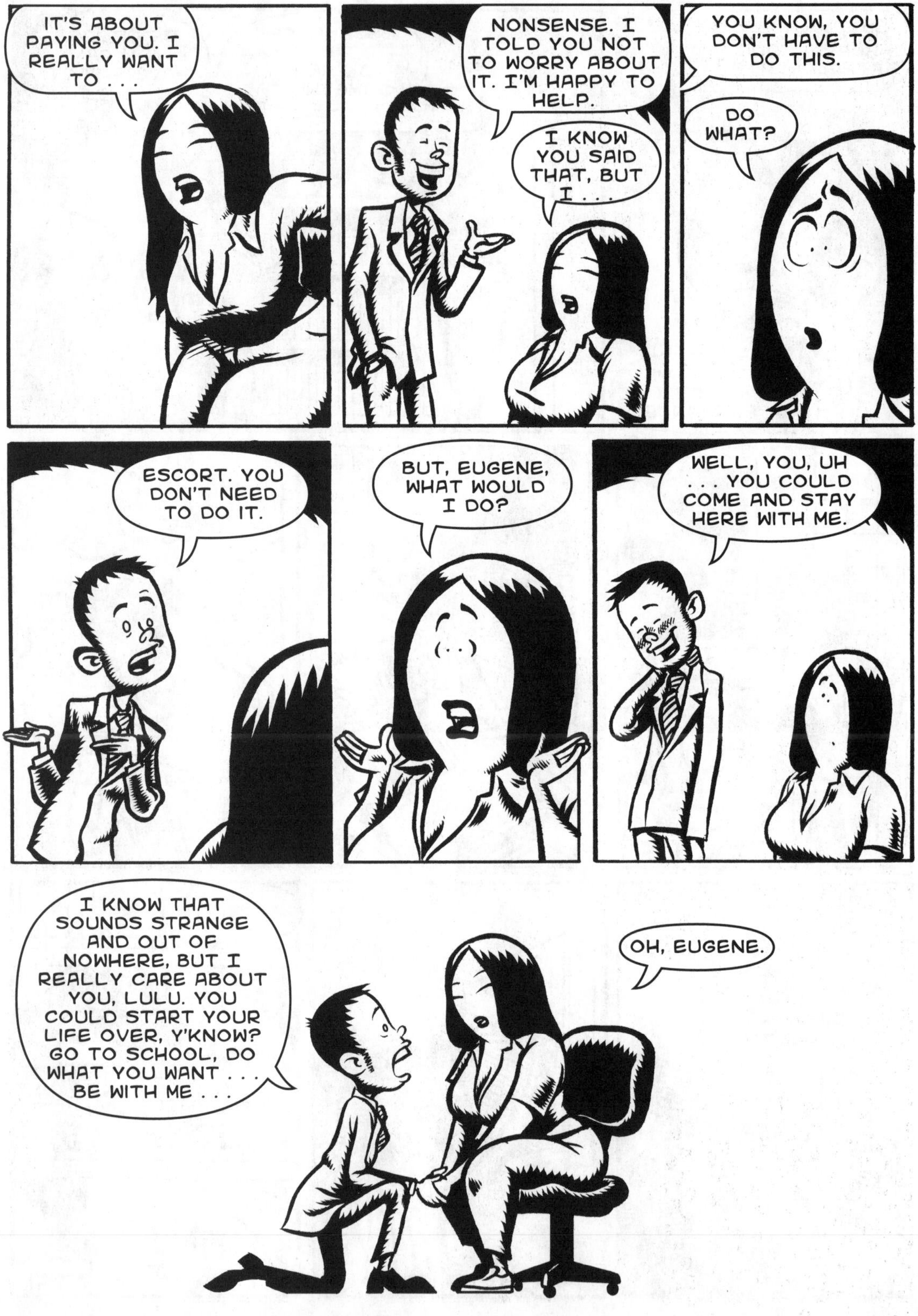
IT'S ABOUT PAYING YOU. I REALLY WANT TO . . .
NONSENSE. I TOLD YOU NOT TO WORRY ABOUT IT. I'M HAPPY TO HELP.
I KNOW YOU SAID THAT, BUT I . . .
YOU KNOW, YOU DON'T HAVE TO DO THIS.
DO WHAT?
ESCORT. YOU DON'T NEED TO DO IT.
BUT, EUGENE, WHAT WOULD I DO?
WELL, YOU, UH . . . YOU COULD COME AND STAY HERE WITH ME.
I KNOW THAT SOUNDS STRANGE AND OUT OF NOWHERE, BUT I REALLY CARE ABOUT YOU, LULU. YOU COULD START YOUR LIFE OVER, Y'KNOW? GO TO SCHOOL, DO WHAT YOU WANT . . . BE WITH ME . . .
OH, EUGENE.

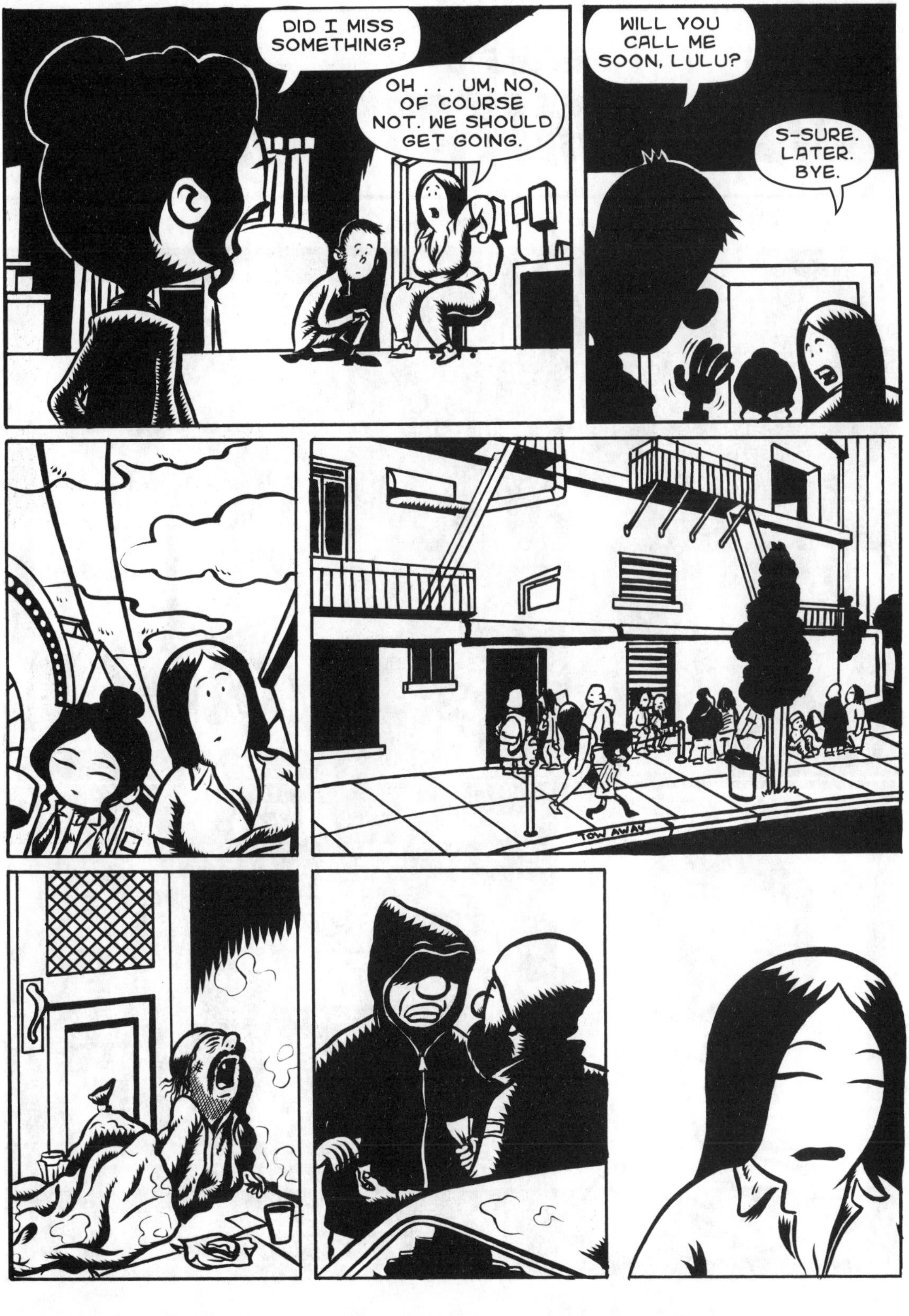
DID I MISS SOMETHING?
OH . . . UM, NO, OF COURSE NOT. WE SHOULD GET GOING.
WILL YOU CALL ME SOON, LULU?
S-SURE. LATER. BYE.
TOW AWAY

WELCOME TO
LULU & MITZY.COM

HOME   GALLERY   CONTACT   RATES   FAQs

LULU

A LATINA GODDESS OF BRICKHOUSE STATURE, LULU IS AS GENTLE AND SOFT AS SHE IS TALL AND STRONG. SHE LOVES INTELLIGENT CONVERSATION, ART, AND THE SENSUAL MUSICAL STYLINGS OF STAB B. STABAHO.

HEIGHT: 6'3"
BREASTS: DDD

MITZY

THIS LITTLE ASIAN HOTTIE IS LIKE A SHOT OF SAKE: SHARP, LIGHT, AND LEAVES YOU VERY THIRSTY HALF AN HOUR LATER. SHE CAN PRETEND TO BE JAPANESE, WHICH MEANS YOU'LL HAVE TO PAY MORE BECAUSE THAT'S TOP OF THE YELLOW-FEVER FOODCHAIN TO YOU BASTARDS WHO FETISHIZE RACE. MITZY IS AS DELICATE AS A CHERRY BLOSSOM BLOWING IN A COOL SPRING BREEZE. SHE ALSO LAYS CLAIM TO MANCHURIA.

HEIGHT: 5'5"
BREASTS: B-ISH

DISCLAIMER!
BY AGREEING TO SEE US, YOU UNDERSTAND THAT OUR FEES ARE FOR COMPANIONSHIP AND TIME ONLY. OUR SERVICES ARE NOT AN OFFER FOR PROSTITUTION. SO STOP SNOOPIN', COPPER!

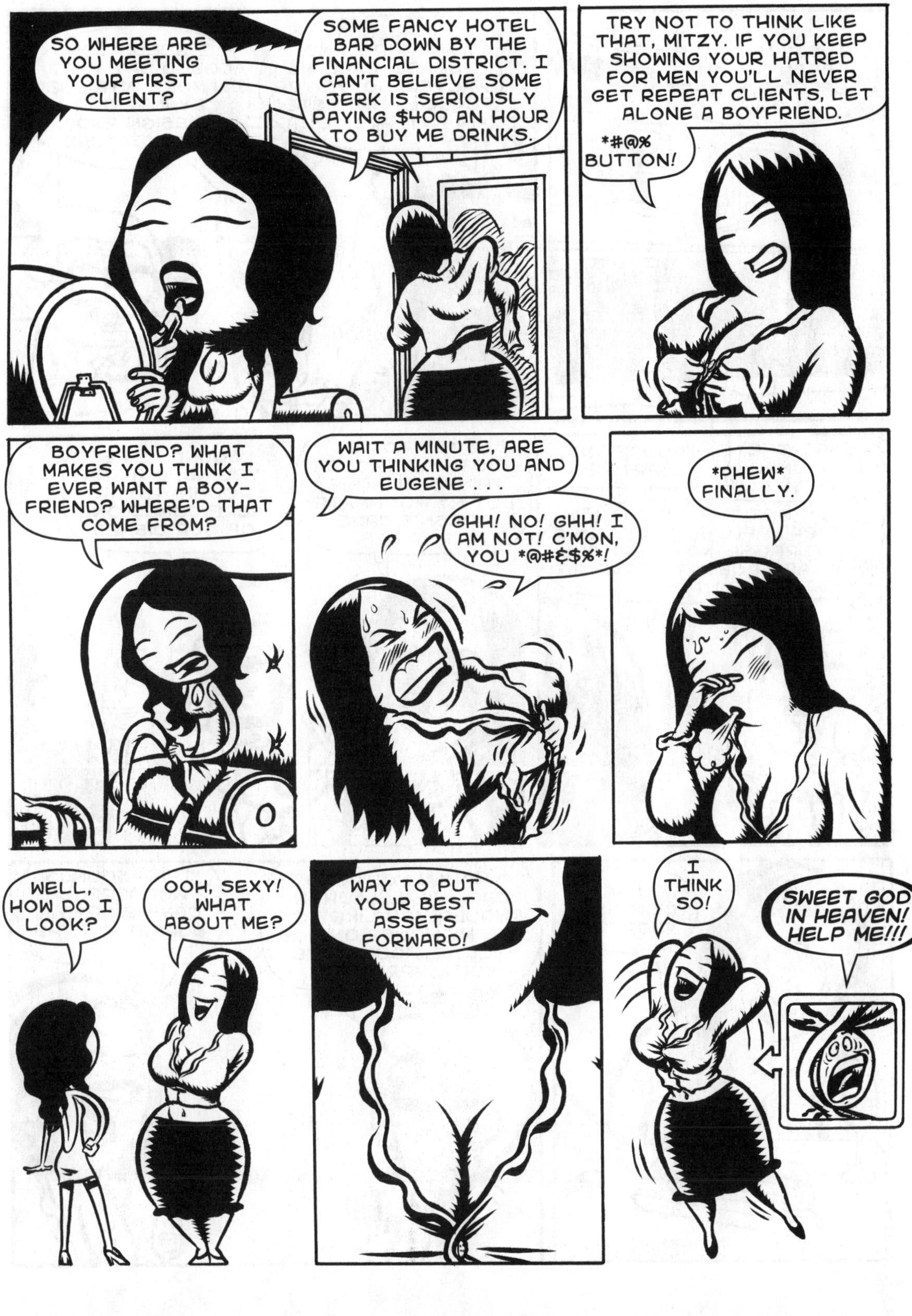
SO WHERE ARE YOU MEETING YOUR FIRST CLIENT?
SOME FANCY HOTEL BAR DOWN BY THE FINANCIAL DISTRICT. I CAN'T BELIEVE SOME JERK IS SERIOUSLY PAYING $400 AN HOUR TO BUY ME DRINKS.
TRY NOT TO THINK LIKE THAT, MITZY. IF YOU KEEP SHOWING YOUR HATRED FOR MEN YOU'LL NEVER GET REPEAT CLIENTS, LET ALONE A BOYFRIEND.
*#@% BUTTON!
BOYFRIEND? WHAT MAKES YOU THINK I EVER WANT A BOY-FRIEND? WHERE'D THAT COME FROM?
WAIT A MINUTE, ARE YOU THINKING YOU AND EUGENE . . .
GHH! NO! GHH! I AM NOT! C'MON, YOU *@#&$%*!
PHEW FINALLY.
WELL, HOW DO I LOOK?
OOH, SEXY! WHAT ABOUT ME?
WAY TO PUT YOUR BEST ASSETS FORWARD!
I THINK SO!
SWEET GOD IN HEAVEN! HELP ME!!!

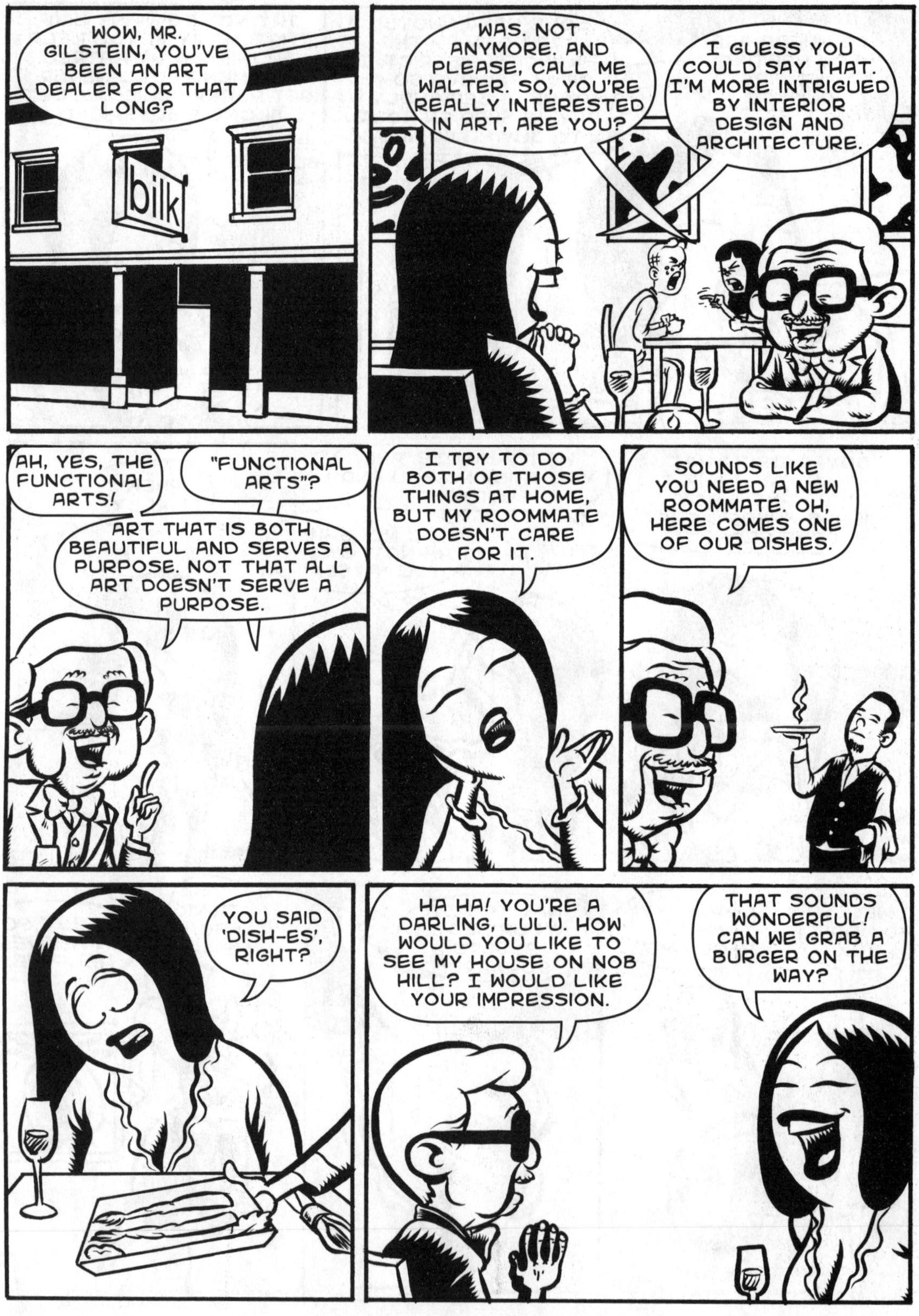
WOW, MR. GILSTEIN, YOU'VE BEEN AN ART DEALER FOR THAT LONG?
bilk
WAS. NOT ANYMORE. AND PLEASE, CALL ME WALTER. SO, YOU'RE REALLY INTERESTED IN ART, ARE YOU?
I GUESS YOU COULD SAY THAT. I'M MORE INTRIGUED BY INTERIOR DESIGN AND ARCHITECTURE.
AH, YES, THE FUNCTIONAL ARTS!
"FUNCTIONAL ARTS"?
ART THAT IS BOTH BEAUTIFUL AND SERVES A PURPOSE. NOT THAT ALL ART DOESN'T SERVE A PURPOSE.
I TRY TO DO BOTH OF THOSE THINGS AT HOME, BUT MY ROOMMATE DOESN'T CARE FOR IT.
SOUNDS LIKE YOU NEED A NEW ROOMMATE. OH, HERE COMES ONE OF OUR DISHES.
YOU SAID 'DISH-ES', RIGHT?
HA HA! YOU'RE A DARLING, LULU. HOW WOULD YOU LIKE TO SEE MY HOUSE ON NOB HILL? I WOULD LIKE YOUR IMPRESSION.
THAT SOUNDS WONDERFUL! CAN WE GRAB A BURGER ON THE WAY?

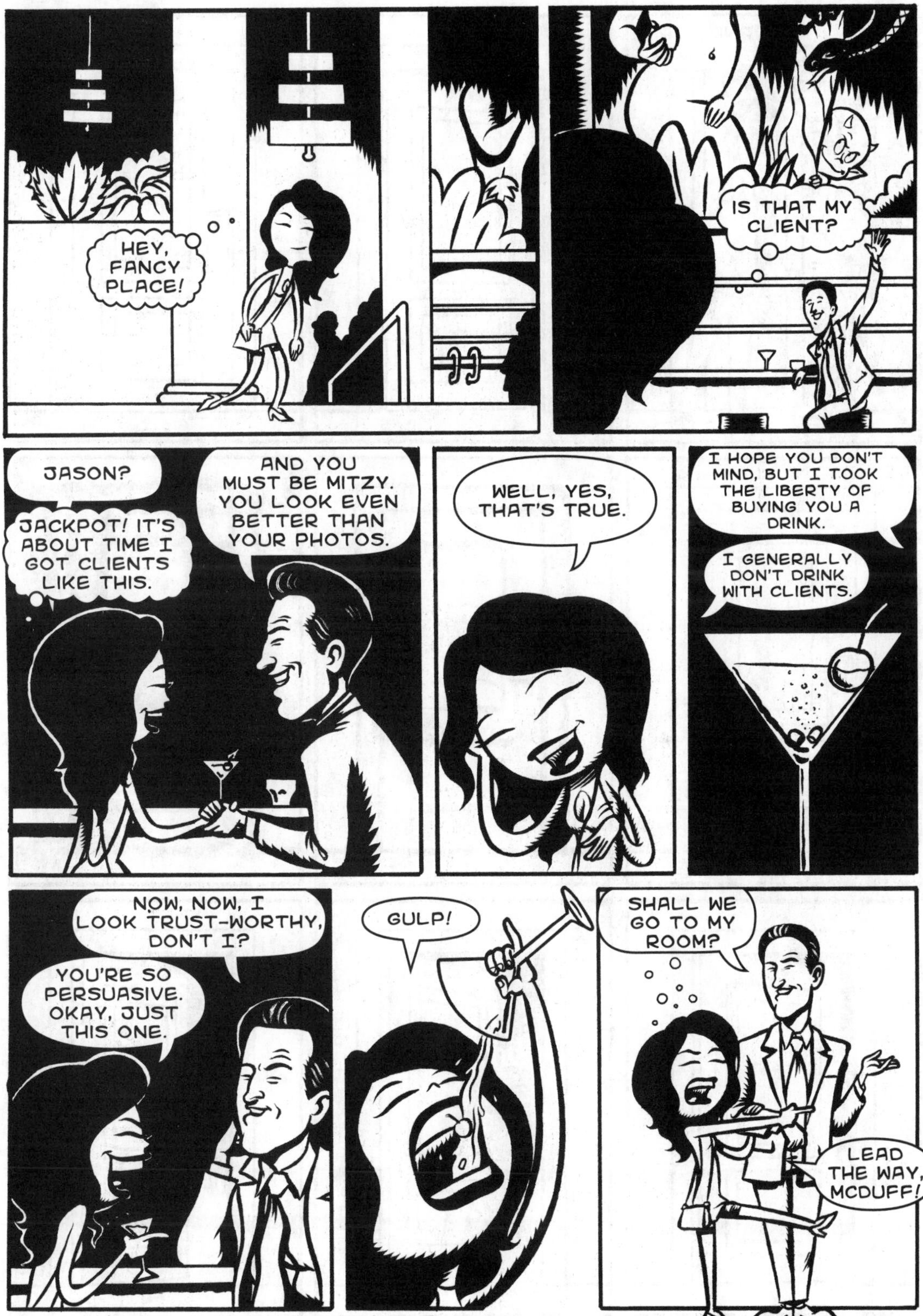
HEY, FANCY PLACE!
IS THAT MY CLIENT?
JASON?
JACKPOT! IT'S ABOUT TIME I GOT CLIENTS LIKE THIS.
AND YOU MUST BE MITZY. YOU LOOK EVEN BETTER THAN YOUR PHOTOS.
WELL, YES, THAT'S TRUE.
I HOPE YOU DON'T MIND, BUT I TOOK THE LIBERTY OF BUYING YOU A DRINK.
I GENERALLY DON'T DRINK WITH CLIENTS.
NOW, NOW, I LOOK TRUST-WORTHY, DON'T I?
YOU'RE SO PERSUASIVE. OKAY, JUST THIS ONE.
GULP!
SHALL WE GO TO MY ROOM?
LEAD THE WAY, MCDUFF!

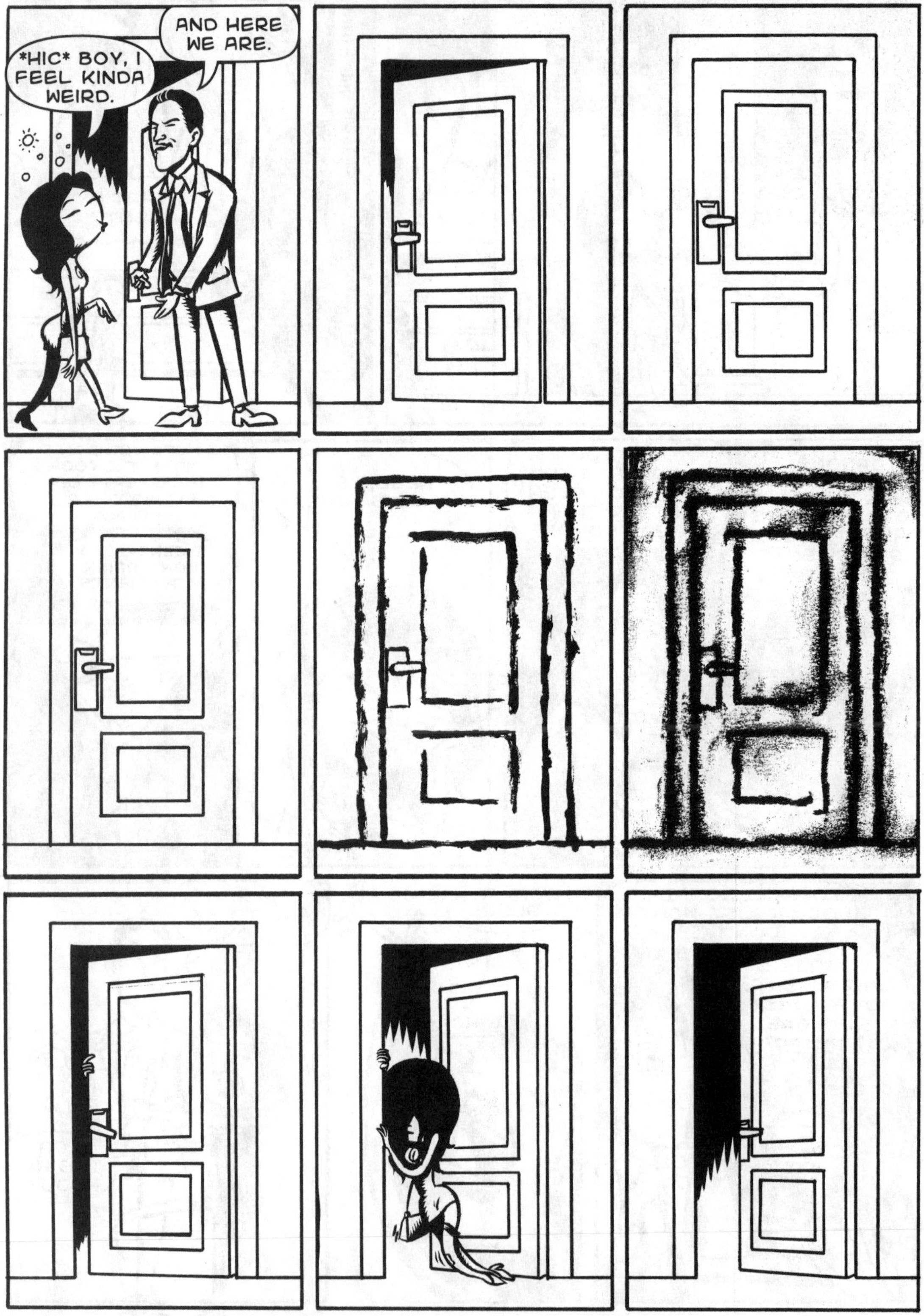
AND HERE WE ARE.
HIC BOY, I FEEL KINDA WEIRD.

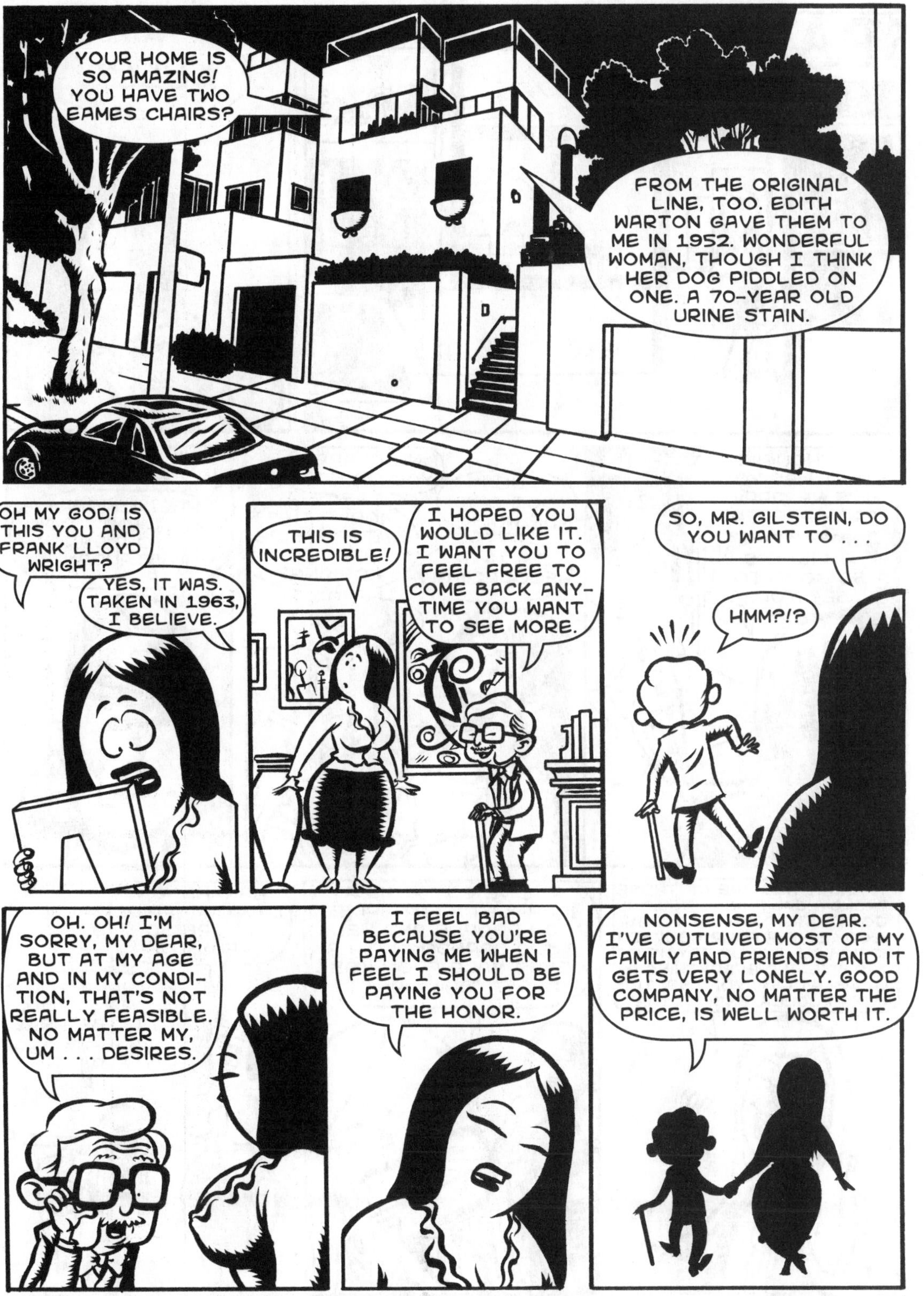
YOUR HOME IS SO AMAZING! YOU HAVE TWO EAMES CHAIRS?
FROM THE ORIGINAL LINE, TOO. EDITH WARTON GAVE THEM TO ME IN 1952. WONDERFUL WOMAN, THOUGH I THINK HER DOG PIDDLED ON ONE. A 70-YEAR OLD URINE STAIN.
OH MY GOD! IS THIS YOU AND FRANK LLOYD WRIGHT?
YES, IT WAS. TAKEN IN 1963, I BELIEVE.
THIS IS INCREDIBLE!
I HOPED YOU WOULD LIKE IT. I WANT YOU TO FEEL FREE TO COME BACK ANY-TIME YOU WANT TO SEE MORE.
SO, MR. GILSTEIN, DO YOU WANT TO . . .
HMM?!?
OH. OH! I'M SORRY, MY DEAR, BUT AT MY AGE AND IN MY CONDI-TION, THAT'S NOT REALLY FEASIBLE. NO MATTER MY, UM . . . DESIRES.
I FEEL BAD BECAUSE YOU'RE PAYING ME WHEN I FEEL I SHOULD BE PAYING YOU FOR THE HONOR.
NONSENSE, MY DEAR. I'VE OUTLIVED MOST OF MY FAMILY AND FRIENDS AND IT GETS VERY LONELY. GOOD COMPANY, NO MATTER THE PRICE, IS WELL WORTH IT.

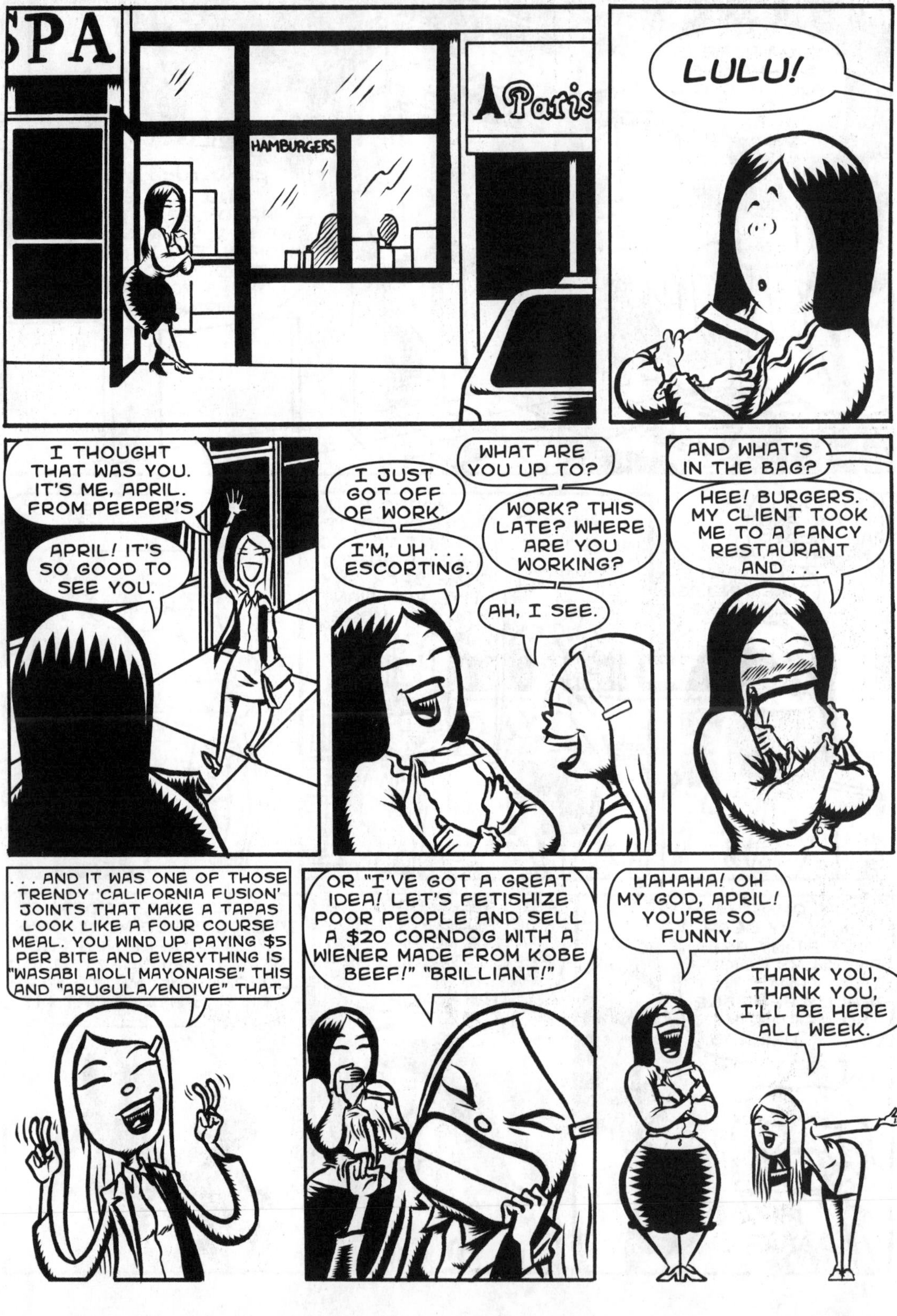
SPA
HAMBURGERS
Paris
LULU!
I THOUGHT THAT WAS YOU. IT'S ME, APRIL. FROM PEEPER'S
APRIL! IT'S SO GOOD TO SEE YOU.
WHAT ARE YOU UP TO?
I JUST GOT OFF OF WORK.
WORK? THIS LATE? WHERE ARE YOU WORKING?
I'M, UH . . . ESCORTING.
AH, I SEE.
AND WHAT'S IN THE BAG?
HEE! BURGERS. MY CLIENT TOOK ME TO A FANCY RESTAURANT AND . . .
. . . AND IT WAS ONE OF THOSE TRENDY 'CALIFORNIA FUSION' JOINTS THAT MAKE A TAPAS LOOK LIKE A FOUR COURSE MEAL. YOU WIND UP PAYING $5 PER BITE AND EVERYTHING IS "WASABI AIOLI MAYONAISE" THIS AND "ARUGULA/ENDIVE" THAT.
OR "I'VE GOT A GREAT IDEA! LET'S FETISHIZE POOR PEOPLE AND SELL A $20 CORNDOG WITH A WIENER MADE FROM KOBE BEEF!" "BRILLIANT!"
HAHAHA! OH MY GOD, APRIL! YOU'RE SO FUNNY.
THANK YOU, THANK YOU, I'LL BE HERE ALL WEEK.

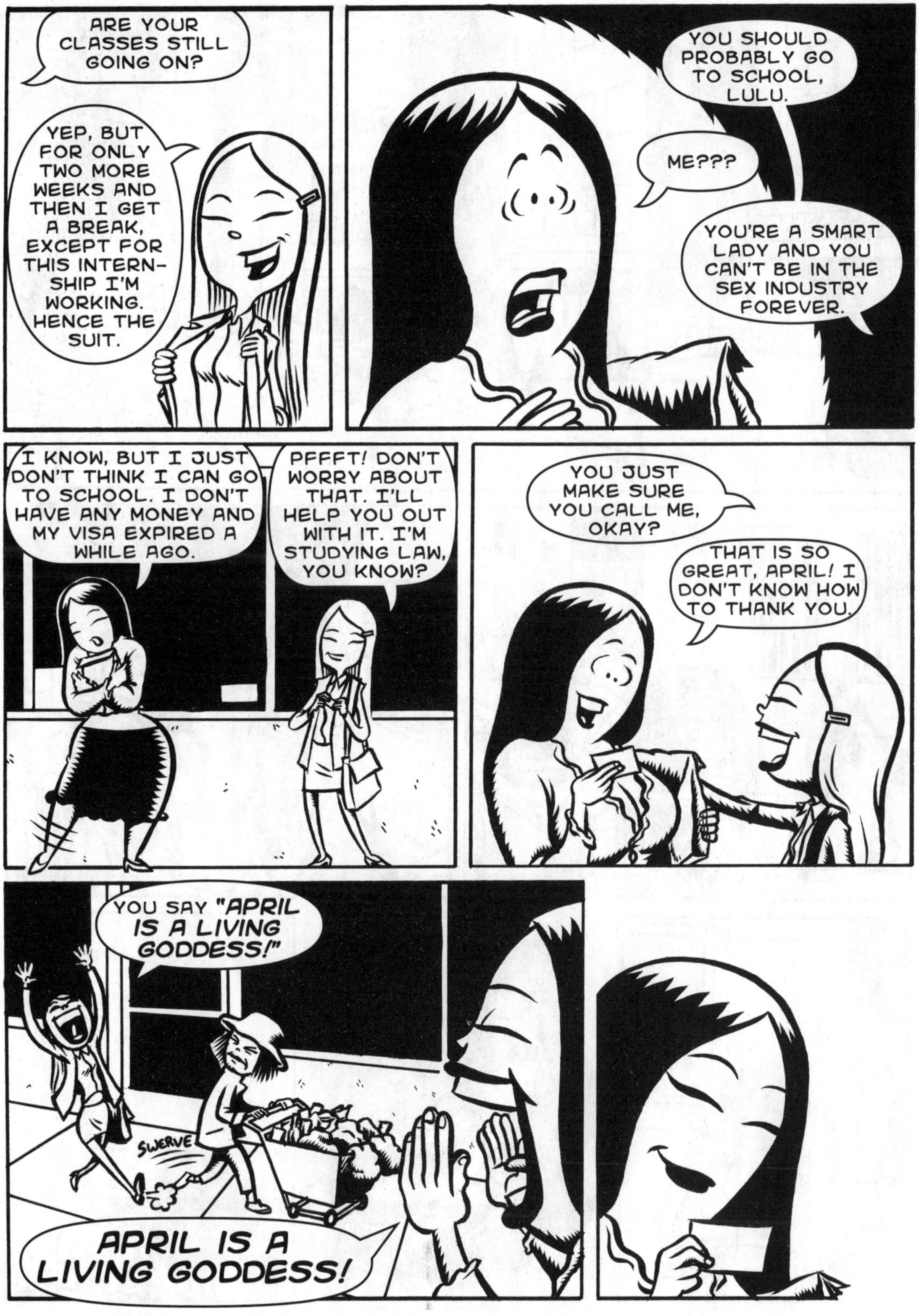
ARE YOUR CLASSES STILL GOING ON?
YEP, BUT FOR ONLY TWO MORE WEEKS AND THEN I GET A BREAK, EXCEPT FOR THIS INTERN-SHIP I'M WORKING. HENCE THE SUIT.
YOU SHOULD PROBABLY GO TO SCHOOL, LULU.
ME???
YOU'RE A SMART LADY AND YOU CAN'T BE IN THE SEX INDUSTRY FOREVER.
I KNOW, BUT I JUST DON'T THINK I CAN GO TO SCHOOL. I DON'T HAVE ANY MONEY AND MY VISA EXPIRED A WHILE AGO.
PFFFT! DON'T WORRY ABOUT THAT. I'LL HELP YOU OUT WITH IT. I'M STUDYING LAW, YOU KNOW?
YOU JUST MAKE SURE YOU CALL ME, OKAY?
THAT IS SO GREAT, APRIL! I DON'T KNOW HOW TO THANK YOU.
YOU SAY "APRIL IS A LIVING GODDESS!"
SWERVE
APRIL IS A LIVING GODDESS!

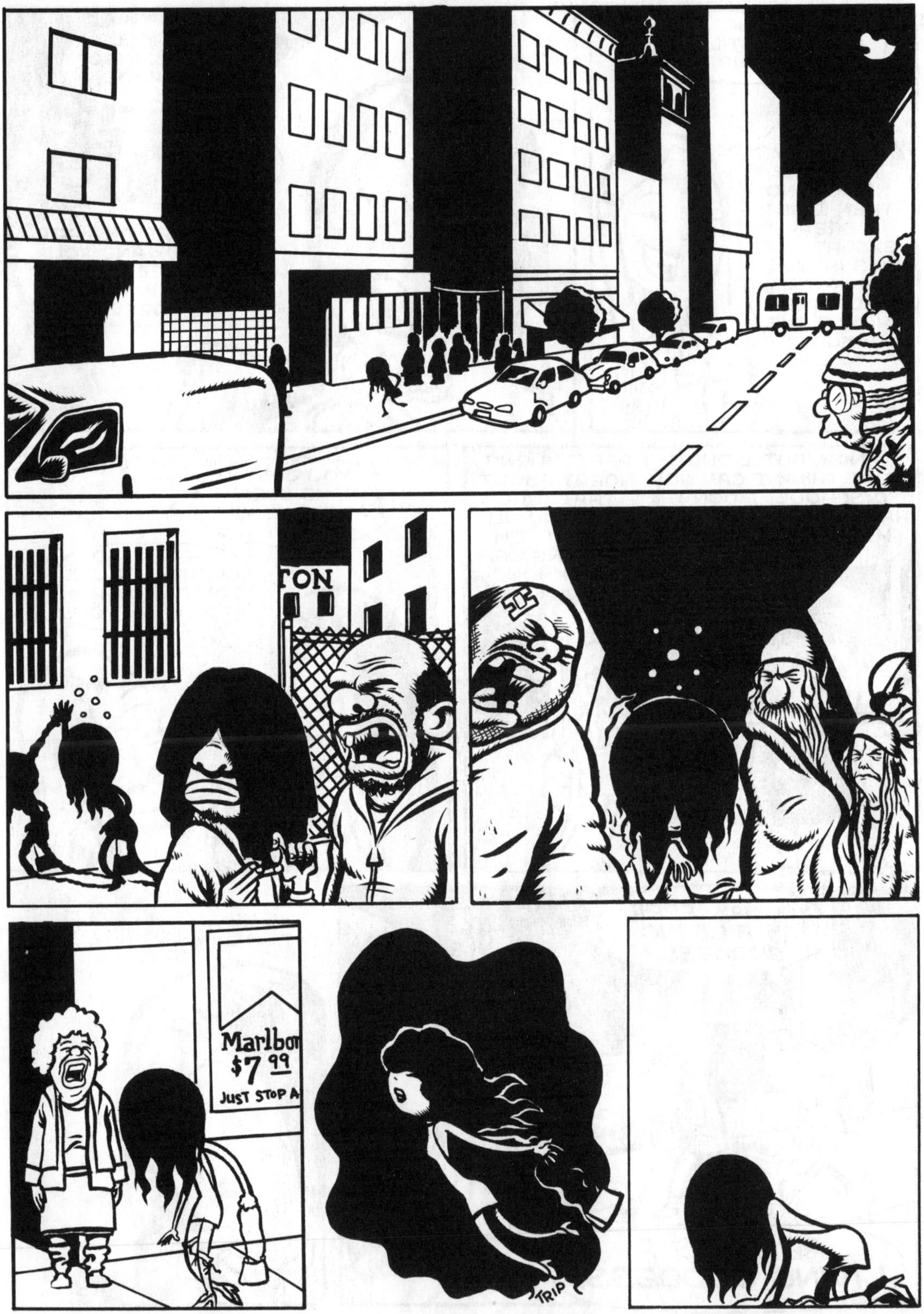
TON
Marlbor
$7 99
JUST STOP A
TRIP

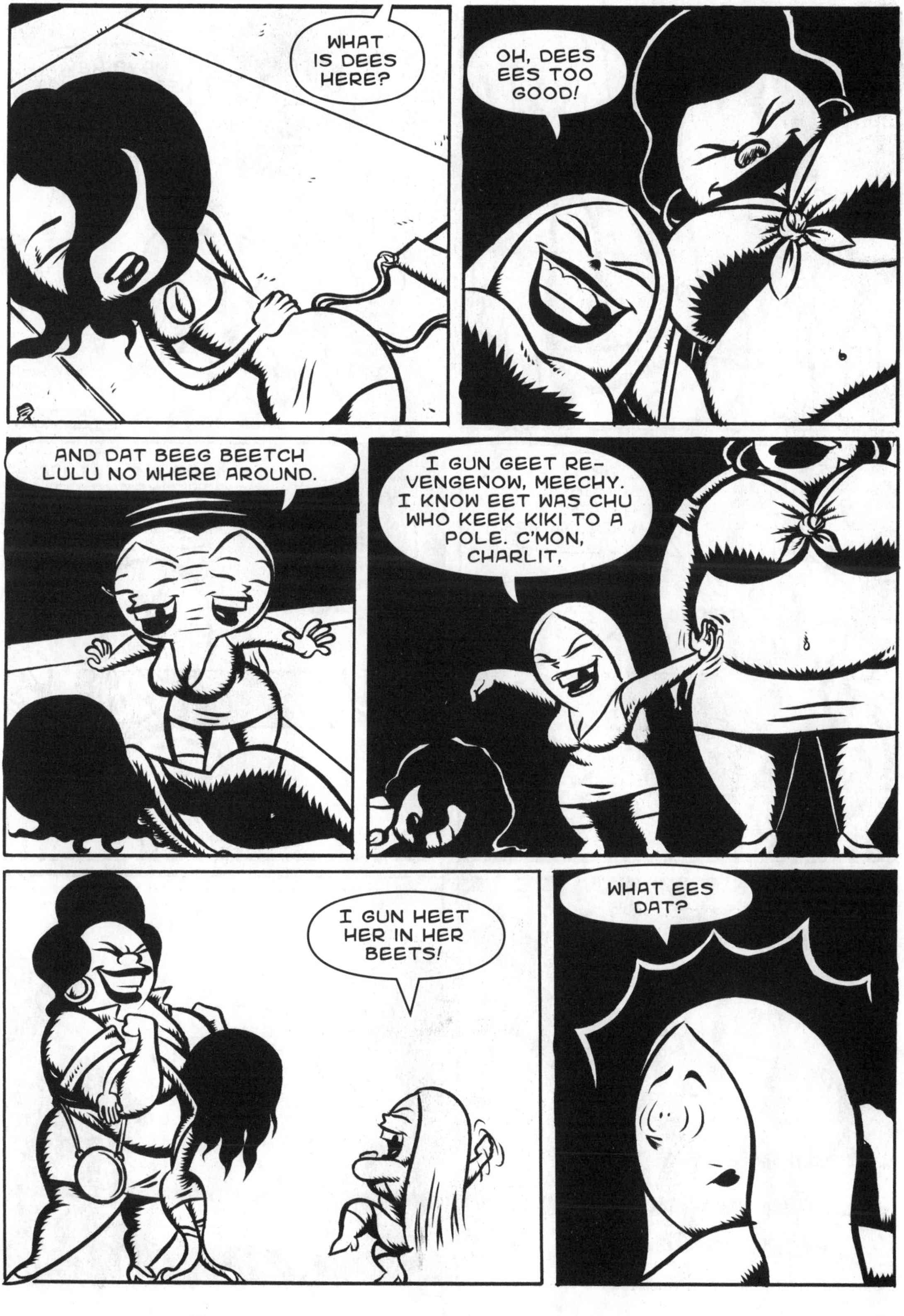
WHAT IS DEES HERE?
OH, DEES EES TOO GOOD!
AND DAT BEEG BEETCH LULU NO WHERE AROUND.
I GUN GEET RE-VENGENOW, MEECHY. I KNOW EET WAS CHU WHO KEEK KIKI TO A POLE. C'MON, CHARLIT,
I GUN HEET HER IN HER BEETS!
WHAT EES DAT?

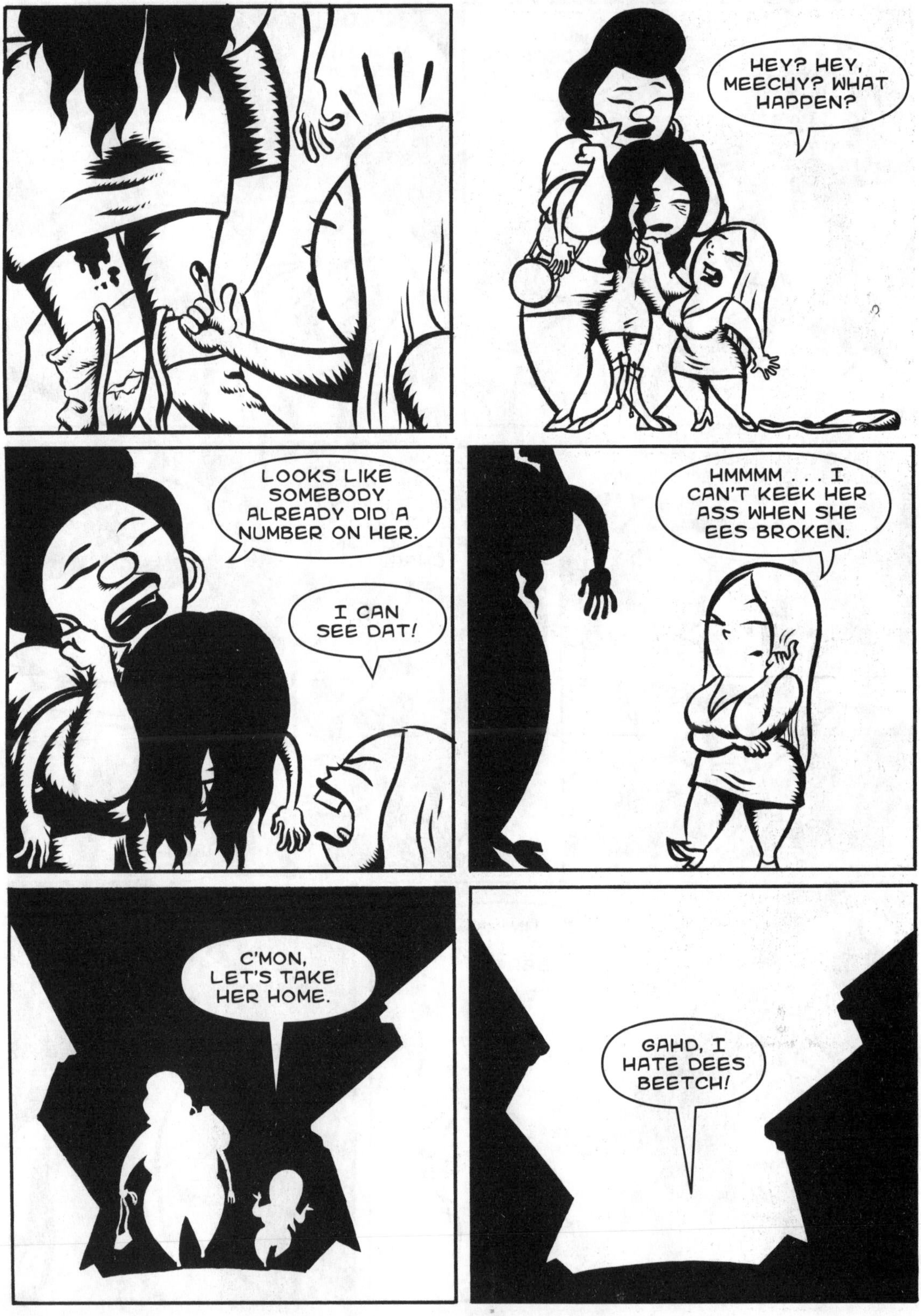
HEY? HEY, MEECHY? WHAT HAPPEN?
LOOKS LIKE SOMEBODY ALREADY DID A NUMBER ON HER.
I CAN SEE DAT!
HMMMM . . . I CAN'T KEEK HER ASS WHEN SHE EES BROKEN.
C'MON, LET'S TAKE HER HOME.
GAHD, I HATE DEES BEETCH!

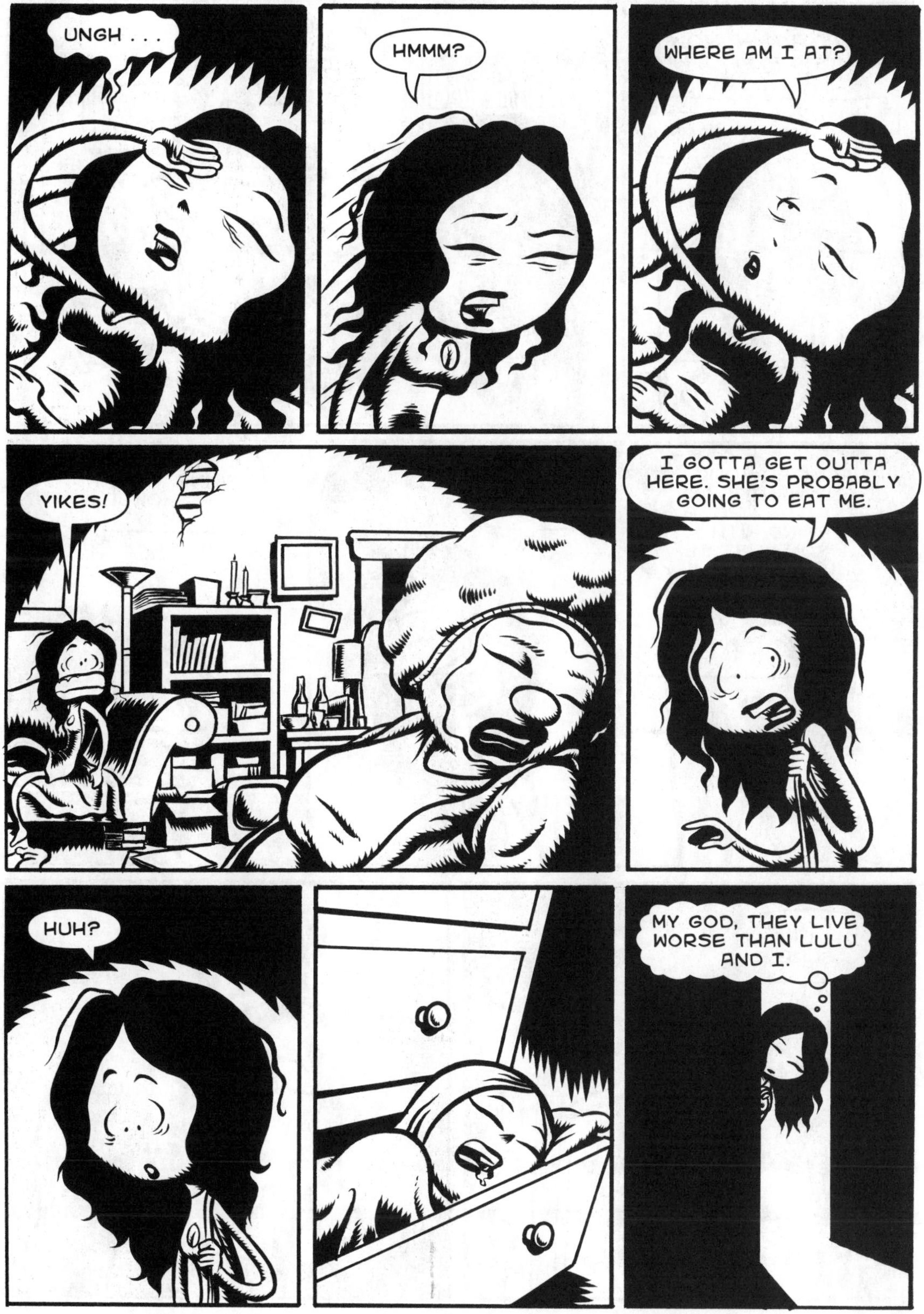
UNGH . . .
HMMM?
WHERE AM I AT?
YIKES!
I GOTTA GET OUTTA HERE. SHE'S PROBABLY GOING TO EAT ME.
HUH?
MY GOD, THEY LIVE WORSE THAN LULU AND I.

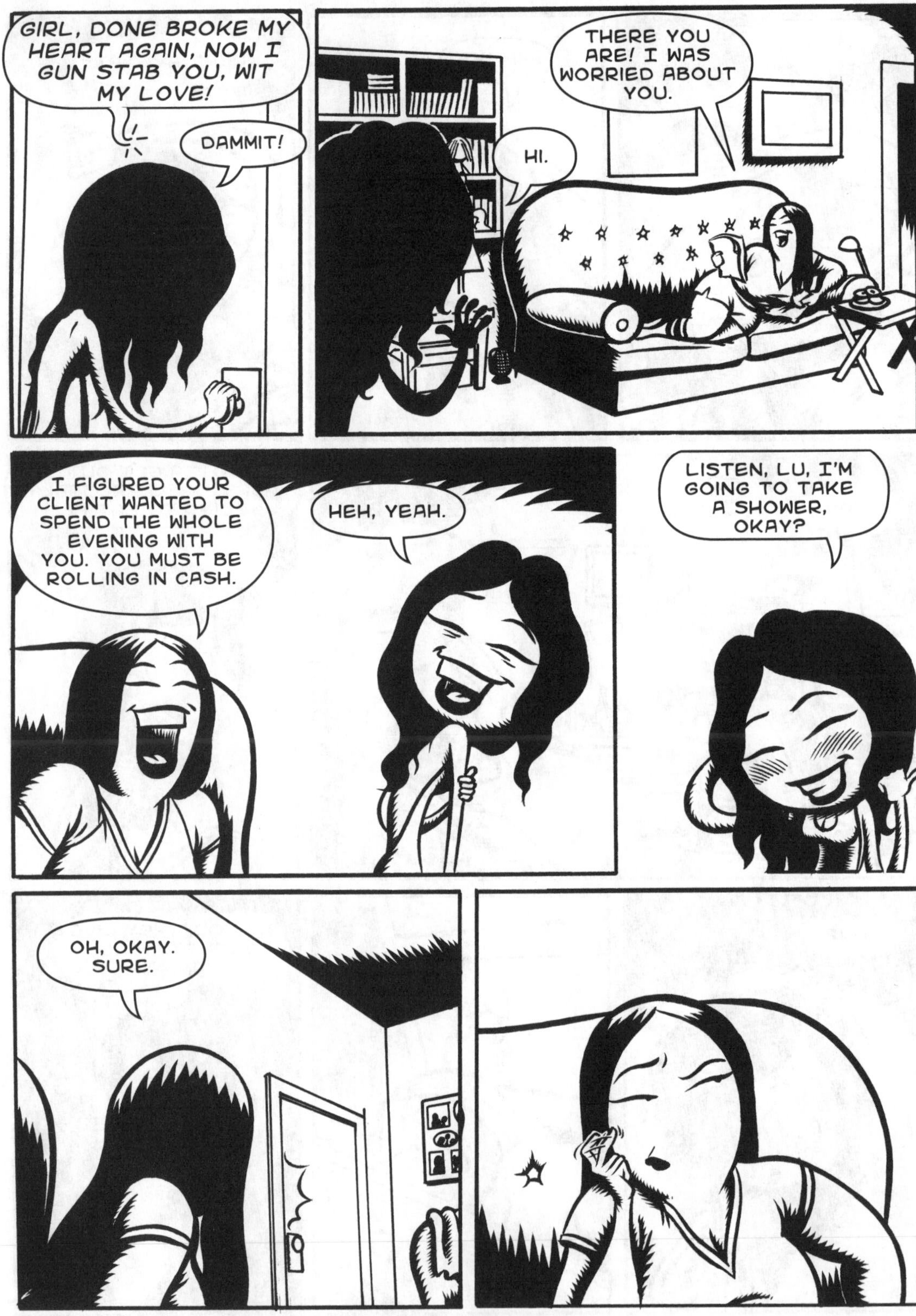
GIRL, DONE BROKE MY HEART AGAIN, NOW I GUN STAB YOU, WIT MY LOVE!
DAMMIT!
HI.
THERE YOU ARE! I WAS WORRIED ABOUT YOU.
I FIGURED YOUR CLIENT WANTED TO SPEND THE WHOLE EVENING WITH YOU. YOU MUST BE ROLLING IN CASH.
HEH, YEAH.
LISTEN, LU, I'M GOING TO TAKE A SHOWER, OKAY?
OH, OKAY. SURE.

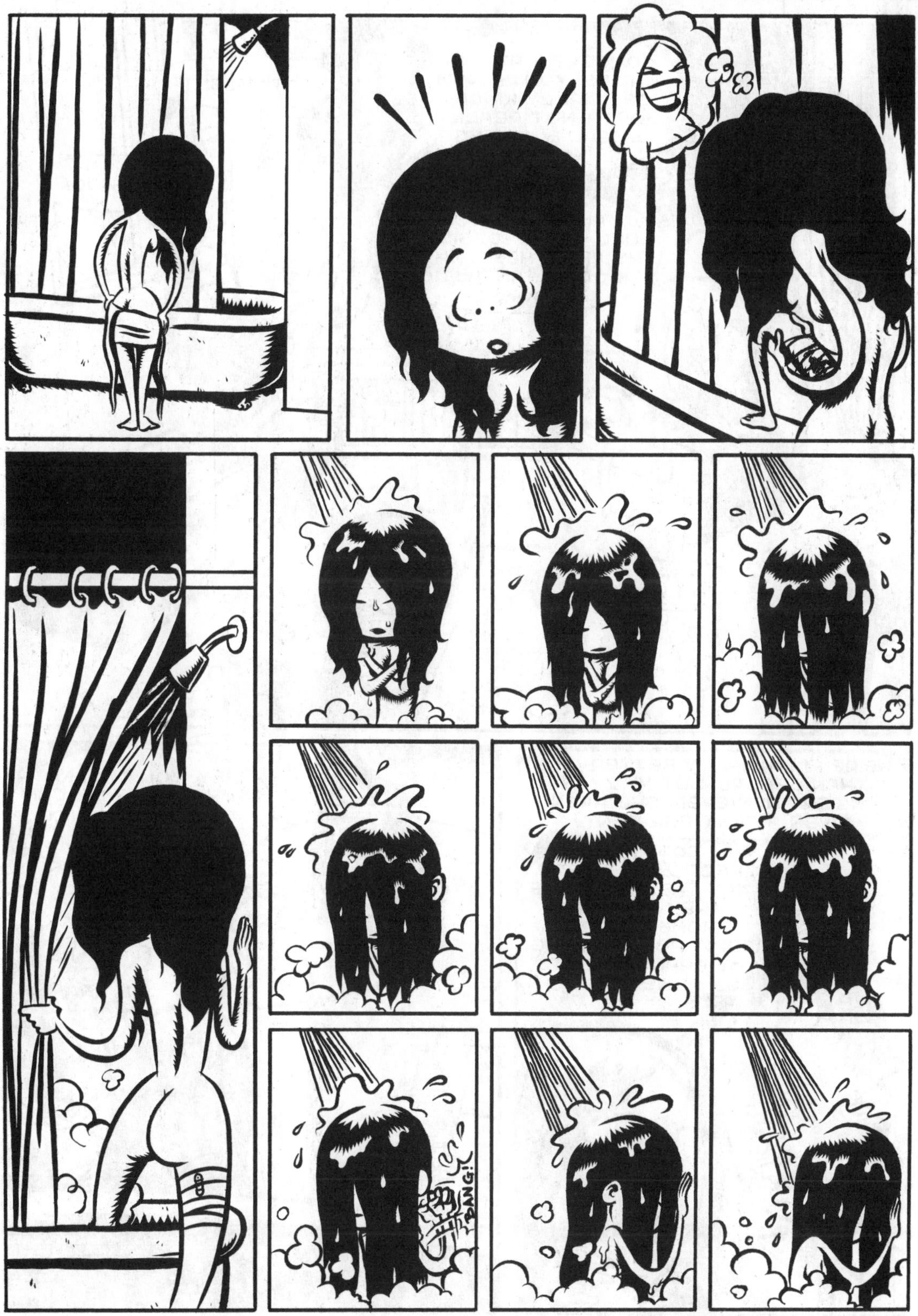
BANG!

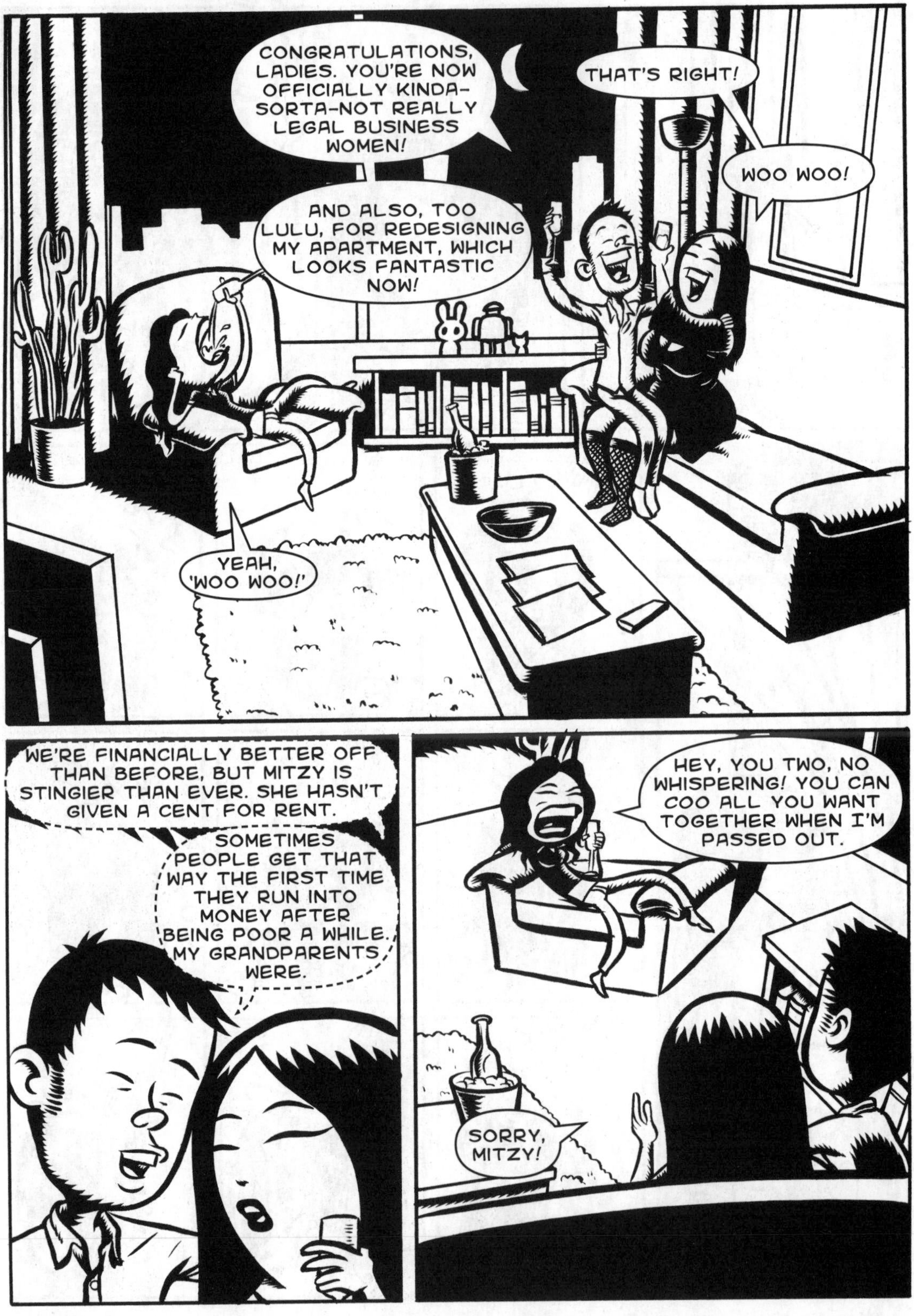
CONGRATULATIONS, LADIES. YOU'RE NOW OFFICIALLY KINDA-SORTA-NOT REALLY LEGAL BUSINESS WOMEN!
THAT'S RIGHT!
WOO WOO!
AND ALSO, TOO LULU, FOR REDESIGNING MY APARTMENT, WHICH LOOKS FANTASTIC NOW!
YEAH, 'WOO WOO!'
WE'RE FINANCIALLY BETTER OFF THAN BEFORE, BUT MITZY IS STINGIER THAN EVER. SHE HASN'T GIVEN A CENT FOR RENT.
SOMETIMES PEOPLE GET THAT WAY THE FIRST TIME THEY RUN INTO MONEY AFTER BEING POOR A WHILE. MY GRANDPARENTS WERE.
HEY, YOU TWO, NO WHISPERING! YOU CAN COO ALL YOU WANT TOGETHER WHEN I'M PASSED OUT.
SORRY, MITZY!

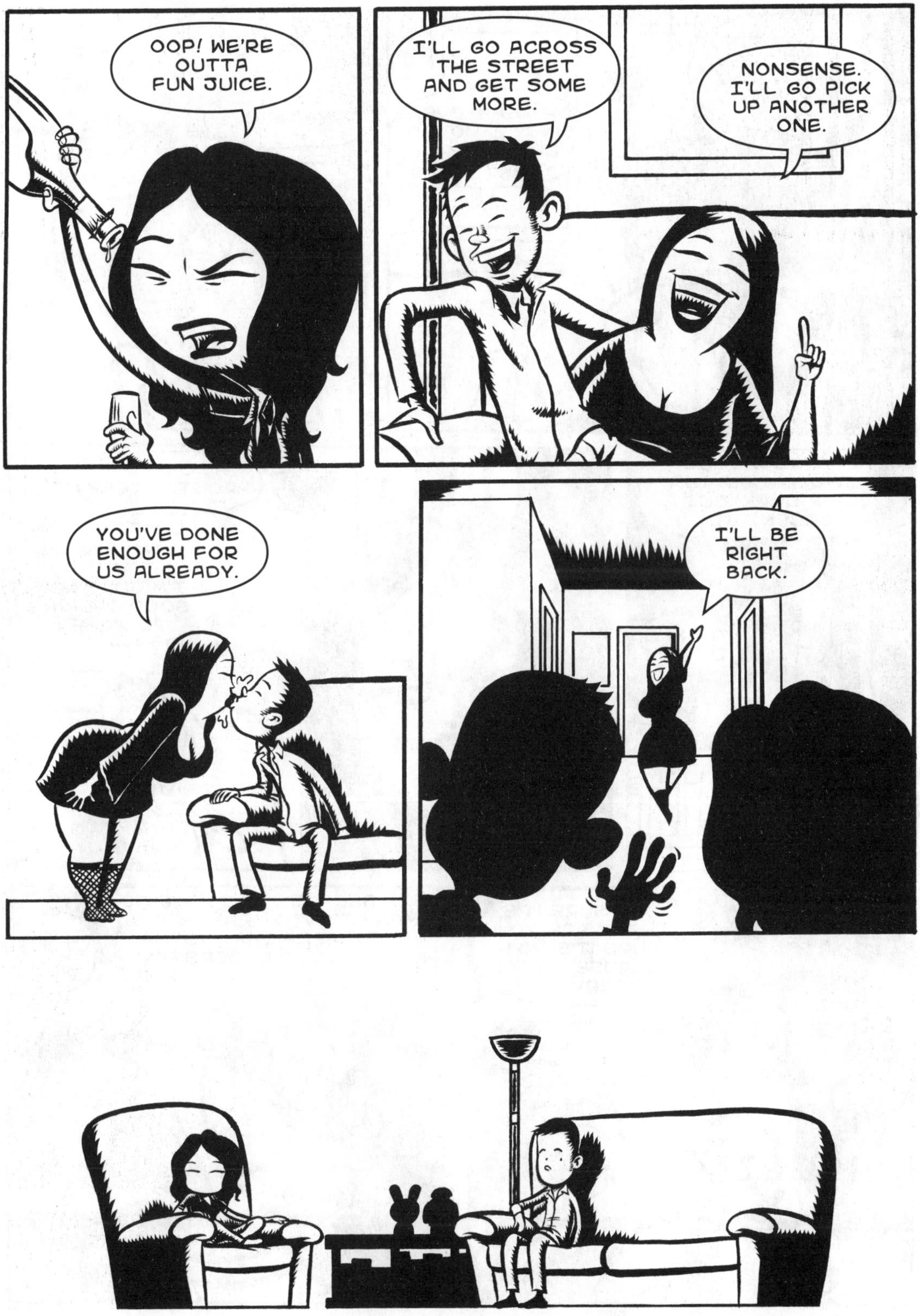
OOP! WE'RE OUTTA FUN JUICE.
I'LL GO ACROSS THE STREET AND GET SOME MORE.
NONSENSE. I'LL GO PICK UP ANOTHER ONE.
YOU'VE DONE ENOUGH FOR US ALREADY.
I'LL BE RIGHT BACK.

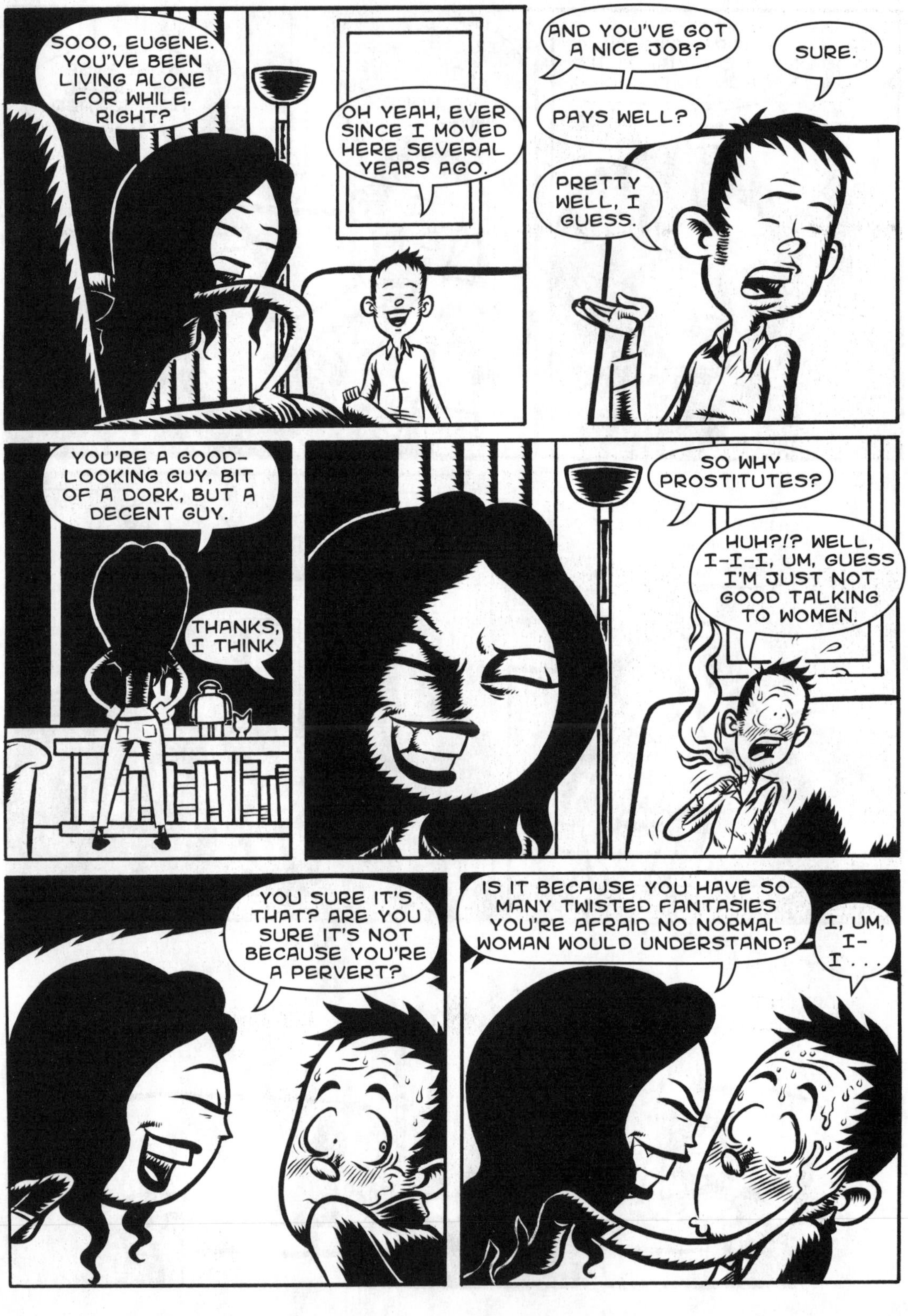
SOOO, EUGENE. YOU'VE BEEN LIVING ALONE FOR WHILE, RIGHT?
OH YEAH, EVER SINCE I MOVED HERE SEVERAL YEARS AGO.
AND YOU'VE GOT A NICE JOB?
SURE.
PAYS WELL?
PRETTY WELL, I GUESS.
YOU'RE A GOOD-LOOKING GUY, BIT OF A DORK, BUT A DECENT GUY.
THANKS, I THINK.
SO WHY PROSTITUTES?
HUH?!? WELL, I-I-I, UM, GUESS I'M JUST NOT GOOD TALKING TO WOMEN.
YOU SURE IT'S THAT? ARE YOU SURE IT'S NOT BECAUSE YOU'RE A PERVERT?
IS IT BECAUSE YOU HAVE SO MANY TWISTED FANTASIES YOU'RE AFRAID NO NORMAL WOMAN WOULD UNDERSTAND?
I, UM, I- I . . .

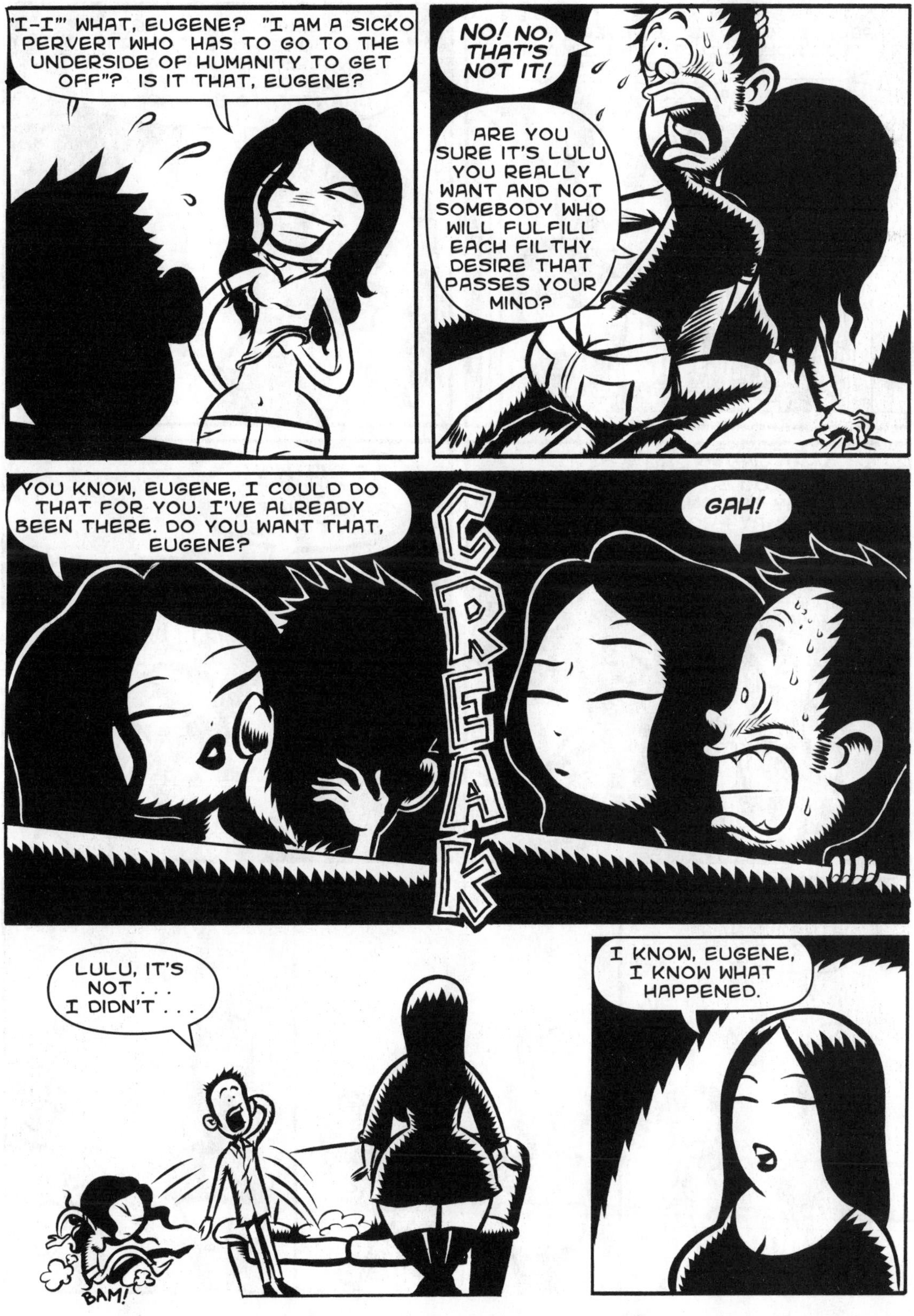
"I-I"' WHAT, EUGENE? "I AM A SICKO PERVERT WHO HAS TO GO TO THE UNDERSIDE OF HUMANITY TO GET OFF"? IS IT THAT, EUGENE?
NO! NO, THAT'S NOT IT!
ARE YOU SURE IT'S LULU YOU REALLY WANT AND NOT SOMEBODY WHO WILL FULFILL EACH FILTHY DESIRE THAT PASSES YOUR MIND?
YOU KNOW, EUGENE, I COULD DO THAT FOR YOU. I'VE ALREADY BEEN THERE. DO YOU WANT THAT, EUGENE?
CREAK
GAH!
LULU, IT'S NOT . . . I DIDN'T . . .
BAM!
I KNOW, EUGENE, I KNOW WHAT HAPPENED.

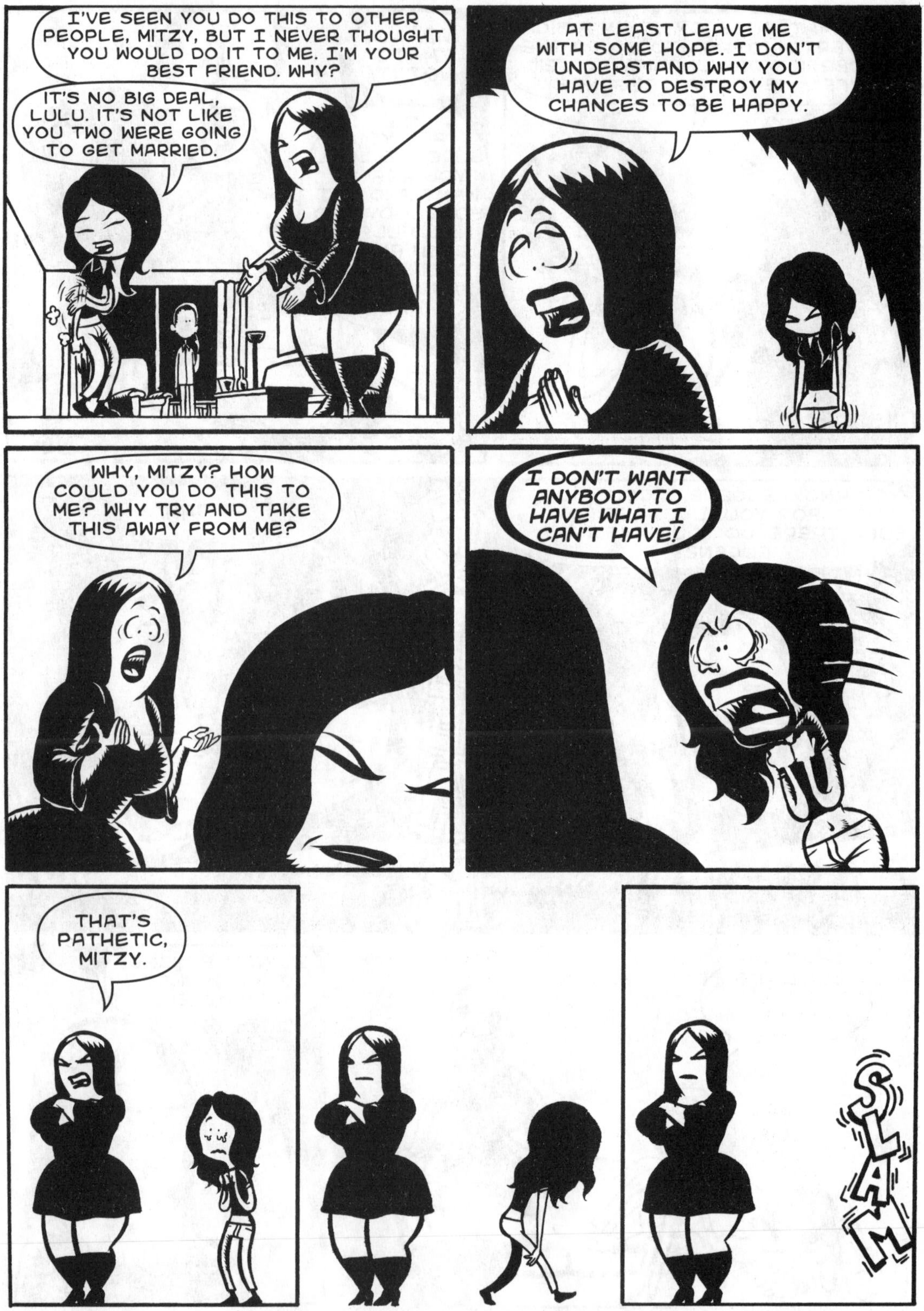
I'VE SEEN YOU DO THIS TO OTHER PEOPLE, MITZY, BUT I NEVER THOUGHT YOU WOULD DO IT TO ME. I'M YOUR BEST FRIEND. WHY?
IT'S NO BIG DEAL, LULU. IT'S NOT LIKE YOU TWO WERE GOING TO GET MARRIED.
AT LEAST LEAVE ME WITH SOME HOPE. I DON'T UNDERSTAND WHY YOU HAVE TO DESTROY MY CHANCES TO BE HAPPY.
WHY, MITZY? HOW COULD YOU DO THIS TO ME? WHY TRY AND TAKE THIS AWAY FROM ME?
I DON'T WANT ANYBODY TO HAVE WHAT I CAN'T HAVE!
THAT'S PATHETIC, MITZY.
SLAM

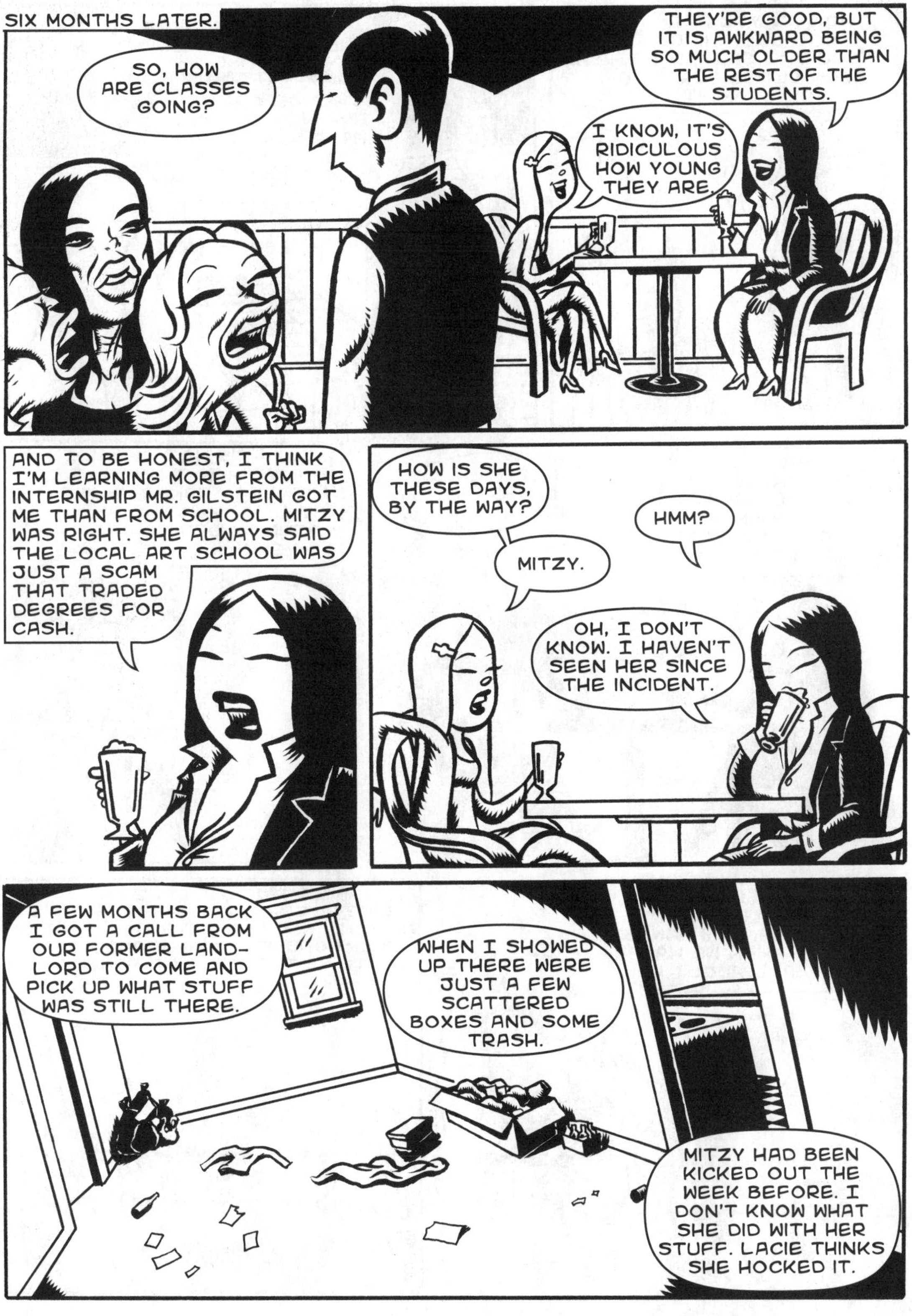
SIX MONTHS LATER.
SO, HOW ARE CLASSES GOING?
THEY'RE GOOD, BUT IT IS AWKWARD BEING SO MUCH OLDER THAN THE REST OF THE STUDENTS.
I KNOW, IT'S RIDICULOUS HOW YOUNG THEY ARE.
AND TO BE HONEST, I THINK I'M LEARNING MORE FROM THE INTERNSHIP MR. GILSTEIN GOT ME THAN FROM SCHOOL. MITZY WAS RIGHT. SHE ALWAYS SAID THE LOCAL ART SCHOOL WAS JUST A SCAM THAT TRADED DEGREES FOR CASH.
HOW IS SHE THESE DAYS, BY THE WAY?
HMM?
MITZY.
OH, I DON'T KNOW. I HAVEN'T SEEN HER SINCE THE INCIDENT.
A FEW MONTHS BACK I GOT A CALL FROM OUR FORMER LAND-LORD TO COME AND PICK UP WHAT STUFF WAS STILL THERE.
WHEN I SHOWED UP THERE WERE JUST A FEW SCATTERED BOXES AND SOME TRASH.
MITZY HAD BEEN KICKED OUT THE WEEK BEFORE. I DON'T KNOW WHAT SHE DID WITH HER STUFF. LACIE THINKS SHE HOCKED IT.

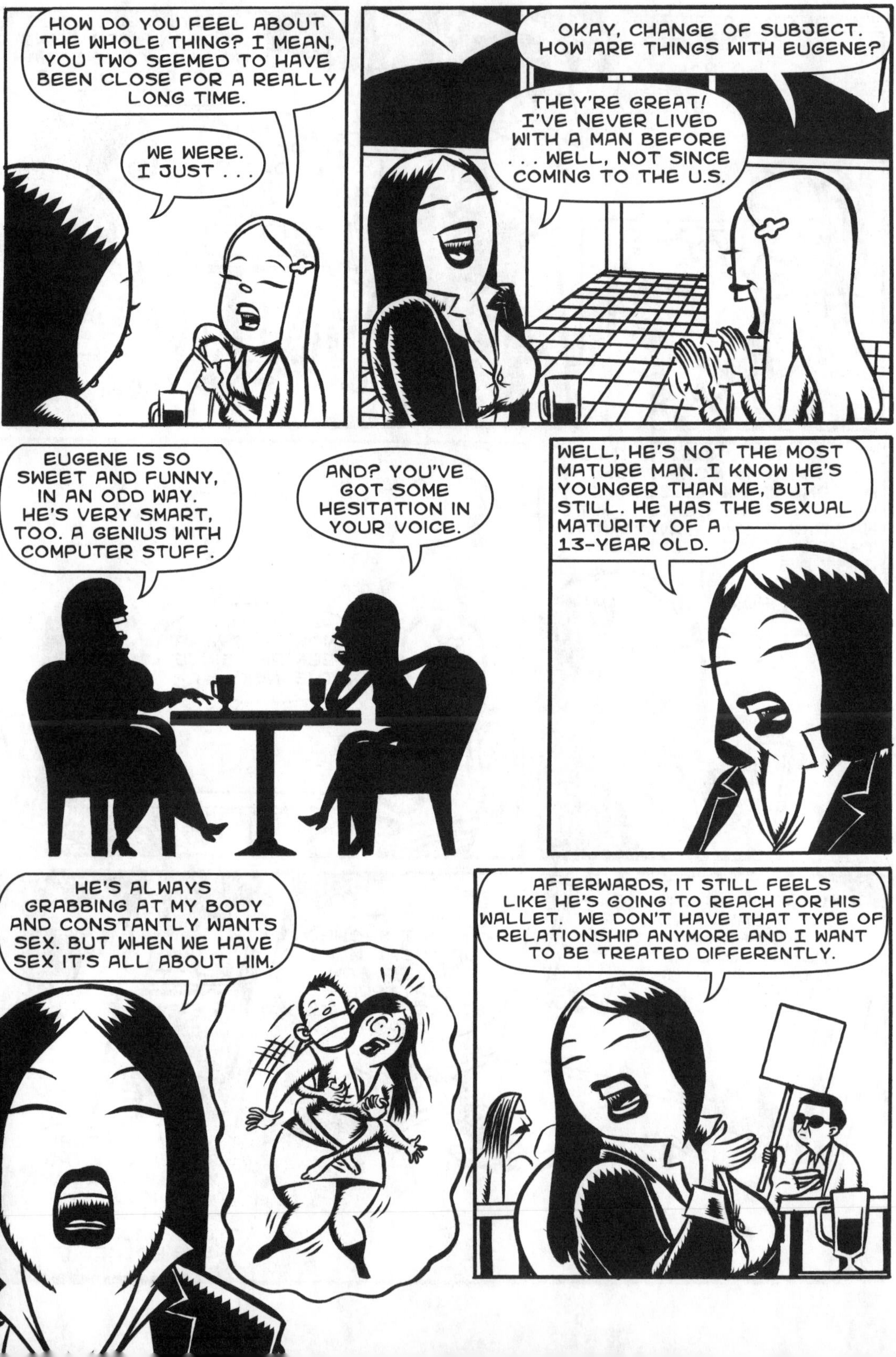
HOW DO YOU FEEL ABOUT THE WHOLE THING? I MEAN, YOU TWO SEEMED TO HAVE BEEN CLOSE FOR A REALLY LONG TIME.
WE WERE. I JUST . . .
OKAY, CHANGE OF SUBJECT. HOW ARE THINGS WITH EUGENE?
THEY'RE GREAT! I'VE NEVER LIVED WITH A MAN BEFORE . . . WELL, NOT SINCE COMING TO THE U.S.
EUGENE IS SO SWEET AND FUNNY, IN AN ODD WAY. HE'S VERY SMART, TOO. A GENIUS WITH COMPUTER STUFF.
AND? YOU'VE GOT SOME HESITATION IN YOUR VOICE.
WELL, HE'S NOT THE MOST MATURE MAN. I KNOW HE'S YOUNGER THAN ME, BUT STILL. HE HAS THE SEXUAL MATURITY OF A 13-YEAR OLD.
HE'S ALWAYS GRABBING AT MY BODY AND CONSTANTLY WANTS SEX. BUT WHEN WE HAVE SEX IT'S ALL ABOUT HIM.
AFTERWARDS, IT STILL FEELS LIKE HE'S GOING TO REACH FOR HIS WALLET. WE DON'T HAVE THAT TYPE OF RELATIONSHIP ANYMORE AND I WANT TO BE TREATED DIFFERENTLY.

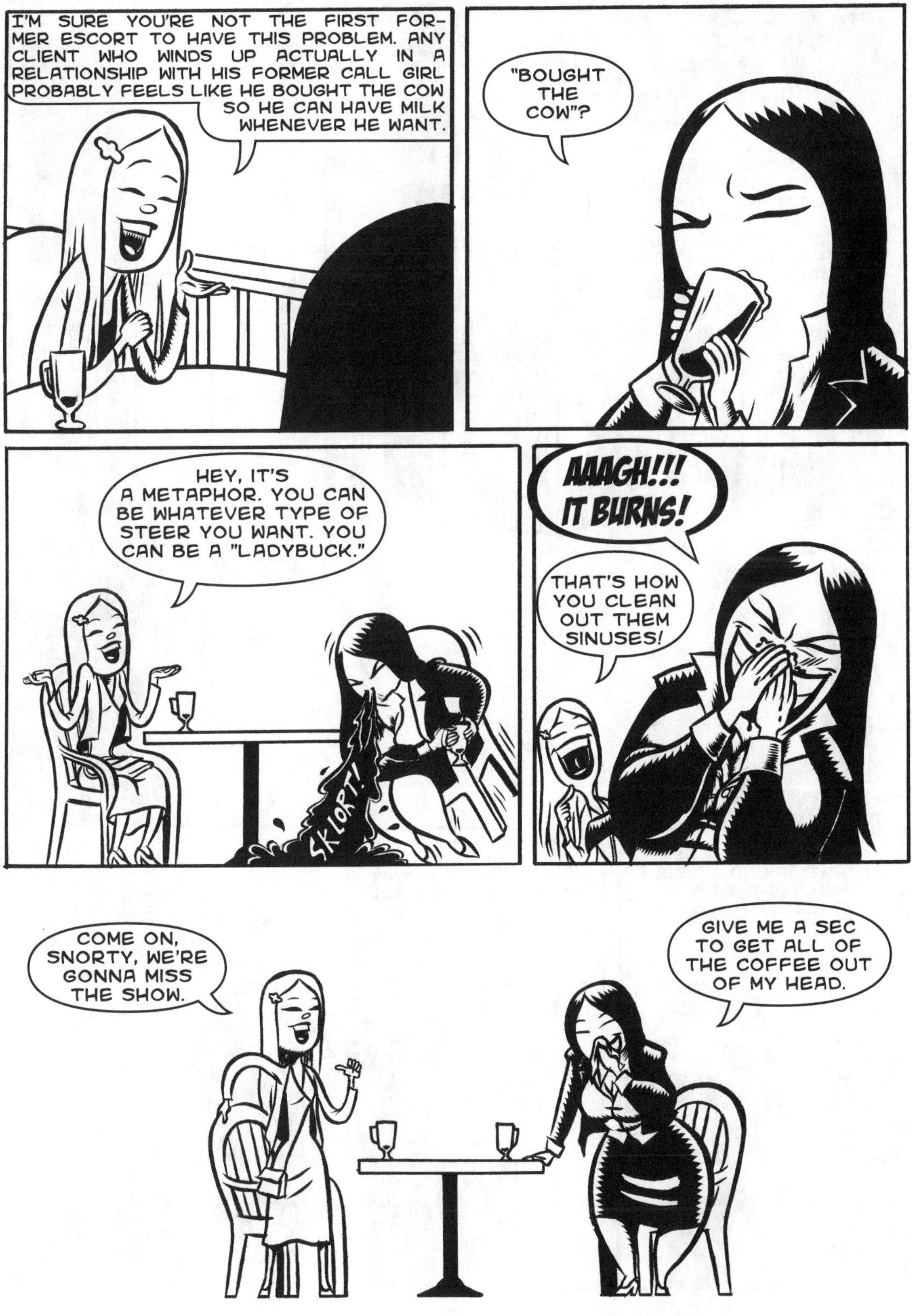
I'M SURE YOU'RE NOT THE FIRST FORMER ESCORT TO HAVE THIS PROBLEM. ANY CLIENT WHO WINDS UP ACTUALLY IN A RELATIONSHIP WITH HIS FORMER CALL GIRL PROBABLY FEELS LIKE HE BOUGHT THE COW SO HE CAN HAVE MILK WHENEVER HE WANT.
"BOUGHT THE COW"?
HEY, IT'S A METAPHOR. YOU CAN BE WHATEVER TYPE OF STEER YOU WANT. YOU CAN BE A "LADYBUCK."
SKLORT!
AAAGH!!! IT BURNS!
THAT'S HOW YOU CLEAN OUT THEM SINUSES!
COME ON, SNORTY, WE'RE GONNA MISS THE SHOW.
GIVE ME A SEC TO GET ALL OF THE COFFEE OUT OF MY HEAD.

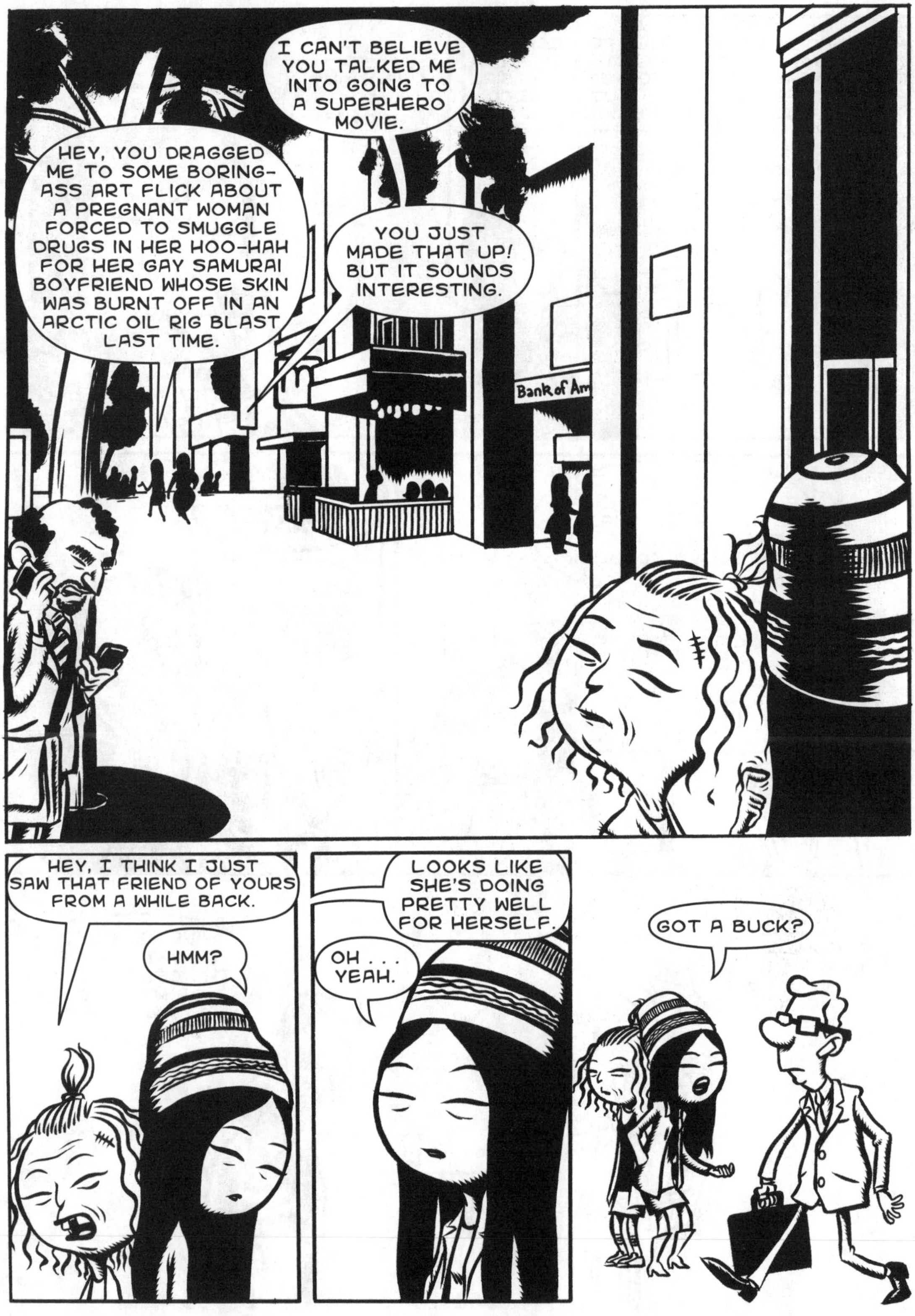
I CAN'T BELIEVE YOU TALKED ME INTO GOING TO A SUPERHERO MOVIE.
HEY, YOU DRAGGED ME TO SOME BORING-ASS ART FLICK ABOUT A PREGNANT WOMAN FORCED TO SMUGGLE DRUGS IN HER HOO-HAH FOR HER GAY SAMURAI BOYFRIEND WHOSE SKIN WAS BURNT OFF IN AN ARCTIC OIL RIG BLAST LAST TIME.
YOU JUST MADE THAT UP! BUT IT SOUNDS INTERESTING.
Bank of Am
HEY, I THINK I JUST SAW THAT FRIEND OF YOURS FROM A WHILE BACK.
HMM?
LOOKS LIKE SHE'S DOING PRETTY WELL FOR HERSELF.
OH . . . YEAH.
GOT A BUCK?

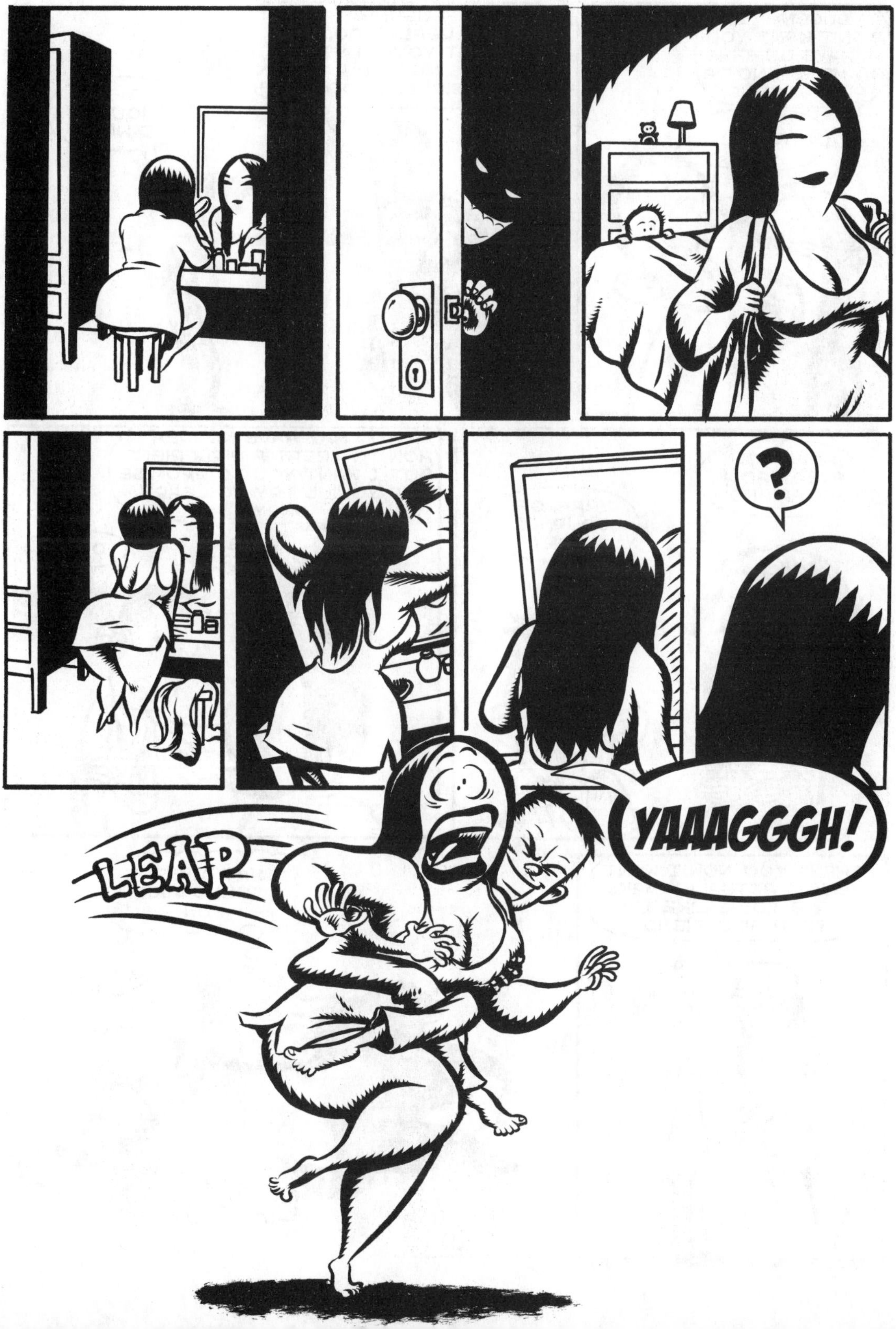
?
YAAAGGGH!
LEAP

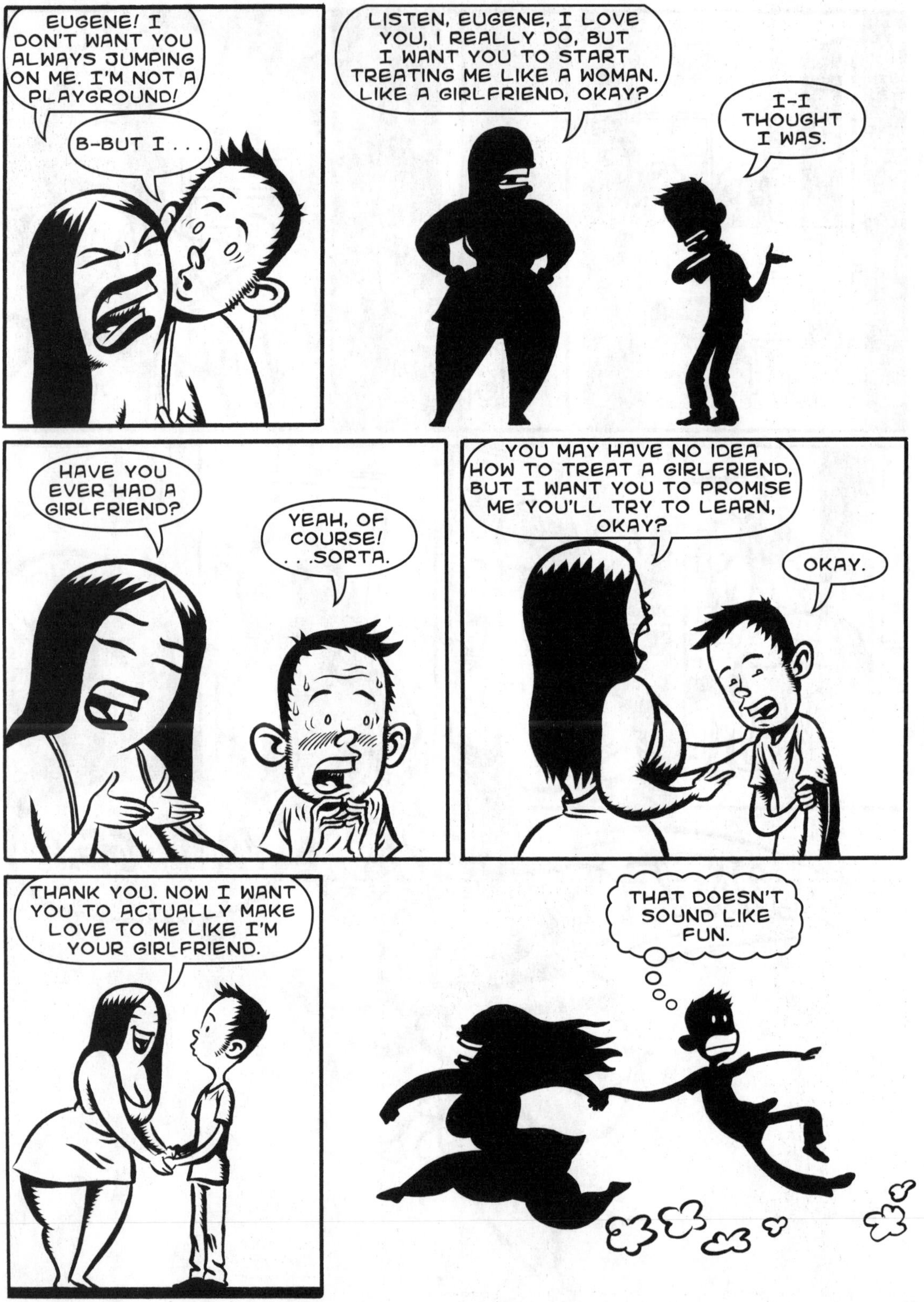
EUGENE! I DON'T WANT YOU ALWAYS JUMPING ON ME. I'M NOT A PLAYGROUND!
B-BUT I . . .
LISTEN, EUGENE, I LOVE YOU, I REALLY DO, BUT I WANT YOU TO START TREATING ME LIKE A WOMAN. LIKE A GIRLFRIEND, OKAY?
I-I THOUGHT I WAS.
HAVE YOU EVER HAD A GIRLFRIEND?
YEAH, OF COURSE! . . .SORTA.
YOU MAY HAVE NO IDEA HOW TO TREAT A GIRLFRIEND, BUT I WANT YOU TO PROMISE ME YOU'LL TRY TO LEARN, OKAY?
OKAY.
THANK YOU. NOW I WANT YOU TO ACTUALLY MAKE LOVE TO ME LIKE I'M YOUR GIRLFRIEND.
THAT DOESN'T SOUND LIKE FUN.

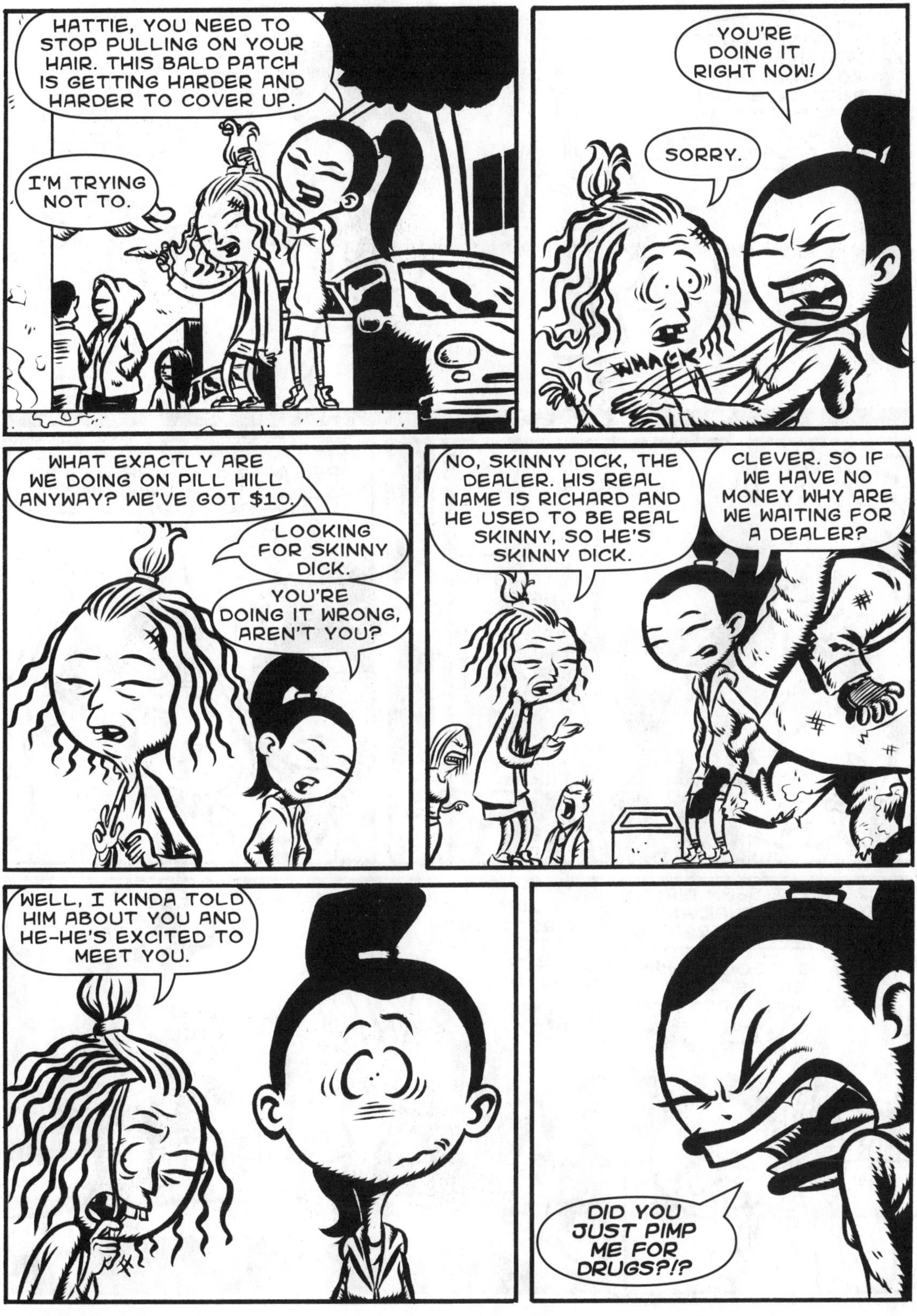
HATTIE, YOU NEED TO STOP PULLING ON YOUR HAIR. THIS BALD PATCH IS GETTING HARDER AND HARDER TO COVER UP.
I'M TRYING NOT TO.
YOU'RE DOING IT RIGHT NOW!
SORRY.
WHACK
WHAT EXACTLY ARE WE DOING ON PILL HILL ANYWAY? WE'VE GOT $10.
LOOKING FOR SKINNY DICK.
YOU'RE DOING IT WRONG, AREN'T YOU?
NO, SKINNY DICK, THE DEALER. HIS REAL NAME IS RICHARD AND HE USED TO BE REAL SKINNY, SO HE'S SKINNY DICK.
CLEVER. SO IF WE HAVE NO MONEY WHY ARE WE WAITING FOR A DEALER?
WELL, I KINDA TOLD HIM ABOUT YOU AND HE-HE'S EXCITED TO MEET YOU.
DID YOU JUST PIMP ME FOR DRUGS?!?

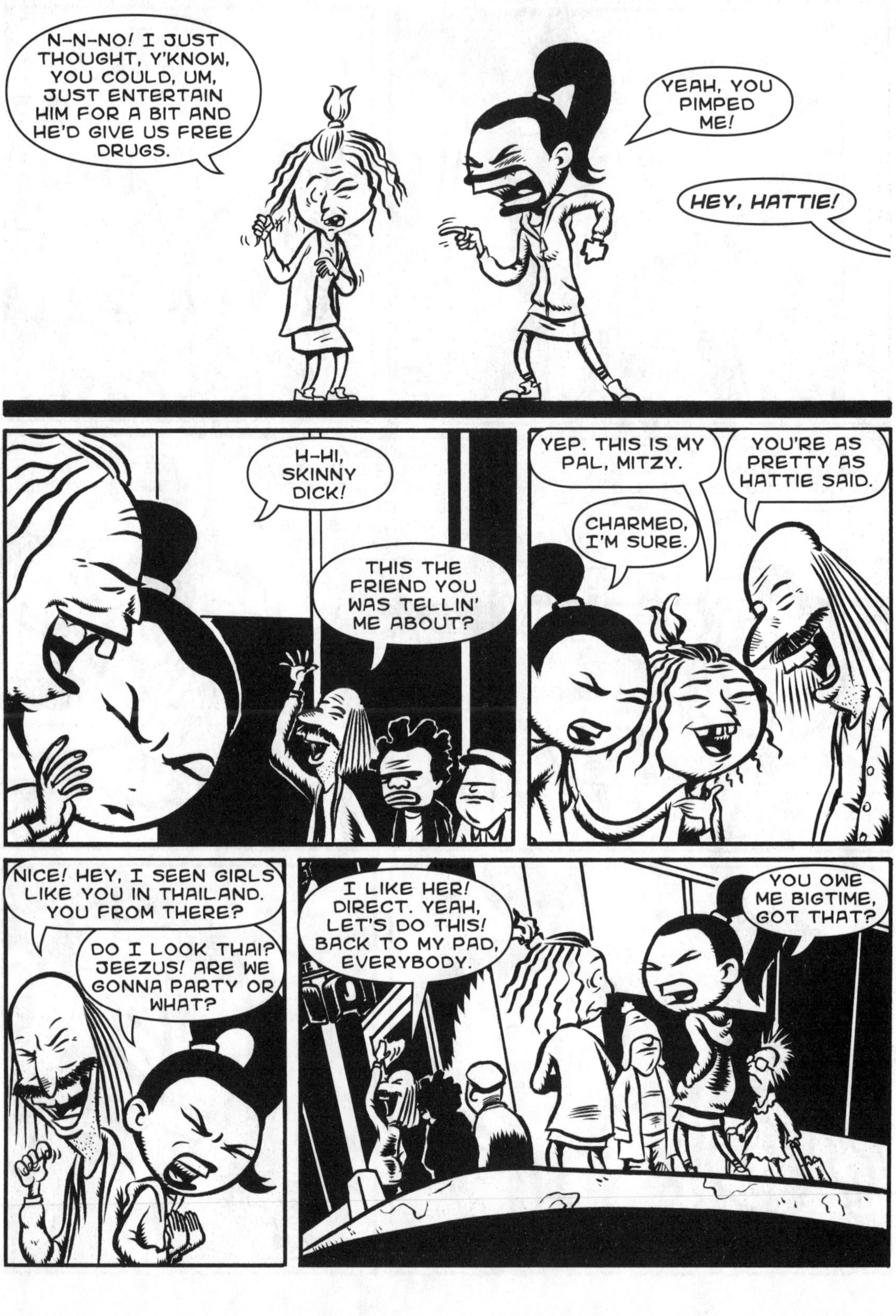
N-N-NO! I JUST THOUGHT, Y'KNOW, YOU COULD, UM, JUST ENTERTAIN HIM FOR A BIT AND HE'D GIVE US FREE DRUGS.
YEAH, YOU PIMPED ME!
HEY, HATTIE!
H-HI, SKINNY DICK!
THIS THE FRIEND YOU WAS TELLIN' ME ABOUT?
YEP. THIS IS MY PAL, MITZY.
CHARMED, I'M SURE.
YOU'RE AS PRETTY AS HATTIE SAID.
NICE! HEY, I SEEN GIRLS LIKE YOU IN THAILAND. YOU FROM THERE?
DO I LOOK THAI? JEEZUS! ARE WE GONNA PARTY OR WHAT?
I LIKE HER! DIRECT. YEAH, LET'S DO THIS! BACK TO MY PAD, EVERYBODY.
YOU OWE ME BIGTIME, GOT THAT?

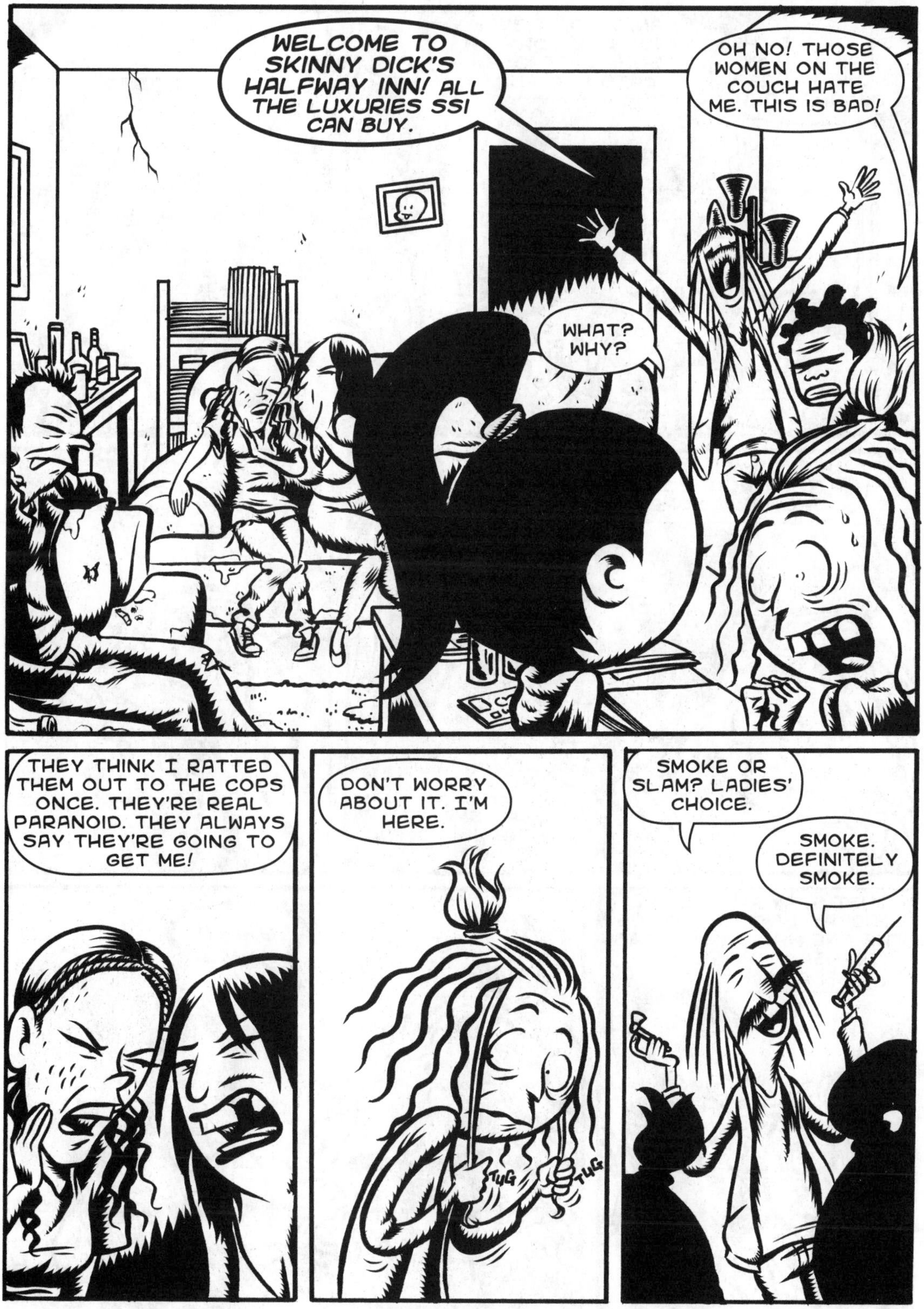
WELCOME TO SKINNY DICK'S HALFWAY INN! ALL THE LUXURIES SSI CAN BUY.
OH NO! THOSE WOMEN ON THE COUCH HATE ME. THIS IS BAD!
WHAT? WHY?
THEY THINK I RATTED THEM OUT TO THE COPS ONCE. THEY'RE REAL PARANOID. THEY ALWAYS SAY THEY'RE GOING TO GET ME!
DON'T WORRY ABOUT IT. I'M HERE.
TUG
TUG
SMOKE OR SLAM? LADIES' CHOICE.
SMOKE. DEFINITELY SMOKE.

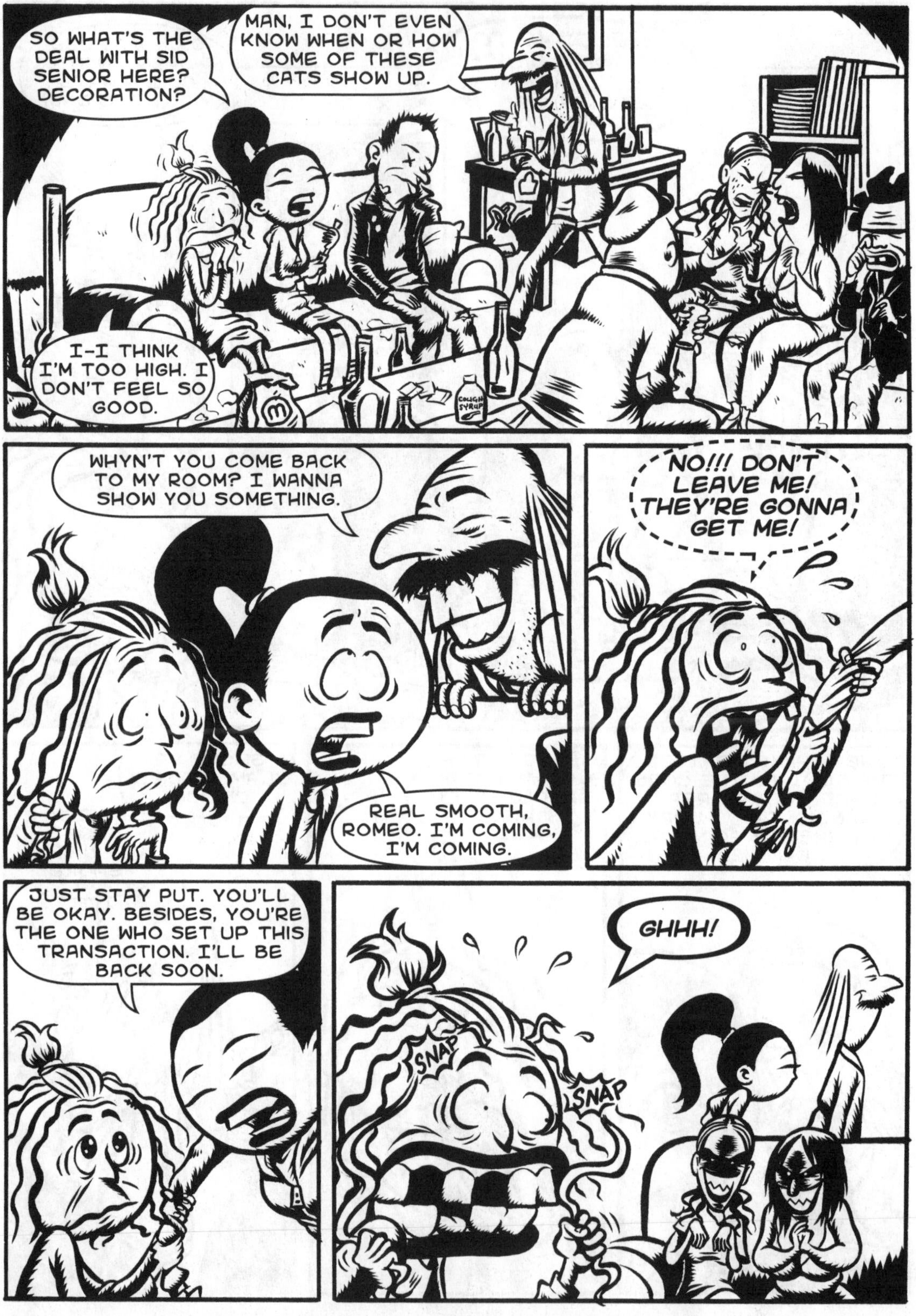
SO WHAT'S THE DEAL WITH SID SENIOR HERE? DECORATION?
MAN, I DON'T EVEN KNOW WHEN OR HOW SOME OF THESE CATS SHOW UP.
I-I THINK I'M TOO HIGH. I DON'T FEEL SO GOOD.
COUGH SYRUP
WHYN'T YOU COME BACK TO MY ROOM? I WANNA SHOW YOU SOMETHING.
REAL SMOOTH, ROMEO. I'M COMING, I'M COMING.
NO!!! DON'T LEAVE ME! THEY'RE GONNA GET ME!
JUST STAY PUT. YOU'LL BE OKAY. BESIDES, YOU'RE THE ONE WHO SET UP THIS TRANSACTION. I'LL BE BACK SOON.
GHHH!
SNAP
SNAP

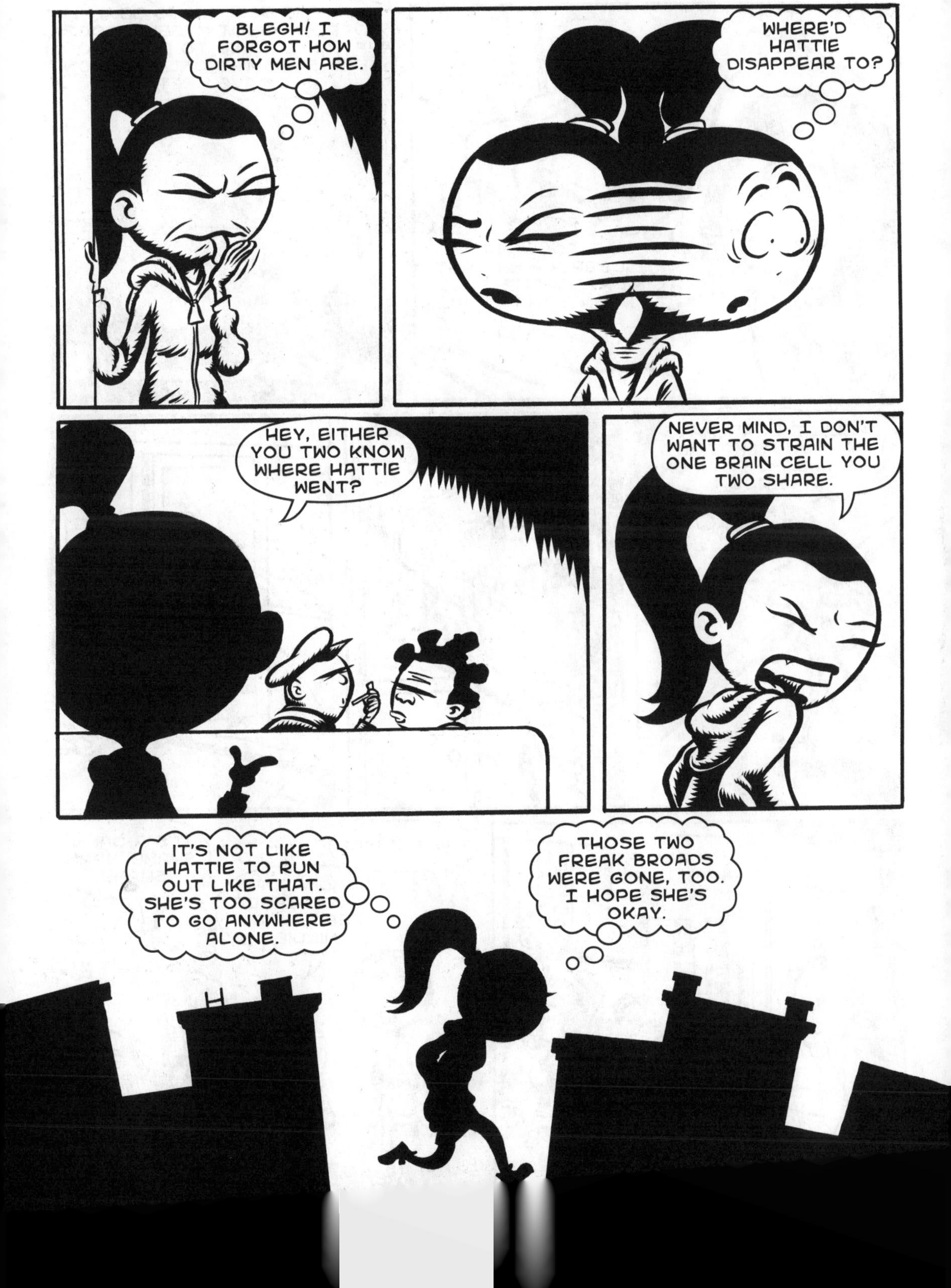
BLEGH! I FORGOT HOW DIRTY MEN ARE.
WHERE'D HATTIE DISAPPEAR TO?
HEY, EITHER YOU TWO KNOW WHERE HATTIE WENT?
NEVER MIND, I DON'T WANT TO STRAIN THE ONE BRAIN CELL YOU TWO SHARE.
IT'S NOT LIKE HATTIE TO RUN OUT LIKE THAT. SHE'S TOO SCARED TO GO ANYWHERE ALONE.
THOSE TWO FREAK BROADS WERE GONE, TOO. I HOPE SHE'S OKAY.

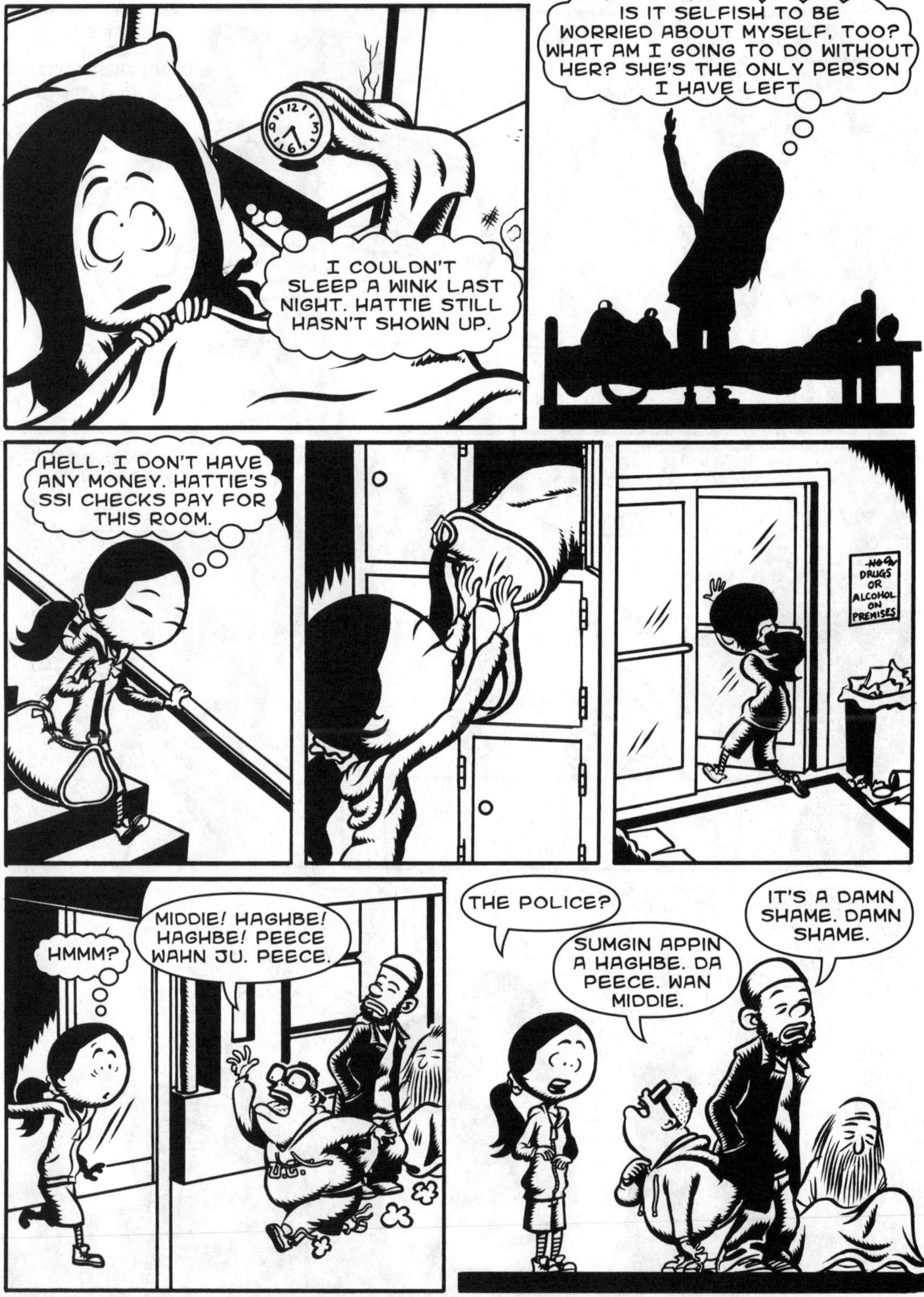
I COULDN'T SLEEP A WINK LAST NIGHT. HATTIE STILL HASN'T SHOWN UP.
IS IT SELFISH TO BE WORRIED ABOUT MYSELF, TOO? WHAT AM I GOING TO DO WITHOUT HER? SHE'S THE ONLY PERSON I HAVE LEFT.
HELL, I DON'T HAVE ANY MONEY. HATTIE'S SSI CHECKS PAY FOR THIS ROOM.
NO DRUGS OR ALCOHOL ON PREMISES
HMMM?
MIDDIE! HAGHBE! HAGHBE! PEECE WAHN JU. PEECE.
THE POLICE?
SUMGIN APPIN A HAGHBE. DA PEECE. WAN MIDDIE.
IT'S A DAMN SHAME. DAMN SHAME.

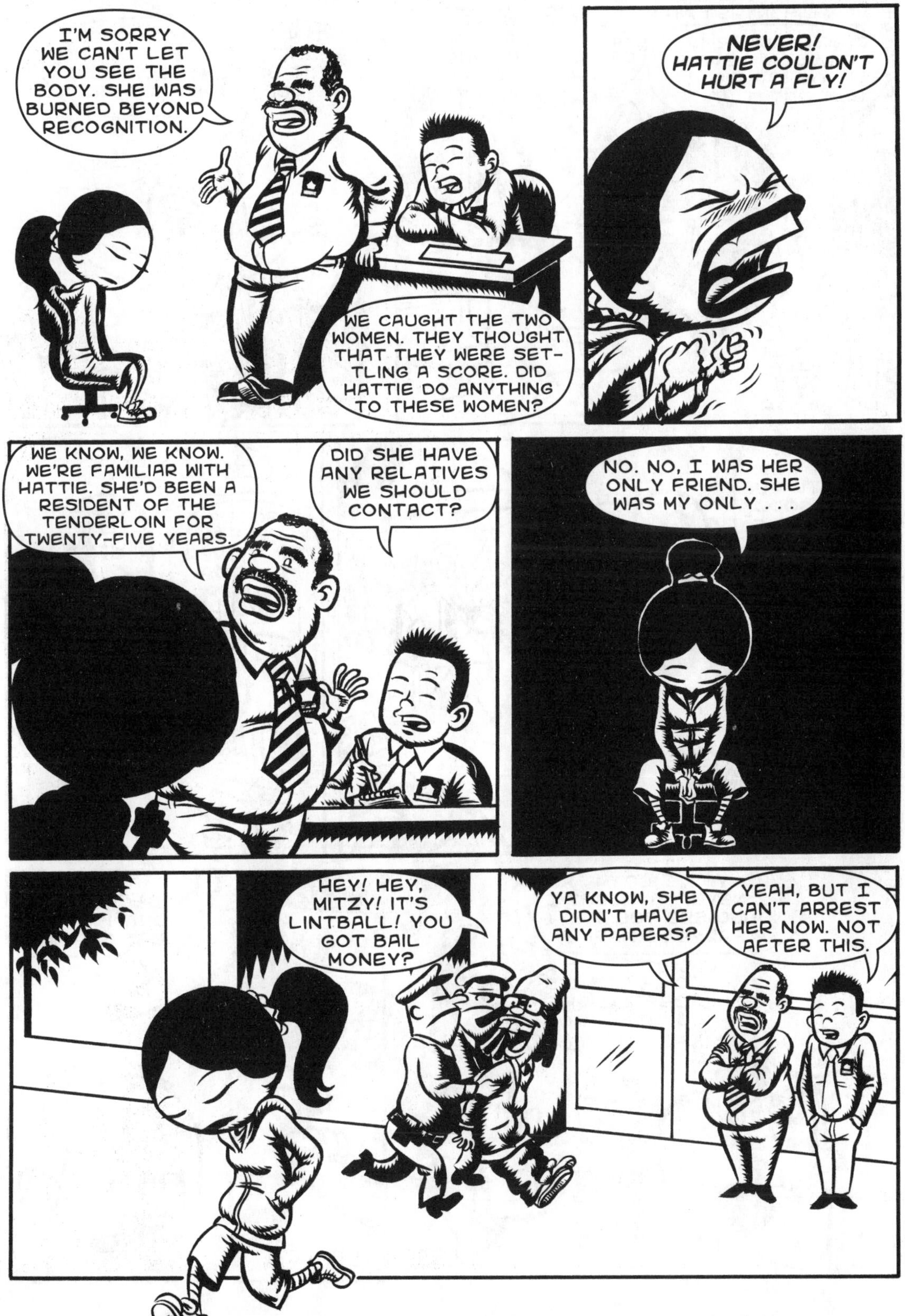
I'M SORRY WE CAN'T LET YOU SEE THE BODY. SHE WAS BURNED BEYOND RECOGNITION.
WE CAUGHT THE TWO WOMEN. THEY THOUGHT THAT THEY WERE SETTLING A SCORE. DID HATTIE DO ANYTHING TO THESE WOMEN?
NEVER! HATTIE COULDN'T HURT A FLY!
WE KNOW, WE KNOW. WE'RE FAMILIAR WITH HATTIE. SHE'D BEEN A RESIDENT OF THE TENDERLOIN FOR TWENTY-FIVE YEARS.
DID SHE HAVE ANY RELATIVES WE SHOULD CONTACT?
NO. NO, I WAS HER ONLY FRIEND. SHE WAS MY ONLY . . .
HEY! HEY, MITZY! IT'S LINTBALL! YOU GOT BAIL MONEY?
YA KNOW, SHE DIDN'T HAVE ANY PAPERS?
YEAH, BUT I CAN'T ARREST HER NOW. NOT AFTER THIS.

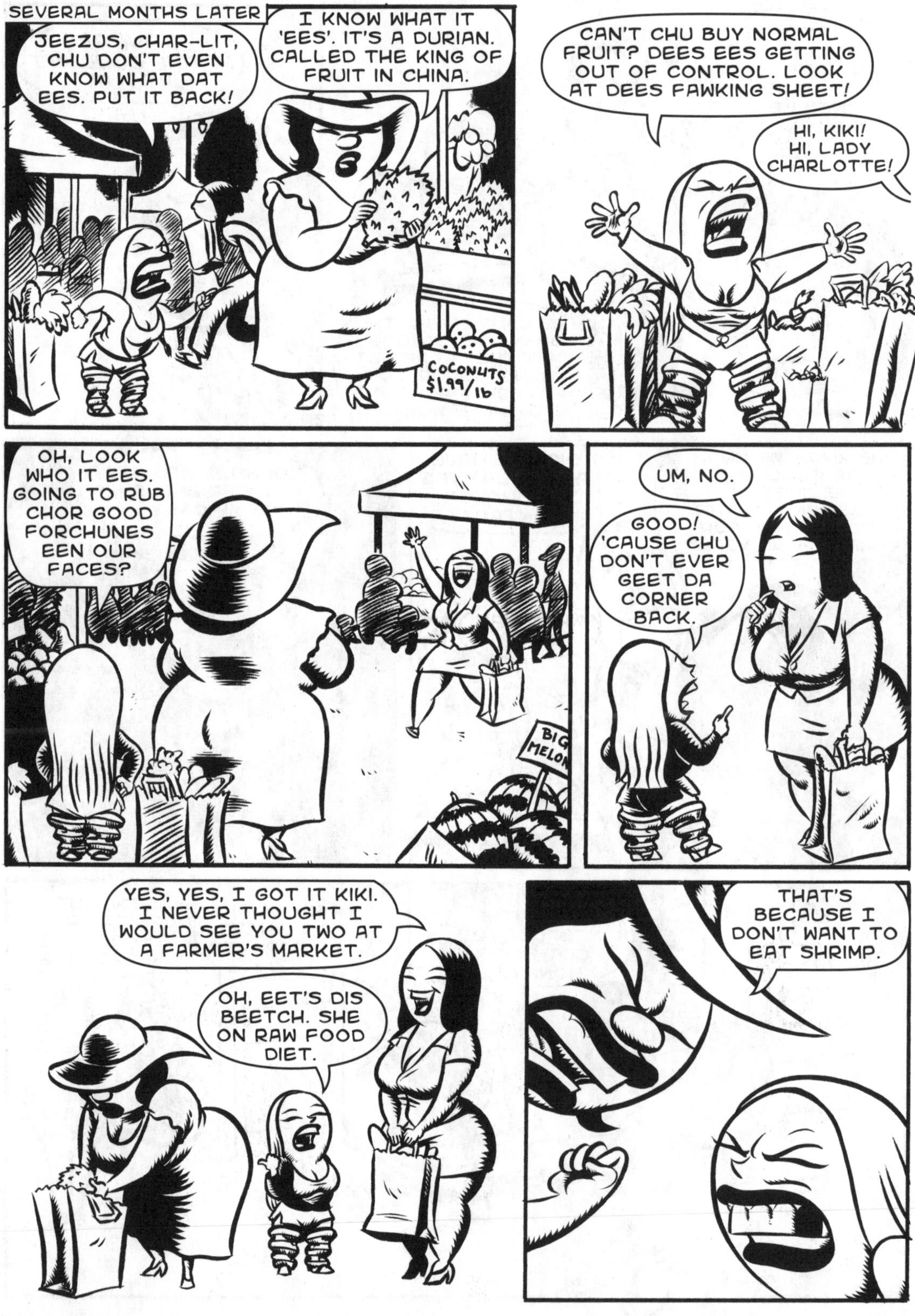
SEVERAL MONTHS LATER
JEEZUS, CHAR-LIT, CHU DON'T EVEN KNOW WHAT DAT EES. PUT IT BACK!
I KNOW WHAT IT 'EES'. IT'S A DURIAN. CALLED THE KING OF FRUIT IN CHINA.
COCONUTS $1.99/lb
CAN'T CHU BUY NORMAL FRUIT? DEES EES GETTING OUT OF CONTROL. LOOK AT DEES FAWKING SHEET!
HI, KIKI! HI, LADY CHARLOTTE!
OH, LOOK WHO IT EES. GOING TO RUB CHOR GOOD FORCHUNES EEN OUR FACES?
BIG MELON
UM, NO.
GOOD! 'CAUSE CHU DON'T EVER GEET DA CORNER BACK.
YES, YES, I GOT IT KIKI. I NEVER THOUGHT I WOULD SEE YOU TWO AT A FARMER'S MARKET.
OH, EET'S DIS BEETCH. SHE ON RAW FOOD DIET.
THAT'S BECAUSE I DON'T WANT TO EAT SHRIMP.

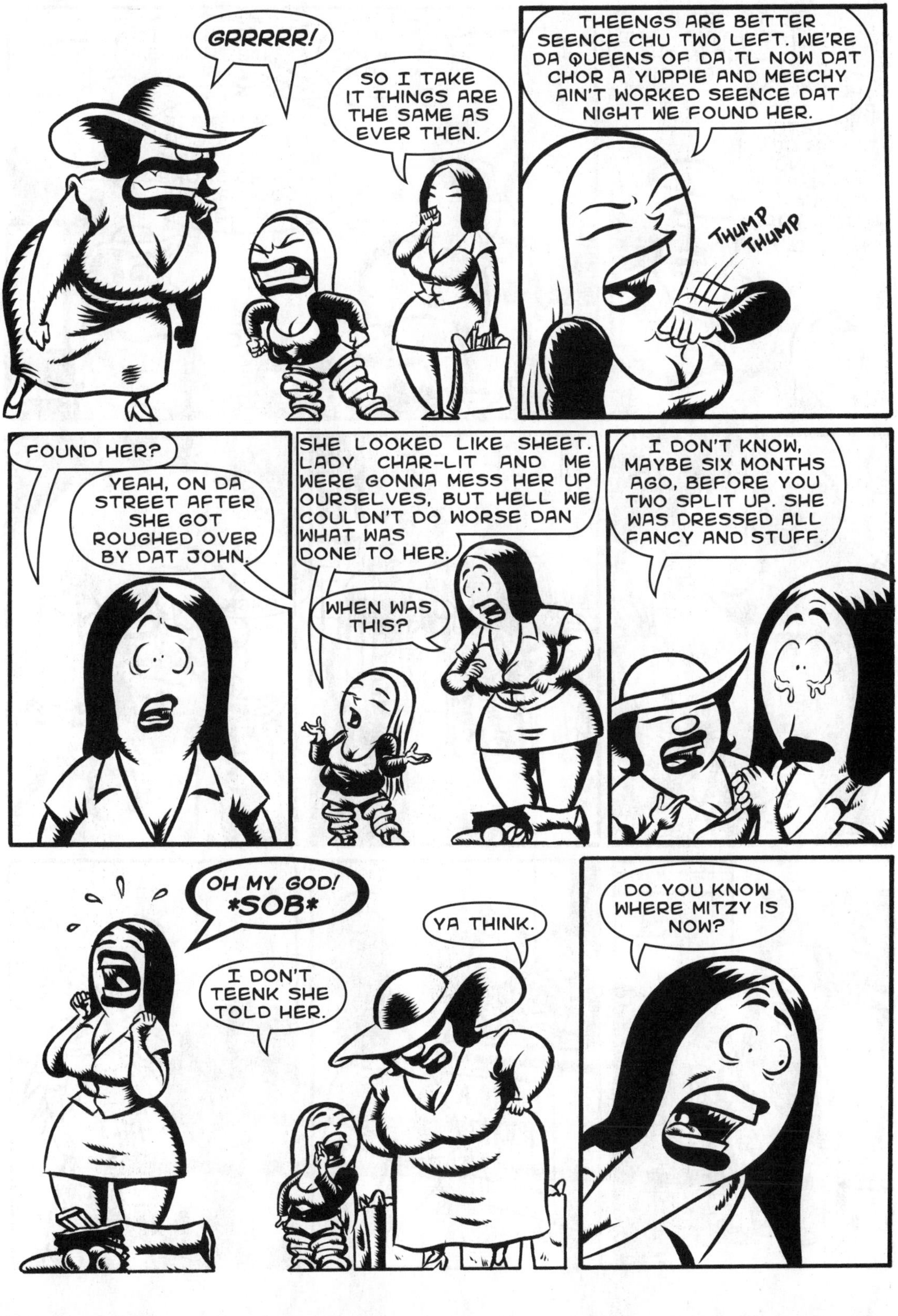
GRRRRR!
SO I TAKE IT THINGS ARE THE SAME AS EVER THEN.
THEENGS ARE BETTER SEENCE CHU TWO LEFT. WE'RE DA QUEENS OF DA TL NOW DAT CHOR A YUPPIE AND MEECHY AIN'T WORKED SEENCE DAT NIGHT WE FOUND HER.
THUMP THUMP
FOUND HER?
YEAH, ON DA STREET AFTER SHE GOT ROUGHED OVER BY DAT JOHN.
SHE LOOKED LIKE SHEET. LADY CHAR-LIT AND ME WERE GONNA MESS HER UP OURSELVES, BUT HELL WE COULDN'T DO WORSE DAN WHAT WAS DONE TO HER.
WHEN WAS THIS?
I DON'T KNOW, MAYBE SIX MONTHS AGO, BEFORE YOU TWO SPLIT UP. SHE WAS DRESSED ALL FANCY AND STUFF.
OH MY GOD! *SOB*
YA THINK.
I DON'T TEENK SHE TOLD HER.
DO YOU KNOW WHERE MITZY IS NOW?

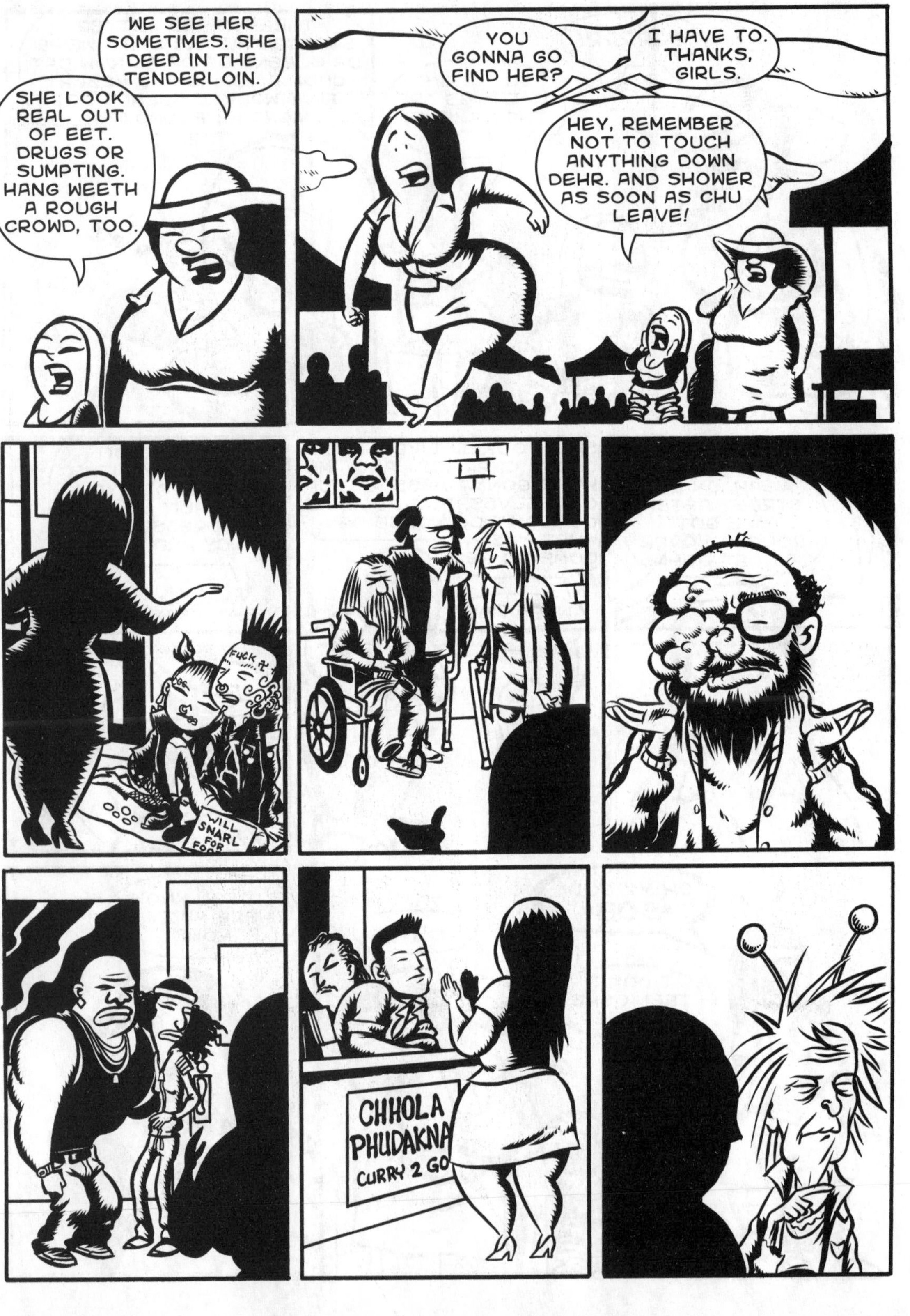
WE SEE HER SOMETIMES. SHE DEEP IN THE TENDERLOIN.
SHE LOOK REAL OUT OF EET. DRUGS OR SUMPTING. HANG WEETH A ROUGH CROWD, TOO.
YOU GONNA GO FIND HER?
I HAVE TO. THANKS, GIRLS.
HEY, REMEMBER NOT TO TOUCH ANYTHING DOWN DEHR. AND SHOWER AS SOON AS CHU LEAVE!
FUCK
WILL SNARL FOR FOOD
CHHOLA PHUDAKNA
CURRY 2 GO

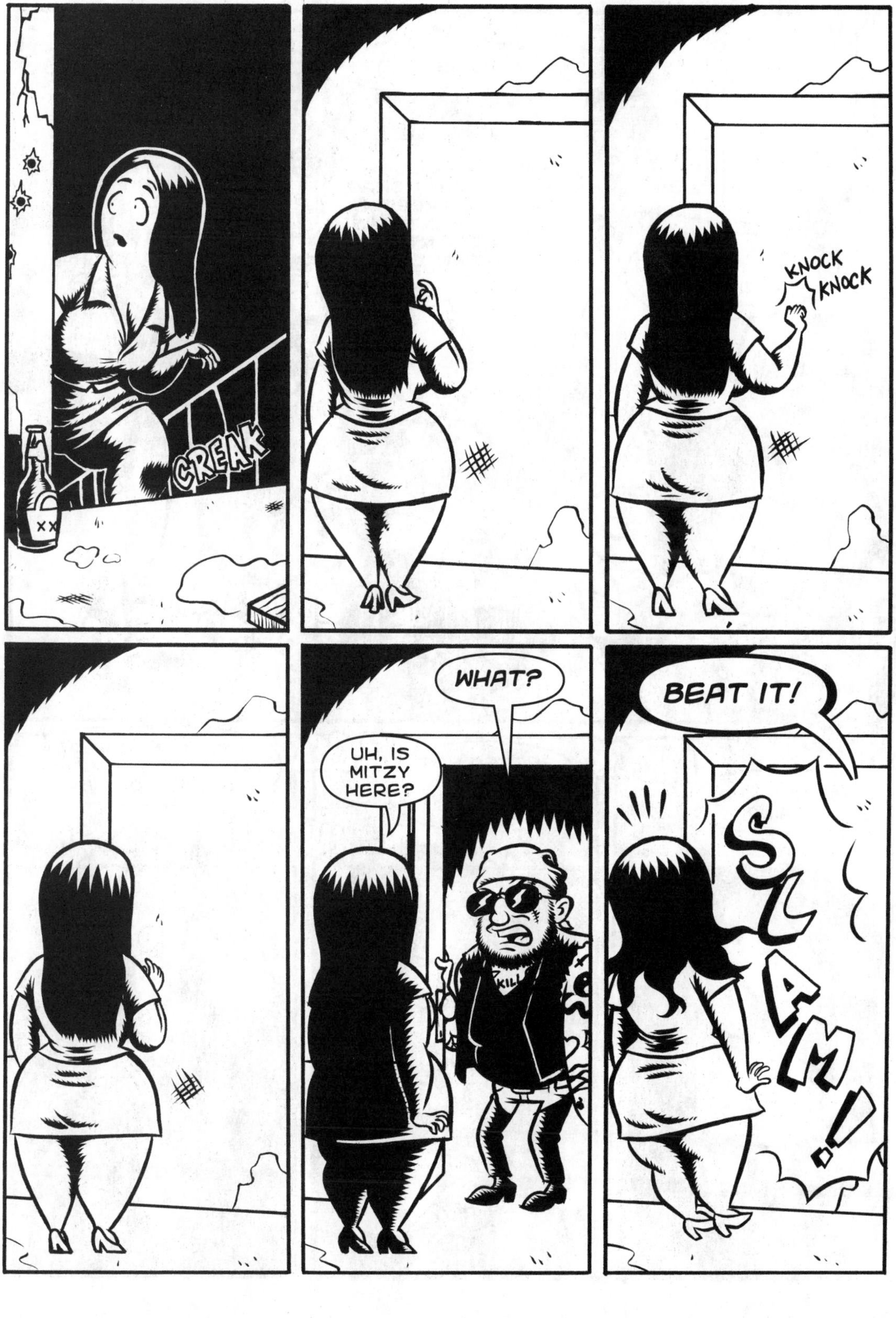
CREAK
KNOCK
KNOCK
WHAT?
UH, IS MITZY HERE?
BEAT IT!
SLAM!

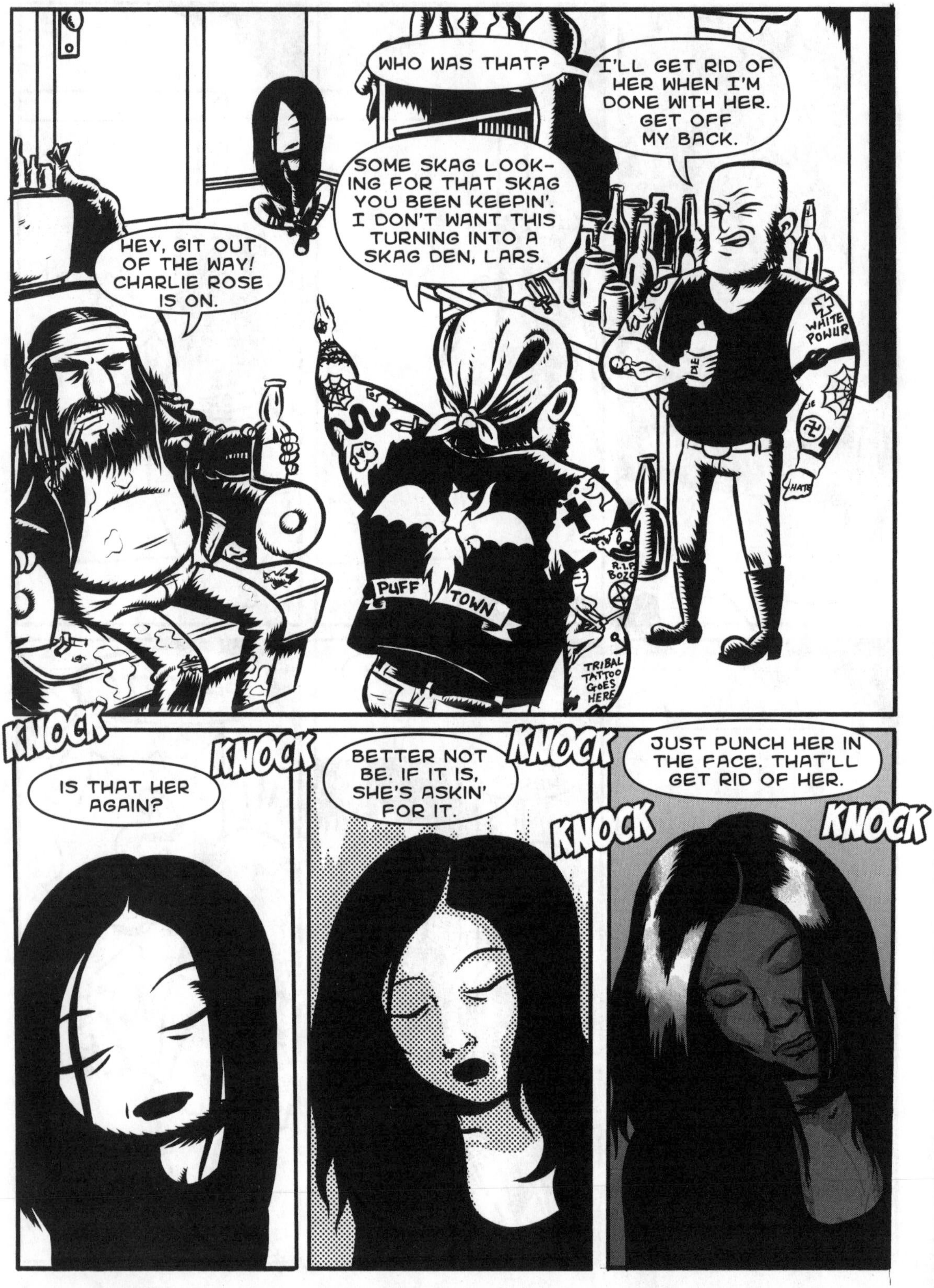
WHO WAS THAT?
SOME SKAG LOOKING FOR THAT SKAG YOU BEEN KEEPIN'. I DON'T WANT THIS TURNING INTO A SKAG DEN, LARS.
I'LL GET RID OF HER WHEN I'M DONE WITH HER. GET OFF MY BACK.
HEY, GIT OUT OF THE WAY! CHARLIE ROSE IS ON.
WHITE POWUR
DIE
HATE
PUFF TOWN
R.I.P. BOZO
TRIBAL TATTOO GOES HERE
KNOCK
IS THAT HER AGAIN?
KNOCK
BETTER NOT BE. IF IT IS, SHE'S ASKIN' FOR IT.
KNOCK
KNOCK
JUST PUNCH HER IN THE FACE. THAT'LL GET RID OF HER.
KNOCK

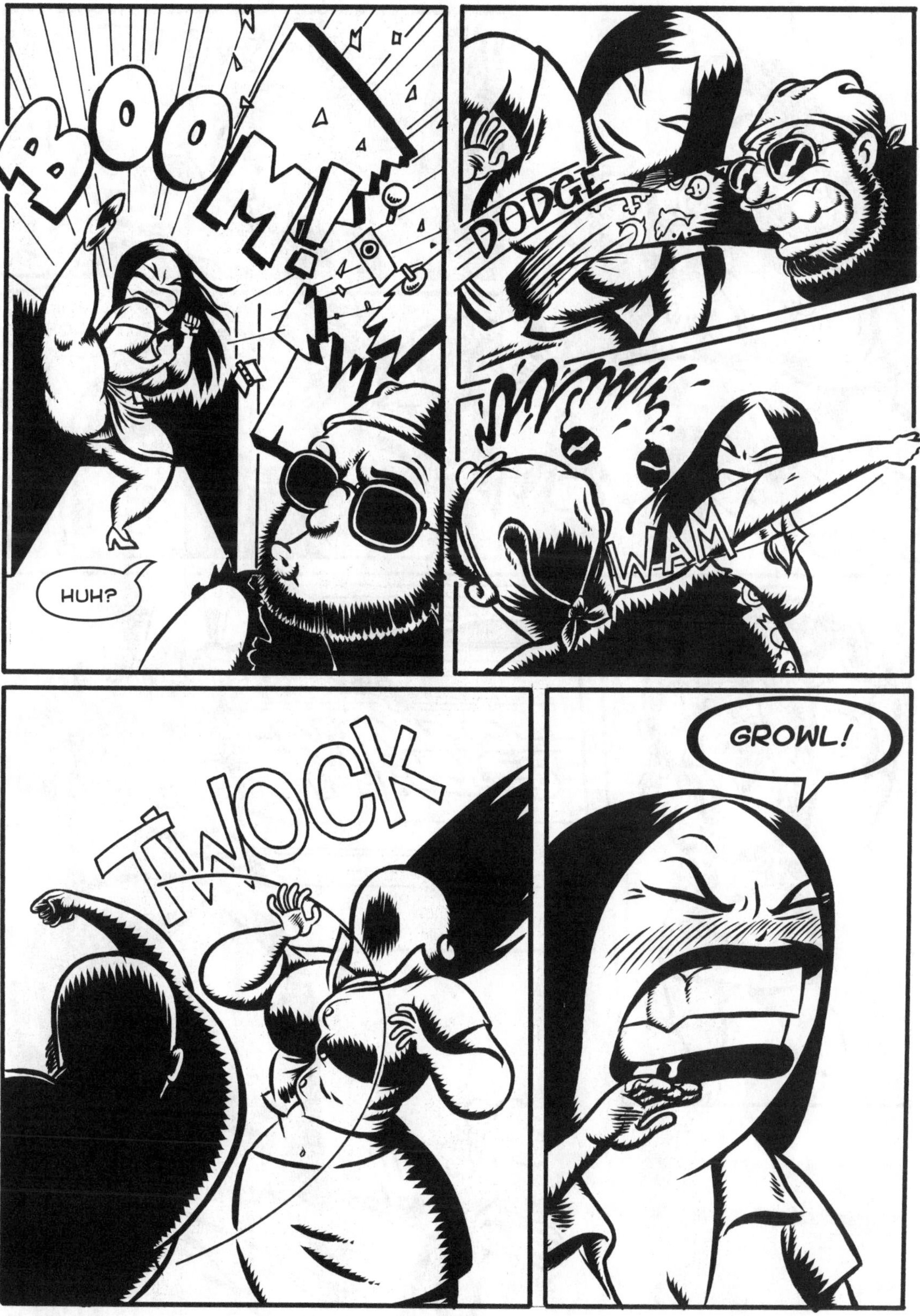
BOOM!
HUH?
DODGE
WAM
TWOCK
GROWL!

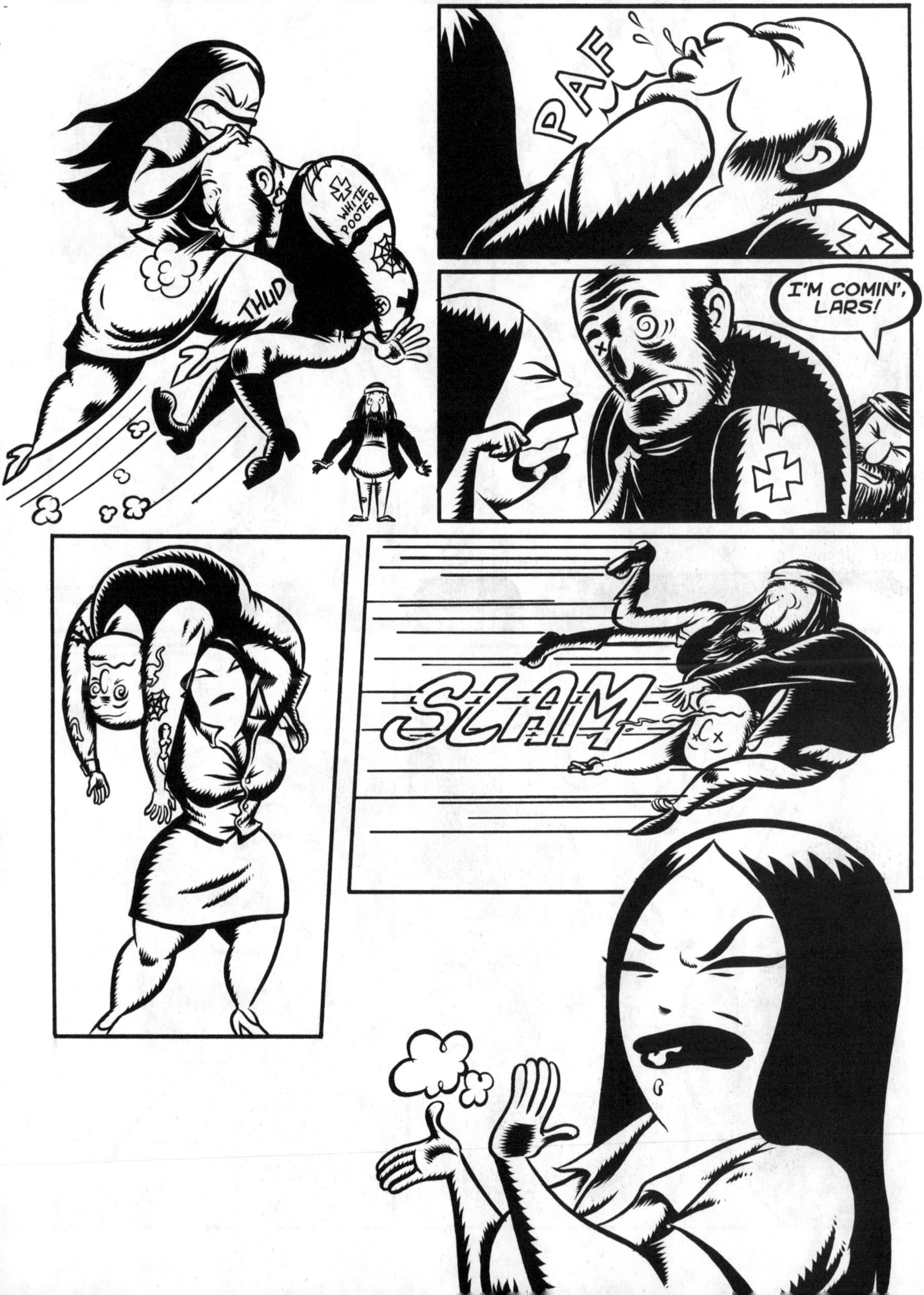
WHITE POOTER
THUD
PAF
I'M COMIN', LARS!
SLAM

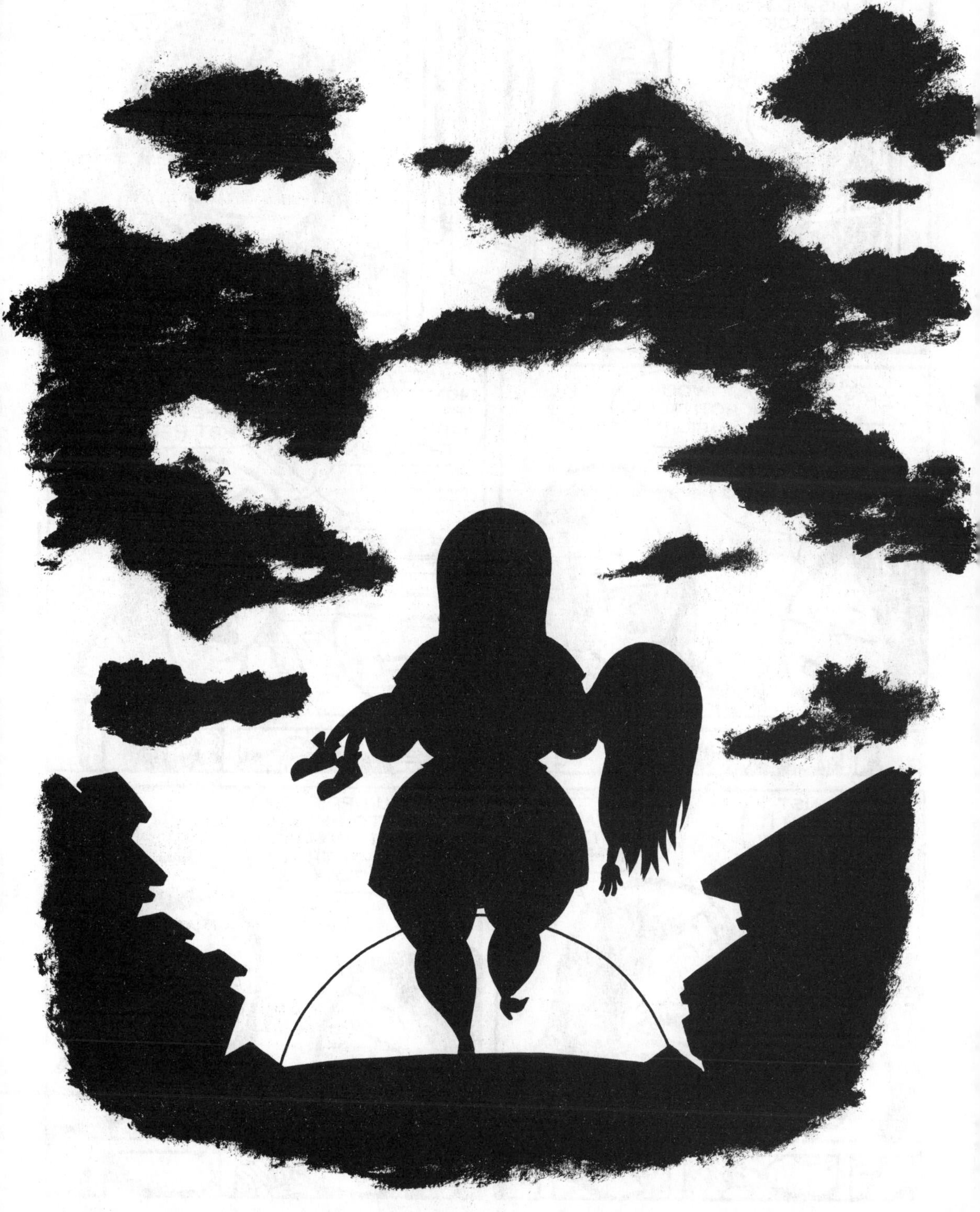

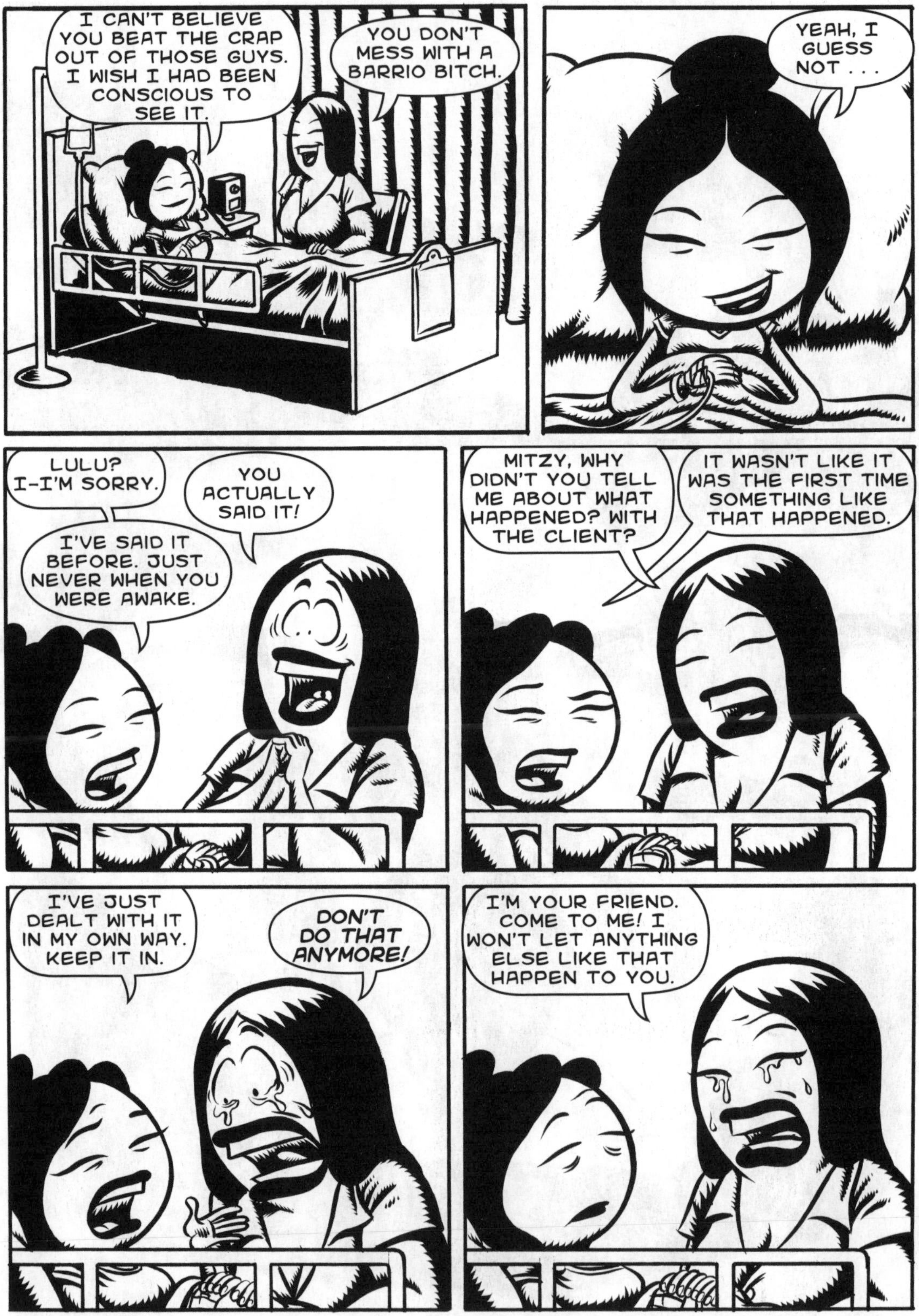
I CAN'T BELIEVE YOU BEAT THE CRAP OUT OF THOSE GUYS. I WISH I HAD BEEN CONSCIOUS TO SEE IT.
YOU DON'T MESS WITH A BARRIO BITCH.
YEAH, I GUESS NOT . . .
LULU? I-I'M SORRY.
YOU ACTUALLY SAID IT!
I'VE SAID IT BEFORE. JUST NEVER WHEN YOU WERE AWAKE.
MITZY, WHY DIDN'T YOU TELL ME ABOUT WHAT HAPPENED? WITH THE CLIENT?
IT WASN'T LIKE IT WAS THE FIRST TIME SOMETHING LIKE THAT HAPPENED.
I'VE JUST DEALT WITH IT IN MY OWN WAY. KEEP IT IN.
DON'T DO THAT ANYMORE!
I'M YOUR FRIEND. COME TO ME! I WON'T LET ANYTHING ELSE LIKE THAT HAPPEN TO YOU.

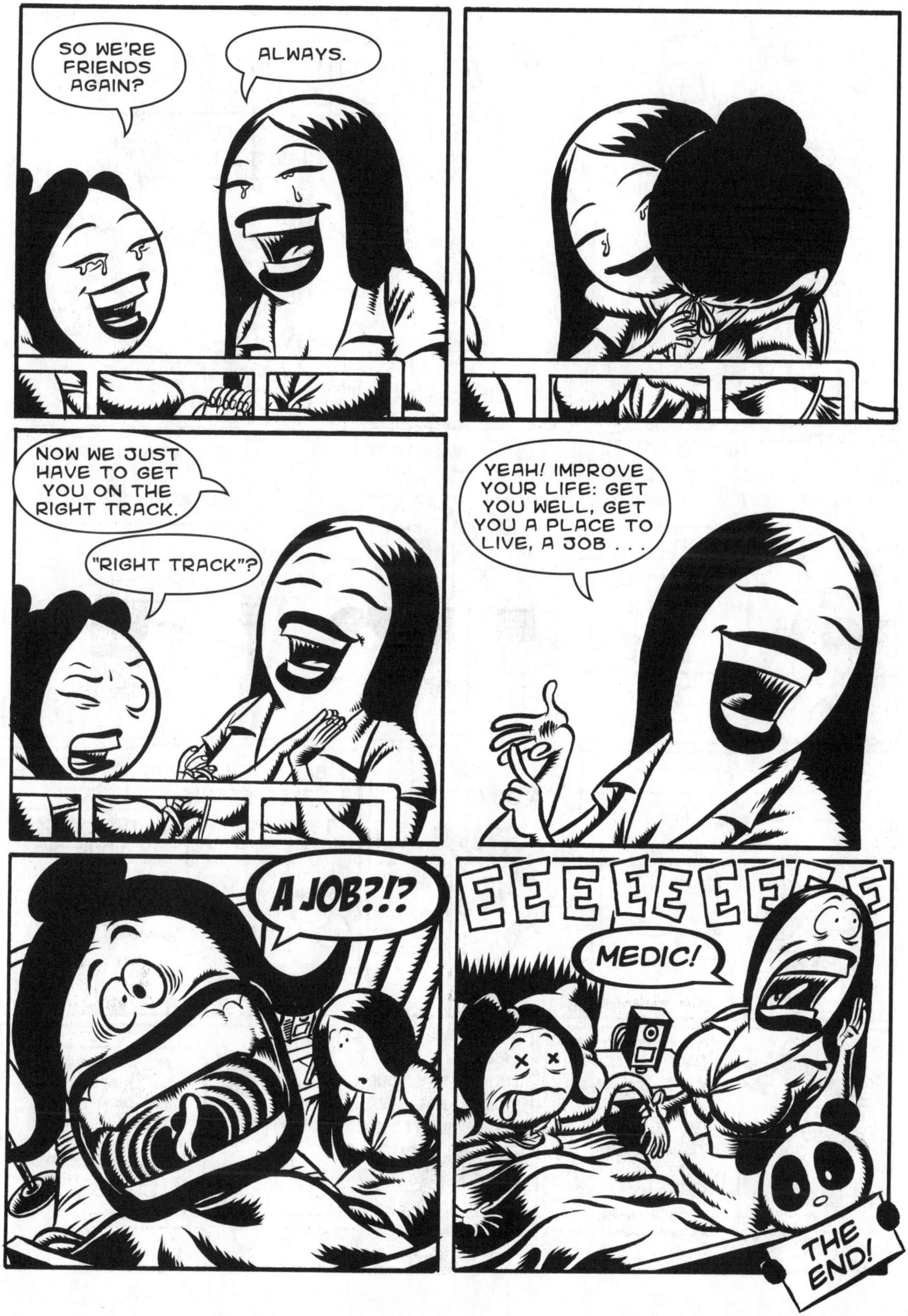
SO WE'RE FRIENDS AGAIN?
ALWAYS.
NOW WE JUST HAVE TO GET YOU ON THE RIGHT TRACK.
"RIGHT TRACK"?
YEAH! IMPROVE YOUR LIFE: GET YOU WELL, GET YOU A PLACE TO LIVE, A JOB . . .
A JOB?!?
EEEEEEEEE
MEDIC!
THE END!

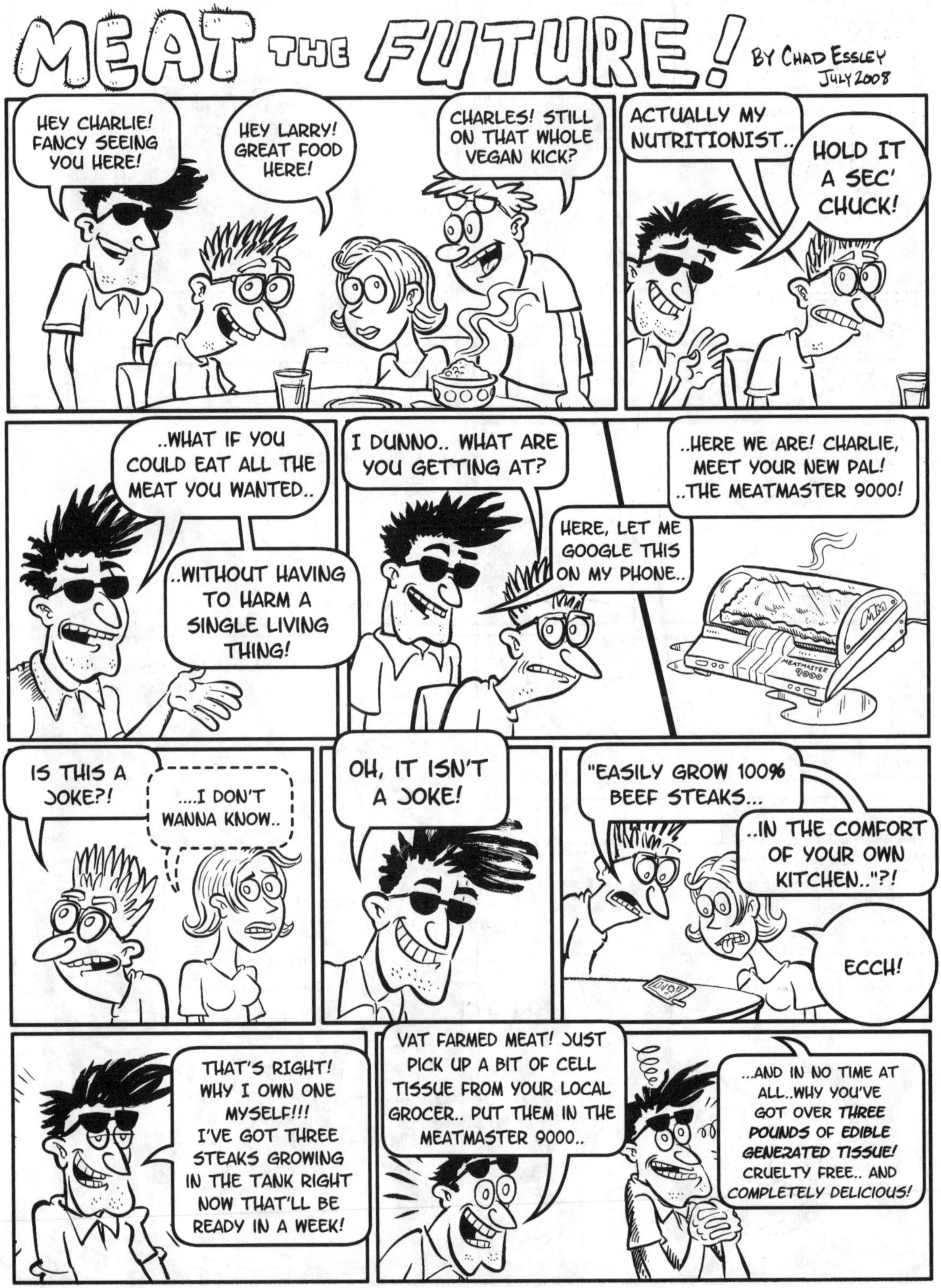
MEAT THE FUTURE!
BY CHAD ESSLEY
JULY 2008
HEY CHARLIE! FANCY SEEING YOU HERE!
HEY LARRY! GREAT FOOD HERE!
CHARLES! STILL ON THAT WHOLE VEGAN KICK?
ACTUALLY MY NUTRITIONIST..
HOLD IT A SEC' CHUCK!
..WHAT IF YOU COULD EAT ALL THE MEAT YOU WANTED..
..WITHOUT HAVING TO HARM A SINGLE LIVING THING!
I DUNNO.. WHAT ARE YOU GETTING AT?
HERE, LET ME GOOGLE THIS ON MY PHONE..
..HERE WE ARE! CHARLIE, MEET YOUR NEW PAL! ..THE MEATMASTER 9000!
MM
MEATMASTER 9000
IS THIS A JOKE?!
....I DON'T WANNA KNOW..
OH, IT ISN'T A JOKE!
"EASILY GROW 100% BEEF STEAKS...
..IN THE COMFORT OF YOUR OWN KITCHEN.."?!
ECCH!
THAT'S RIGHT! WHY I OWN ONE MYSELF!!! I'VE GOT THREE STEAKS GROWING IN THE TANK RIGHT NOW THAT'LL BE READY IN A WEEK!
VAT FARMED MEAT! JUST PICK UP A BIT OF CELL TISSUE FROM YOUR LOCAL GROCER.. PUT THEM IN THE MEATMASTER 9000..
...AND IN NO TIME AT ALL..WHY YOU'VE GOT OVER THREE POUNDS OF EDIBLE GENERATED TISSUE! CRUELTY FREE.. AND COMPLETELY DELICIOUS!

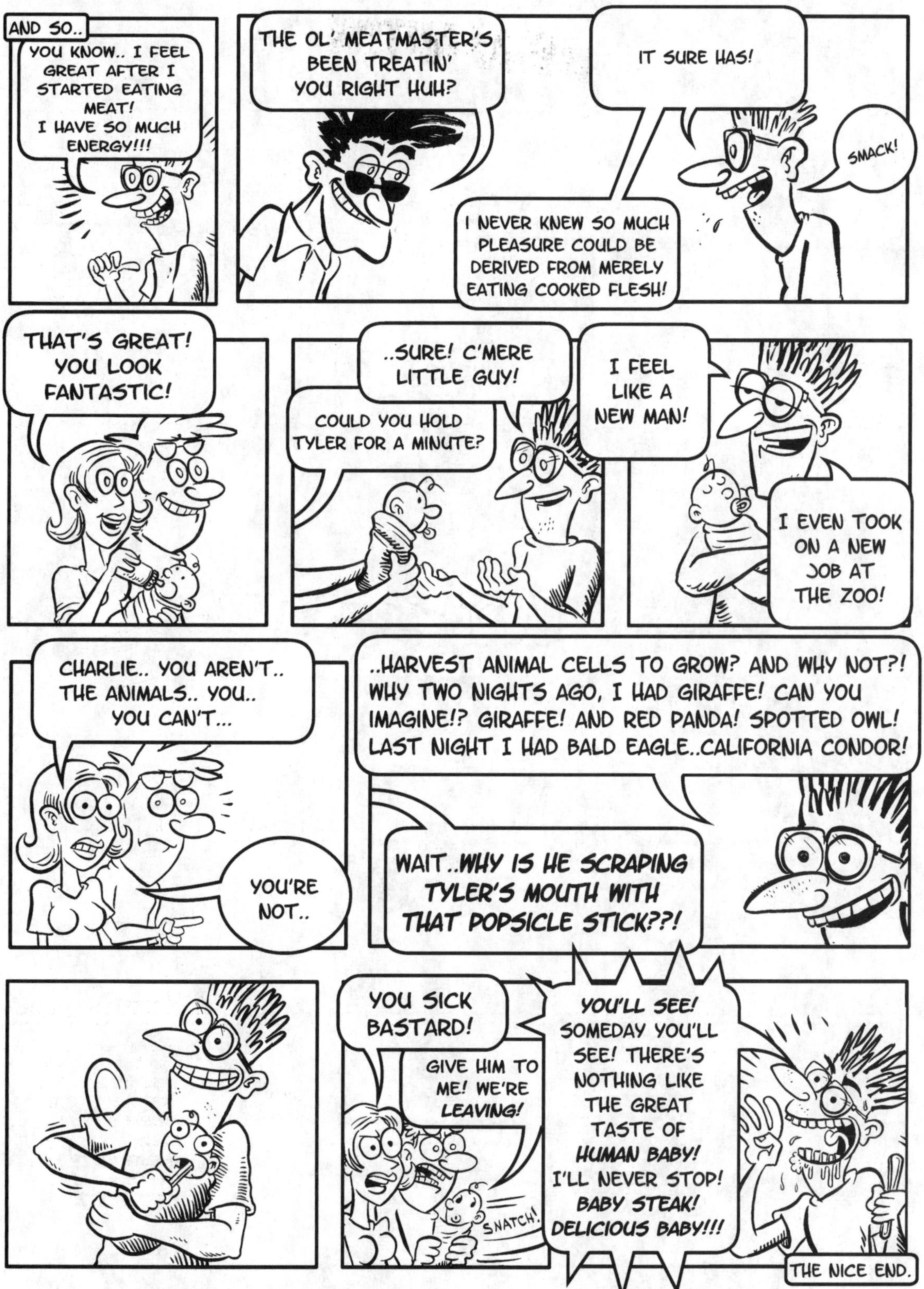
AND SO..
YOU KNOW.. I FEEL GREAT AFTER I STARTED EATING MEAT! I HAVE SO MUCH ENERGY!!!
THE OL' MEATMASTER'S BEEN TREATIN' YOU RIGHT HUH?
IT SURE HAS!
SMACK!
I NEVER KNEW SO MUCH PLEASURE COULD BE DERIVED FROM MERELY EATING COOKED FLESH!
THAT'S GREAT! YOU LOOK FANTASTIC!
COULD YOU HOLD TYLER FOR A MINUTE?
..SURE! C'MERE LITTLE GUY!
I FEEL LIKE A NEW MAN!
I EVEN TOOK ON A NEW JOB AT THE ZOO!
CHARLIE.. YOU AREN'T.. THE ANIMALS.. YOU.. YOU CAN'T...
YOU'RE NOT..
..HARVEST ANIMAL CELLS TO GROW? AND WHY NOT?! WHY TWO NIGHTS AGO, I HAD GIRAFFE! CAN YOU IMAGINE!? GIRAFFE! AND RED PANDA! SPOTTED OWL! LAST NIGHT I HAD BALD EAGLE..CALIFORNIA CONDOR!
WAIT..WHY IS HE SCRAPING TYLER'S MOUTH WITH THAT POPSICLE STICK??!
YOU SICK BASTARD!
GIVE HIM TO ME! WE'RE LEAVING!
SNATCH!
YOU'LL SEE! SOMEDAY YOU'LL SEE! THERE'S NOTHING LIKE THE GREAT TASTE OF HUMAN BABY! I'LL NEVER STOP! BABY STEAK! DELICIOUS BABY!!!
THE NICE END.

UNDATED PHOTO OF
THE CREATOR.

S. EDDY BELL WAS BORN IN FLINT, MICHI-
GAN AND RELOCATED TO PORTLAND IN
1998. SINCE THEN HE HAS LIVED FOR
PERIODS OF TIME IN SEATTLE AND LOS
ANGELES, BUT CURRENTLY RESIDES IN
SAN FRANCISCO WITH HIS WIFE, THE YO,
AND A CAT NAMED MILK.

HE HAS WORKED IN ANIMATION, INTER-
NET MEDIA, AND PUBLISHING, LEAVING
A MARK IN NONE OF THOSE FIELDS
WORTH MENTIONING. *LULU & MIZTY:
BEST LAID PLANS* IS HIS FIRST PUB-
LISHED GRAPHIC NOVEL.

ACKNOWLEDGEMENTS

MANY THANKS TO MY WIFE, MY PARENTS, BRIAN VANDIVER,
COIRE REILLY, DYLAN WOOTERS, AND CHAD ESSLEY FOR
THEIR SUPPORT AND INSIGHT. ALSO, THANKS TO DAN VADO
AT SLG FOR TAKING A CHANCE ON THIS BOOK.

A VERY SPECIAL THANKS TO SAN FRANCISCO'S TENDERLOIN
DISTRICT. ITS COLORFUL INHABITANTS AND LOCALES
INSPIRED ME TO DEVELOP LULU AND MITZY. THE REST OF
SAN FRANCISCO MAY CHOOSE TO IGNORE YOU OR SLIGHT
YOU, BUT MAY THEY NEVER GENTRIFY YOUR SPIRIT.

VISIT S. EDDY AT WWW.FICTIONBOX.COM